ENGLISH AND SCOTTISH EARTHENWARE

1660-1860

Animals grouped in a corner alcove: (Top shelf) Ralph Wood retriever and setter, height 7½ inches, and lion in natural colour on green and brown plinth, height 9¾ inches, length 12 inches. (Second shelf) Whieldon figures: pair of buffaloes in cream ware mottled in warm glazes, splashed on one side with blue, height 6 inches; owl in deep rich brown glaze, height 9 inches. (Third shelf) Ralph Wood figures: camel in rich brown glaze, height 9 inches; plaque of two lions surmounted by an armorial design height 10½ inches; and elephant in natural colours, height 7½ inches. (Bottom shelf) Whieldon figures: recumbent horse in green, blue and manganese glazes, height 6 inches; dog and cat with mottled glazes in green, brown and yellow, height 7 inches; stag in white splashed with chocolate brown height 13 inches; and hind at graze in natural colourings, height 4 inches.

G. BERNARD HUGHES

ENGLISH AND SCOTTISH
EARTHENWARE
1660–1860

ABBEY FINE ARTS
LONDON

ABBEY FINE ARTS
146 — 152, HOLLOWAY ROAD, LONDON, N. 7

CONTENTS

LIST OF ILLUSTRATIONS

7

6. Stoneware: tankard decorated with horizontal mouldings and applied reliefs; tankard decorated with a hare-hunting scene; punch bowl of Nottingham grey stoneware; wine bottle or bellarmine (*all in the Victoria and Albert Museum*)

7. Brown salt-glazed stoneware: two spirit flasks (*by courtesy of Joseph Bourne & Son Ltd.*); tobacco jar, two spirit flasks and two jugs (*by courtesy of Doulton & Co. Ltd.*)

8. Swan and cygnet in salt-glazed stoneware painted in enamels, *and* basket dish in salt-glazed stoneware; a collection of early English pottery from Lambeth, Fulham and Nottingham (*all in the Victoria and Albert Museum*)

9. Staffordshire salt-glazed stoneware teapots (*all in the Victoria and Albert Museum*)

10. White salt-glazed stoneware jug enamelled with musicians (*in the British Museum*); pear-shaped jug in white salt-glazed stoneware (*in the Victoria and Albert Museum*); two teapots and a jug in Staffordshire salt-glazed stoneware, decorated with stamped reliefs (*in the Victoria and Albert Museum*)

11. Teapot in agate ware; posset pot marbled in white; marbled slip ware dish; teapot in blue, white and brown agate ware (*all in the Victoria and Albert Museum*)

12. A collection of Whieldon figures (*in the collection of Viscount Mackintosh of Halifax*); *and* an all-white pew group in salt-glazed stoneware (*in the Glaisher Collection, Fitzwilliam Museum, Cambridge*)

13. Early equestrian figures of soldiers, by John Astbury, Ralph Wood and Thomas Whieldon (*in the collection of Viscount Mackintosh of Halifax*)

14. Staffordshire pottery figures of the late 18th century

15. Group of Ralph Wood figures (*in the collection of Viscount Mackintosh of Halifax*)

16. Three Ralph Wood figures in white earthenware with clear glaze (*in the collection of Viscount Mackintosh of Halifax*)

17. Ralph Wood Toby jugs (*in the collection of Viscount Mackintosh of Halifax*)

18. Wedgwood cream-coloured earthenware (*in the Wedgwood Museum*)

19. Wedgwood busts and figures in black basaltes (*by courtesy of Delomosne & Son*)

20. Wedgwood black basaltes. Three-burner lamp (*in the Wedgwood Museum*); a water vase decorated with gilded copper (*by courtesy of Gered Ltd.*); a collection of ornamental basaltes (*in the collection of Sir John Wedgwood*)

35 Loving cups: decorated with transfer printing; with ovoid bowl encircled with shallow flutes; in hard white earthenware decorated with black transfer designs (*all in the collection of Mr. Clifford Chubb*)

36. Cream-coloured earthenware mug transfer-printed in black (*in the Victoria and Albert Museum*); vase of reddish-brown earthenware covered with lustrous black glaze; Liverpool double-handled mug in pearl ware; pair of greyhounds in Jackfield ware

37. Wedgwood terra cotta (*in the Wedgwood Museum*)

38. Mason's ironstone china (*in the Hanley Museum and Art Gallery*)

39. Staffordshire blue underglaze transfer-printed ware: earthenware plate printed with Spode's "Temple" pattern (*in the collection of Mr. Gresham Copeland*); a plate with Spode's "Italian" pattern *and* an early example of Spode printing (*in the Spode-Copeland Museum*); stone china plate printed with "William Penn's Treaty" (*in the collection of Miss Rita Philpott*); dish with openwork rim and an early Anglo-Chinese design by John Davenport

40. Table ware decorated with blue transfer-printed willow pattern designs

41. Statuette in brown salt-glazed stoneware *and* statuette in terra cotta (*by courtesy of Doulton & Co. Ltd.*); early Victorian terra cotta tobacco jar (*in Eastbourne Museum*); mantelpiece in Mason's ironstone china (*in the Hanley Museum and Art Gallery*)

42. Pottery figures of soldiers of the Napoleonic wars *and* the coat of arms of George IV in Staffordshire pottery (*by courtesy of Drury & Drury*)

43. Architectural ornaments in earthenware (*in the Brighton Museum*); dish painted in ultramarine under the glaze *and* Middlesbrough pottery with bluish-grey ground (*both in the collection of Mr. Kenneth Glover*)

44. Tazza in imitation majolica *and* vase of enamelled earthenware hand-painted in black and yellow (*both in the Victoria and Albert Museum*)

45. Rack plate in Portobello pottery (*in the Royal Scottish Museum*); Staffordshire figure of Dick Turpin (*Victoria and Albert Museum*); Portobello Toby jug; dark brown Portobello jug with printed design (*in the collection of Lady Broun Lindsay of Colstoun*)

46. Portobello pottery figures (*in the Royal Scottish Museum*)

The illustrations kindly lent by the Viscount Mackintosh of Halifax appeared in his book *Early English Pottery*, 1938

LIST OF PLATES

Line drawings

INTRODUCTION

THE early story of pottery in the British Isles is of primitive methods and coarse, homely products. Monasteries
and great houses operated their own potteries but towns
and villages depended on local potters. Utility earthenware,
individualistic but seldom adventurous, might be made
wherever clay and wood fuel were available, only the lead
for the scanty glazing being obtained from further afield.
But a master potter would rarely possess facilities for firing
more than one small oven a week, his products most likely
consisting of green-glazed buff earthenware, brown-glazed
red earthenware, and slip ware.

As a foreword to this book it is interesting perhaps to
take a brief glance at these early beginnings, but they must
be recognised as beginnings only: the triumph of English
and Scottish earthenwares, as contrasted with those of the
rest of the world, is the fact that they advanced spectacu-
larly to become numbered among Britain's most successful crafts for their design, fabric, ornament and for the
techniques that made such excellence possible to men
deliberately serving the least moneyed and the least
critical. This book is devoted to the details of this advance
with particular reference to the interests of today's collectors.

For the average collector the earliest likely finds will date
to the 1770s, but some of the early work reviewed here
continued to be produced into the nineteenth century, and
the shrewd collector will find that comparison of early and
later techniques and styles can guide his dating of slipware,
for example, or tin-enamelled earthenware, or Nottingham
ware. Mid-nineteenth-century reproductions abound, catalogued now, as then, as Elizabethan. An obvious confusion
for the tyro is the existence of English majolica, scarcely

13

even superficially resembling the old Continental treasure, but well worth collecting for what it is.

Even when a piece is marked it is often only a knowledge of manufacturing processes and their first introduction and development that can establish a date—and the vast majority of pieces in any average collection are bound to lack even this slender clue to identity or age.

From the late thirteenth century earthenware plates, dishes, salt cellars, jugs and cups are mentioned in inventories. The majority were plain surfaced, but surviving examples preserved in museums may be patterned with crude heads, strips and dots of clay, geometric indentations and impressed motifs. "White table ware", really dirty grey in colour, was also potted from pipe clay, such as the "12 dozen white cups, 10/-" bought for the marriage feast of Gervys Clifton and Mary Neville in 1530. For the same occasion were bought "64 great earthenware pots, 3/4".

Contemporaneously slipware was made, characteristic of early Staffordshire where several types of earthenware clay were found within half a mile of Burslem. These were described by Doctor Robert Plot, first keeper of the Ashmolean Museum, who visited Burslem in 1677 and nine years later published his *Natural History of Staffordshire*. "These", he wrote, "are to be distinguished by their colours and used as followeth:

"1. Bottle clay, of a bright whitish streaked yellow colour.

"2. Hard-fire clay of a duller whitish colour, and fuller interspered with a dark yellow, which they use for black wares, being mixed with the

"3. White-clay, so-called although of a blewish colour and used for making a yellow-coloured ware, because yellow is the lightest colour they make any ware of.

"All of which they call *throwing clays*, because they are of the closer texture and will work on the wheel;

"which none of the other three clays, they call slips, will any of them doe, being of looser and more friable natures; these mixed with water they make into a consistance thinner than a syrup, so that being put into a bucket it will run out through a quill; this they call *Slip*, and is the substance wherewith they paint their wares; whereof the

"1. sort is called the Orange slip, which before it is worked, is of a

greyish colour mixt with orange ball, and gives the ware when
annealed an orange colour.

"2. The White slip is of a dark blewish colour, yet makes the ware
yellow, which being the lightest colour they make any of, they call it
the white slip.

"3. The Red slip is made of a dirty reddish clay which gives wares
a black colour".

Collectors group their earthenware into three easily distinguished classes, each sub-divided into numerous types.
The earliest group, pre-dating 1728, but continuing in production for many years afterwards, was almost entirely
from local clays; in 1728 calcined flint began to be added to
strengthen and whiten the yellowish body to cream colour;
the third or industrial group dates from 1775 when Cornish
clay and china stone were first incorporated with local clays
or substituted for them.

At least twenty different types of earthenware were then
in active manufacture. Sixteen of these are listed in the 1784
inventory of Richard Frank and Son, Earthen and Stone
Pot Works, Water Lane, Bristol: black ware, red china
ware; tortoiseshell ware; blue and white sprigged ware;
blue and white stoneware; Staffordshire ware; Dutch ware;
Delph ware; copperplate tiles; Nottingham ware; blue china
glazed ware; enamelled china glaze ware; common enamelled ware; copperplate ware; cream colour ware; white stoneware; and brown stoneware. In addition Staffordshire was
making fine stonewares: basaltes, jasper and cane-colour.
These were succeeded in the nineteenth century by at least
thirty types of stronger earthenwares resulting from the
continuing advance of technical knowledge. Aesthetically
it is easy to deplore some of the results, governed as they
were by a desperate price-cutting competition that sent innumerable potters bankrupt. But in earthenwares more
than in most nineteenth-century products the traditional
rules of craftsmanship were remembered and upheld as
long-trained expert fingers turned moist clay to men's
service and delight.

Chapter One

TIN-ENAMELLED EARTHENWARE

COLOURED ornaments rarely brightened modest English houses until the days of Elizabeth I, when earthenware covered with opaque white enamel decorated in cobalt blue and made lustrous with lead glaze was introduced to England by potters from the Dutch town of Delft. The name delft eventually became a generic term for this earthenware, which was really a development of majolica adapted to compete with imported oriental porcelains.

The first of this earthenware to be made in England was produced at Norwich, where two Flemish potters set up a kiln in 1567 to make "gally paving tiles and vessels for apothecaries and others". One of them, Jacob Janson, with four Flemish colleagues, is recorded as potting in Aldgate, London, in 1571. By the end of the century other potters of tin-enamelled earthenware were established at Lambeth on the south bank of the Thames. During the next hundred and fifty years the trade flourished also in Fulham, Vauxhall, Battersea, Pedlars' Acre, Southwark and along the riverside as far as Deptford.

This English tin-enamelled earthenware was in no way comparable with the Dutch delft, imported in a wide range of domestic articles, plain and decorated in cobalt blue. The ware eventually to become known as English delft was not made until 1671, when John Ariens van Hamme was granted a patent for "makinge tiles and porcelain and other earthenwares after the way practised in Holland". Unfortunately no detailed account of the processes involved was included with the published specification. The granting of this fourteen-year monopoly was followed a few months

17

later by a proclamation of Charles II "prohibiting the importation of any kind or sort of painted earthenware whatsoever". Van Hamme appears to have licensed his process to others, for several potters of similar enamelled earthenware were established in Lambeth by 1676. Soon the trade extended to Bristol, and later to Liverpool, Wincanton in Somerset, Wednesbury in South Staffordshire, Dublin and elsewhere.

Fine earthenware clays were exported from England to Holland when the delft ware potters blended them with two or three native clays. The Dundry clay of Bristol was in great demand by the Dutch potters: other west country pockets of similar clay were also exploited. The Dutch blending clays contained calcium carbonate. Several authorities have stated that collectors can distinguish between Dutch and English tin-enamelled earthenware by testing the body with dilute hydrochloric acid: on Dutch ware the acid effervesces because calcium carbonate is present, whereas there is no reaction on English ware. This is not entirely correct. True, there is a quick reaction on the Dutch ware, the acid sinking quickly into its porous body. The English body, also containing lime in its composition, is hard, and the effervescence takes much longer to commence and even then is considerably less vigorous than with the Dutch.

Dutch processes differed from the English in some respects. The decoration was applied to the unfired enamel on the biscuit, and the glaze contained protoxide of lead or gold foam, a refuse product of the gold refineries. This made it harder and more evenly textured than the English lead glaze. In England the decoration was painted over the vitrified enamel. The earlier processes were much the same.

Suitable clays were carefully washed and blended. Kilns capable of reaching higher temperatures appear to have been used in England, for the basic earthenware is more vitreous and denser of texture than the Dutch, which is comparatively soft and porous and can be scratched with a knife. Deep vessels required to be wreathed to prevent the hazard of collapse in the kiln. This was the term given to the spiral ridging visible on the inner wall of pieces such as drug pots, pedestals for food warmers, vases and so on.

This slight unevenness was intended to strengthen the body which softened at one period during firing and tended to collapse beneath its own weight. The slight variation in thickness provided by wreathing was sufficient to prevent this.

After shaping the ware was fired to a biscuit in a kiln of equable temperature, thus preventing shrinkage and reducing the wastage caused by warping. This biscuit was vigorously brushed to remove dust and then dipped into white tin oxide enamel held in suspension by water. Hugh Owen has suggested that this was composed of 50 parts tin oxide, 65 parts frit, $\frac{1}{2}$ part smalt, and $\frac{8}{100}$ parts of red copper. The frit was prepared by fusing together 50 parts sand, 6 parts salt and 3 parts soda. The whole was ground to an impalpable powder with water. This formula closely resembles one published by Blancourt in 1699. The dipped ware was set aside to air-dry which left the surface coated with a layer of white powder.

The Dutch potters painted directly over this powder, afterwards sprinkling it with a thin coating of powdered glaze. The biscuit with its coating of enamel, decoration and glaze was then fired a second time, the heat converting the powder into an opaque film of white enamel, thicker and smoother than was possible by the English method. A great amount of this was absorbed into the porous biscuit carrying with it fine particles of enamel deeply into its texture, thus effectively concealing the red tint of the body. This skilful combination of enamel, colour and glaze produced a brilliance almost equal to that of the over-glaze enamels on oriental porcelains.

The English potters of tin-enamelled earthenware applied their enamel to the biscuit and then fired a second time, before painting and glazing. The denser and more vitreous texture of the ware prevented the enamel from penetrating as in Dutch tin-enamelled earthenware: in consequence the surface was less even. The coating of white enamel was thick enough to conceal firecracks and minor flaws in the reddish surface of the earthenware, but, because it did not sink in, the enamel might show a pinkish tinge. The enamelled tiles were now ready for hand-painting, usually in cobalt blue.

After further air-drying the ware was lightly coated with powdered lead glaze known as smithum, sprinkled from a short, stiff brush with hair bristles. It was then fired for the last time. The heat caused the glaze to spread over the enamel like a smooth clear varnish, and in fact it was so termed by the potters themselves. Surface lustre has vastly diminished on existing examples, the effect of atmospheric action during several generations.

It will be seen that the English tin-enamelled earthenware did not reproduce the qualities of the Dutch body: in fact it was not true delft, but a much harder, more durable ceramic and considerably less costly. Decorations were usually carried out on small-scale mass-production lines. These patterns were outlined on the tin-enamelled surface by pouncing fine charcoal powder through a pin-pricked paper stencil, the decorator completing the design with speedy freehand work. Zaffre, a preparation of cobalt oxide, was ground with oil of lavender on a marble slab and applied with pencil brushes made by the decorators themselves from ox bristles. Shading effects were accomplished with various qualities of the same pigment. The flat tints of zaffre sometimes appear as though the colour had curdled during firing: such a defect is a sign of overfiring, rarely found on Dutch delft. Fine work was carried out with the much more costly cobalt product known as smalt. The less popular violet or puce decoration was obtained by using manganese oxide as a pigment.

Rims of flat ware made after about 1750 might be decorated in powder blue or powder puce, more rarely in brown or yellow, used as a ground for round, fan-shaped and shell-shaped reserves. This effect was produced not by powdering but by spattering colour upon the glaze with a brush: its alternative term is "spattered ground ware". This was done by a resist process described by W. J. Pountney in *Old Bristol Potteries:*

"The article having been once fired and then dipped in the enamel, or painted with it, and dried, was then treated in the following manner. Small pieces of paper, cut to the desired shape, were pasted on the flange in the requisite position. Another circular piece of paper covered the whole of the centre of the dish. The painter then took his brush, containing a moderate supply of liquid colour, which he tapped on his mahlstick, thus causing a sprinkling to go over that part of the dish not covered with paper. This he repeated until he got an evenly sprinkled surface, which then formed the ground colour. He would then remove the paper and paint in the designs upon the vacant spaces left on the enamel."

Tin-enamelled earthenware was very rarely marked. Only by a few named and dated pieces and the researches of local antiquarians has it been possible to attribute distinguishing features.

English tin-enamelled earthenware was for long referred to as Dutch or Flemish ware in recognition of the original source of supply. Mortimer's *Husbandry*, 1707, recorded that "fireplaces set with Dutch tiles are the new fashion, facings being set with single, double or triple rows". Chambers' *Cyclopaedia*, 1727, noted that "Flemish tyles are now commonly used plastered up in the jaumbs of chimney-corners"

The ware became known as white and painted earthenware in the 1680s and was so designated at a trial in 1693 concerning supplies of potter's clay. This term continued in use throughout the first half of the eighteenth century. R. Campbell's London *Tradesman*, 1747, refers to the "delf ware" at Lambeth as being "made of clay wrought and cleansed from all its Impurities", and then goes on to list these as "white potters" to distinguish them from the stoneware men. The ware began to be known as "delft" early in the eighteenth century, the earliest reference given by the *Oxford English Dictionary* dating to 1714. More usually the ware was known as "delf".

The van Hamme pottery in Lambeth no doubt introduced from Holland painters experienced in decorating tin-enamelled earthenware. Examination of pieces attributed to Lambeth suggests that there was little uniformity in the clays used which were brought by coastal vessels from various sites in the West Country. Lambeth tin-enamelled earthenware differs in this respect from that of Bristol, Liverpool and Wednesbury, where blended local clays were used.

When Z. C. von Uffenbach visited London in 1710 he

recorded in his diary: "On 21 July Monday morning we went first to see the porcelain sheds at Foxhall. The articles made here are very coarse and heavy. The work is no different from that I saw in Delft and Berlin, excepting here the clay is washed in great vats in the yard, dried in the sun, and then prepared for manufacture." The enamel on early Lambeth ware is usually white: in the eighteenth century a faintly bluish-green tint distinguishes it from the bluish-purple of Bristol. There is sometimes a pinkish tone where the colour of the earthenware is not fully obscured around the edges of the rim.

The extensive range of productions included plates, wall plaques, mugs, jugs, wine serving bottles, punch bowls, puzzle jugs, wine bin labels, food warmers, posset pots, candlesticks, water fountains, fuddling cups, vases, brick-shaped bulb pots or flower holders with loose grids and tiles. The cleanliness and light-reflecting properties of tiles caused them to be widely used in the domestic quarters of homes, in cellars and in the vaults of public resorts. Apothecaries' pill slabs were made in large numbers, often taking the form of a heraldic escutcheon painted in blue with the arms of the Apothecaries' Company and perforated to hang when not in use. Drug pots and ointment pots are found in numerous sizes and shapes.

Collectors wrongly assume that they will find few opportunities of acquiring examples of English tin-enamelled earthenware, the general belief being that manufacture ceased in the mid-eighteenth century. But in fact tin-enamelled earthenware was potted in Lambeth throughout the first quarter of the nineteenth century, and examples of early delft come to light with surprising frequency. In 1959 I noted an unrecognised 250-year-old wall plaque lying on a kitchen floor.

Demand was such that in 1811 Richard Waters, near Lambeth Church, felt it worth while to expend £300 in taking out a patent for forming "delf-ware pots and other articles by compression of the clay between suitable moulds". John Wagstaff in the 1790s acquired a delft-ware pottery at Mortlake that had operated continuously since the late seventeenth century. Delft ware continued to be manufactured here until 1821. In the Victoria and Albert Museum is a punch bowl, 21 inches in diameter, painted in blue with birds and flowers, made at this pottery.

The flourishing trade in tin-enamelled earthenware at Bristol appears to have stemmed from a pottery founded at Brislington, three miles from Bristol, by Robert Collins, a potter from Southwark who settled there in the 1650s. Tin-enamelled earthenware potters operated at Brislington until the 1770s. In 1682 Edward Ward moved from Brislington to Temple Back, Bristol, three years before the van Hamme patent lapsed. Among the early potters of Bristol tin-enamelled earthenware were Thomas Frank who succeeded Edward Ward in 1697 and moved to Redcliffe Back in 1706, and Woodes Rogers who founded a pottery at Limekiln Lane during the same year. Bristol was probably responsible for the majority of decorated tin-enamelled earthenware made in England during the first half of the eighteenth century. Each potter inevitably worked to a different formula in which improvements were made from time to time. Professor Church has described Frank's basic earthenware as "having a buff-coloured body, harder, denser and a trifle redder and darker in tint than the body of competing potters".

Some authorities state that tin-enamelled earthenware potted at Bristol was thicker in section than that at Liverpool. Mr. Boswell Lancaster's examination of authenticated examples at my request did not confirm this: each group potted thinly in its late productions. Texture of the enamel on some pieces attributed to Bristol of the post-1740 period suggests that one or more of the potters was using the newly-improved kiln invented by Perrott of Bristol. This applies to the enamel of uniform texture stained a greenish blue tint and attributed to Joseph Flower whose pottery was established in 1743. In another series the enamel is stained yellow, but the effect is not very successful. Bristol enamel as a general rule was whitened by the addition of cobalt and displays an almost imperceptible tinge of blue.

Bristol decorations were rarely equal to those of Lambeth although undoubtedly far more skilful paintings were made, such as Joseph Flower's drawings in the style of line engravings. Painting technique, for the most part, betrays the meticulous care of the copyist or the work of painters hurrying against time. Symmetrical flowers are characteristic. Colours are chiefly in shades of cobalt blue: the blackish indigo tint dates from the mid-1750s when zaffre from English-made cobalt was sold at Bristol, probably continuing in use until 1770. Other colours include green, dull yellow, brownish orange and occasionally manganese purple and pale turquoise blue: early colours are softer than those of Lambeth.

Bianco-sopra-bianco, or white-over-white, is an attractive type of decoration that was fashionable from the mid-1740s. It was produced at Bristol, Lambeth and Liverpool. So far as Bristol is concerned the first examples are attributed to Joseph Flower's pottery. Against a ground of pale blue tin-enamel, known to the trade as bleu agate and sometimes converted to a pale greyish hue by overfiring, were painted scroll borders in an opaque enamel of intense whiteness made at a glass-house. In the centre might be painted a bird or other motif in colours.

Several Bristol decorators have been identified. The most important was Joseph Flower, who established a pottery at Redcliffe Back in 1743. He made "starch blue" and lavender plates with broad white flowers on the rims in the *bianco-sopra-bianco* manner, and centres of landscapes in blue or purple-blue, olive green and brownish orange. The same blue with borders of white flowers was used inside bowls containing ships in blue with touches of colour for such details as flags. Pountney, after examining a large number of *bianco-sopra-bianco* borders, concluded that the presence of a pomegranate in the design showed it to be from the hand of Joseph Flower. Flower's decorators produced easily-painted conical trees.

John Bowen, one of Flower's assistants, confined himself to painting in blue on white with great economy of brushwork, creating a style in which stately ladies and gentlemen strolled amid tall trees and houses. He also painted views with a river in the foreground, a building in the middle distance and mountains beyond. His ships are notable for their accuracy of detail.

1. (left to right) Puzzle jug and tyg both in earthenware covered with a dark brown lead glaze; the jug 6½ inches high, the tyg 2⅞ inches high. Baluster jug in buff earthenware partly glazed in green lead glaze, height 12¾ inches. Thirteenth or fourteenth century.

1a. Earthenware slip ware with trailed decoration: (left) dish inscribed on the rim "RALPH TOFT 1677", diameter 18 inches; (right) four-handled tyg, height 10⅛ inches.

John Niglett, probably a free-lance decorator from the early 1720s to the late 1760s, devised a colour scheme in mahogany red, blue, sage green and bright yellow, which was much in demand by potters. He favoured designs with a Chinese flavour. His patterns include various arrangements of "Long Lizas", boys, rocks and palisades, a crude adaptation of the K'ang H'si style. Michael Edkins, a later free-lance decorator, also favoured Chinoiserie, both in blue and in polychrome.

Tile-making was an important branch of work for tin-enamelled earthenware potters. Fireplace tiles abounded in hundreds of designs, but the majority of tiles were issued in the white for walls. Owen mentions two sets of nine tiles, each set painted with a dog and a cat as guardians of the hearth—the dog's collar being inscribed "Bristol 1752".

Wall pictures were also made, composed of 5-inch-square tiles arranged as close together as possible to form a square or oblong. These were painted singly to form an all-over design, and included landscapes, sea-views, birds, insects and formal arrangements of flowers in urns adapted from flower prints. Tile pictures made attractive house and trade signs. In Guildhall Museum is the sign of the "Cock and Bottle Tavern", Cannon Street, London. This is painted in blue with an old English game cock and a globe-and-shaft bottle covering twenty-four 5-inch tiles and enclosed in an elaborate scrollwork border $2\frac{1}{2}$ inches wide. One-piece tiles for setting in the chimney breast above the fireplace were made measuring a yard or more in width and a foot deep. The potting of perfectly flat panels of such dimensions in tin-enamelled earthenware would involve many difficulties in the eighteenth century. The number of wasters would make such a project costly.

Plates for wall and rack decoration were made at Bristol and at the other centres of the tin-enamelled earthenware trade until the nineteenth century. At first they were circular or oval with wide convex rims painted with oblique strokes in blue, as stylised rope work, prompting the twentieth-century name of "blue dash chargers". A plate for hanging on the wall may be distinguished by a flat ring on the back resembling a foot rim designed to take a suspending cord. The ring may be grooved for the cord, or pierced with two holes made by pushing round pegs of wood through the unfired clay: they burnt away in the course of firing, but prevented distortion of the holes. The pegs left fragments of displaced clay at the edge of each hole, a detail omitted from reproductions. Ornament included such motifs as portraits of monarchs in their coronation robes, ranging from Charles II in the Boscobel oak to George III, equestrian figures of military leaders, Biblical scenes, ships, windmills, trade guild coats of arms, inscriptions and flowers such as vigorously-painted groups of guelder roses, pinks and tulips. During the eighteenth century decorative plates figured on cupboard tops, on farmhouse dressers and those hanging shelves known as delf racks. These plates might be circular, octagonal or scalloped, with bouge and flat rim, the picture covering the entire ground. A feature found on Bristol plates is the cracked ice pattern dating to the 1770s. Tea-table wares were attempted late in the eighteenth century, but were clumsy and unpopular.

At Wincanton in Somerset a pottery was established in the late 1730s to specialise in tin-glazed earthenware. Nathaniel Ireson, brick maker and quarry owner, discovered suitable clays on his ground and took into partnership Thomas Lindslee from the Limekiln Lane Pottery, Bristol. Downman and Gunn when excavating the site unearthed a mass of perfect plates, a dozen in all, that had been discarded because they had run together in the kiln. It was thus proved that Wincanton ware is faintly pink coloured, and other fragments showed that the enamel was tinged with blue. A frequent characteristic is the large quantity of pinholes in the enamel, and wire marks. A decorative motif used during its last years was the spatterdash manganese ground between reserves. The pottery closed in 1748. In the Edinburgh Museum is a jug painted in blue with a Masonic coat of arms and the name Joseph Clewitt, a Wincanton mason whose tombstone is carved with an identical coat of arms.

It has not yet been determined with accuracy when tin-enamelled earthenware was first made in Liverpool, but it was probably early in Queen Anne's reign. A news paragraph in *The Post Boy*, 23rd May 1710, refers to the establishment of a new pottery in Liverpool for "fine white and painted pots and other vessels and tiles". The clay was brought by sea from Carrickfergus, Ireland, and produced a light buff body, but fragments excavated from pottery sites show that a pinkish body was also made. Productions resembled those of other centres with additional specialities of barrel mugs, jugs, char pots resembling wine coasters in shape with fish painted on the outer surfaces, and transfer-printed tiles.

These date from the late 1750s, and their production in a new style of decoration at less than half the price virtually ousted hand-painted English and Dutch tiles from the market. Many writers wrongly believe that tiles decorated by the transfer-printing process were first produced by John Sadler and Guy Green of Liverpool. It has not been observed by them that the *Journal of the House of Commons*, 1st November 1753, records a petition by Henry Delamain, a potter of tin-enamelled earthenware, Strand, Dublin, in which he stated that he had "perfected the Art of Printing Earthen Ware with as much Beauty, Strong Impression, and Dispatch as it can be done on paper". Delamain was at that time also a partner in the Battersea enamel works established earlier in that year and the first firm to develop and make successful use of the transfer-printing process. It seems reasonable to conjecture, in view of his petition, that Delamain was decorating tin-enamelled earthenware with transfer-printing, particularly as he resigned from the Battersea enterprise in 1754. Delamain died in 1757, and his wife continued as a successful potter until her death four years later. No example of Dublin printing is known.

Sadler & Green in Liverpool had meanwhile established a profitable business at the "Printed Ware Manufactory", Harrington Street, where a wide variety of goods were decorated. Designs were in various shades of black, red, brown, green and purple. The black varied from a rich full colour, sometimes tinged with purple, to a greenish grey hue brought about by inefficient firing. In some instances the transfer was over-painted in colours—yellow, blue and green in varying shades. The ware was then refired in a muffle kiln. Much tin-enamelled earthenware in the white, tiles in particular, was supplied to Green at this period by Zachariah Barnes, Old Haymarket, Liverpool. He issued hand-painted tiles decorated with butterflies, birds, flowers, landscapes, ships and so on in polychrome.

Liverpool punch bowls were highly regarded. Here were potted the giants, a most difficult technical feat in the eighteenth century. The obstacles in the way of making a 28-inch punch bowl, such as the famous one destroyed by German bombs, were immense, owing to the liability of collapse or distortion in the kiln. This specimen was exceptionally thick of fabric, the section at the bowl base measuring 1 inch, tapering to $\frac{3}{4}$ inch at the rim. The same potter was probably responsible for the famous punch bowl at "Ye Olde Cheshire Cheese" in Fleet Street, London, for the points of resemblance in both potting and decoration are numerous. This 23-inch diameter giant is decorated on the outside with a blue conventional floral design and on the inside with an infant Bacchus, vine leaves and bunches of grapes. The principal makers of punch bowls in Liverpool were Seth and John Pennington and Zachariah Barnes.

F. W. Hackwood, the Black Country historian, has recorded in *Wednesbury Workshops* the existence of two tin-enamelled earthenware potteries at Wednesbury, South Staffordshire. The pockets of local clays adjacent to the solid limestone hills of Sedgeley Beacon and Wren's Nest contain the essential calcium carbonate. Confirmation is found in an advertisement in *Aris's Birmingham Gazette*, 1748, offering for sale eight acres of land "whereon is erected a water-mill with two overshot wheels, 28 feet high, one part of which hath been used for grinding corn. . . . Also to be sold at the same time and place, a pair of millstones, two mills for grinding enamels and a dressing mill". The reference to the two mills for grinding enamels shows that a considerable quantity of enamel was prepared, more than would have been necessary for the newly-established enamel box trade. The glass was available at nearby Stourbridge. Local collectors possess examples of Wednesbury tin-enamelled earthenware.

Chapter Two

STONEWARE is an almost vitrified pottery composed of ordinary plastic clay and silica fired at a temperature so high that they become fritted into a hard substance. Clay possessing the necessary properties and containing silica in correct quantities was not universally available: the potting of stoneware therefore was confined to certain districts. Its partial vitrification ensured a closeness of texture that made it hard as stone—hence its name—and impervious to liquids. It will emit a ringing sound when struck and displays an almost glassy texture when fractured. Stoneware is usually coloured, as plastic clays contained impurities which caused them to burn to tints such as yellowish to dark brown, greyish or bluish, the exact hue depending upon the impurities and method of firing.

The ware was hardened and salt-glazed at a single firing, the finished surface until the 1840s resembling in texture the granular surface of an orange skin. This hard glaze was produced by throwing into the kiln common salt, which vaporised and settled in minute drops on the surface of the silica-rich stoneware, forming a film of transparent glaze that did not obliterate even the finest scratch. The brown surface colour of the glaze was produced by placing the pieces in the kiln as close together as possible without touching, a method known as "smothering".

Salt-glazed stoneware vessels were first imported into England from Germany in the early sixteenth century. They came under the name of Cologne ware because the Rhine valley potters sent their products to that town for marketing. A profitable trade was developed that eventually became a monopoly under the control of Garnet Tynes of Acon. In 1570 William Simpson of London applied to Queen Elizabeth for the transfer of this monopoly to give him the sole right to import "Cologne drinking stone pottes". In addition he contracted "to drawe the making of such like pottes into some decayed town within the realm, wherebie manie a hundred poor men may be sett at work". The annual licence fee was probably too high, for there is no evidence that he received the patent or that he potted salt-glazed stoneware.

Charles I granted two industrial patents for the manufacture of salt-glazed stoneware in England, but it is not known if, in fact, potteries were established. In 1626 Thomas Rous and Abraham Cullyn received a patent permitting them to "put in use the arte and feate of frameing, workeing, and makeing of all manner of potte, jugge, and bottelle, commonly called or knowne by the names of stone potte, stone jugge and stone bottelle". In 1635, five years before the expiry of the Rous-Cullyn patent, a further patent was granted to David Ramsey and Arnold Ayliff for "Makeinge and Dyeinge of all sortes of Panne Tyles, Stone Juggs, Bottles of all sizes . . . and other Earthen Commodities within this our Realme, which now are made by Straungers in Forraigne Partes".

Although it has not been established that salt-glazed stoneware was made in England until 1671, jugs exist with their rims deeply mounted in silver struck with Elizabethan hall-marks. Doctors of the period advocated the use of silver or silver-rimmed drinking vessels to escape the diseases then associated with promiscuous drinking from porous wood, earthenware and ·base metals. Museum authorities who have inspected these agree that the stoneware is of German origin. But William Burton, a practical stoneware potter, was of the opinion that shape, body and mottling of the glaze differ from those of the German and Flanders stoneware.

John Dwight (1640–1703) was the first potter proved to have made salt-glazed stoneware in England. Apparently educated for the Church, he left Christ Church College, Oxford, in June 1661, when he was appointed "registrar and scribe" to Brian Walton, Bishop of Chester. Dwight continued this work under successive bishops, finally under Bishop Hall who, in those days of plurality of livings, was also rector of Wigan where he resided. Dwight remained at Wigan during 1669–70 and then turned his energies towards becoming a master potter.

In April of the following year John Dwight, described as a gentleman, was granted a patent in his own name stating that he had discovered "the Mistery of Transparent Earthenware, commonly knowne by the Names of Porcelaine or China, and Persian Ware, as alsoe the mistery of the Stone Ware vulgarly called Cologne Ware; and that he designed to introduce a Manufacture of the said Wares into our Kingdome of England where they have not hitherto been wrought or made." A patent is a legal document, then costing over £300. It would not have been possible for such a patent to have passed the scrutiny of the Lord Chief Justice had the ceramics described formerly been potted in England. It is reasonable to assume, then, that earlier patentees had failed to market a saleable stoneware.

Dwight established a pottery at Fulham in 1671, possibly acquiring plant already in operation. That he was highly successful is proved by an *Indenture of Agreement* with the Glass Sellers' Company, dated 25th March 1676. Here Dwight is shown to be so associated with Windsor Sandys that they were undoubtedly in partnership: Sandys was probably the financing partner.

The Glass Sellers controlled design in the London pottery trade until early Georgian days. Sandys and Dwight were required not to deviate from Company "standards or patterns" as well as to comply with rules laid down regarding "stuff, size and workmanship". A Freeman of the Company was employed as an inspector at their London warehouse "to see that the same is properly done". All native-made ceramics passed through this warehouse before being sent to the London shops. In December 1676 Sandys and Dwight were assisted by a Company proclamation prohibiting the retail sale of foreign "painted earthenwares" —that is, painted delft and enamelled stonewares.

Dr. Robert Plot, the first keeper of the Ashmolean

Museum, wrote of his friend John Dwight in his *Natural History of Oxfordshire*, 1677: "that the ingenious John Dwight hath discovered the mystery of the stone or Cologne wares (such as d'Alva bottles, jugs, noggins) hereto fore made only in Germany, and by the Dutch brought over to England in great quantities; and hath set up a manufacture of the same, which (by methods and contrivances of his own altogether unlike those used by the Germans) in three or four years hath he brought it to greater perfection than it has attained where it has been used for many ages, insomuch as the Company of Glass Sellers of London, who are the dealers of that commodity, have contracted with the inventor to buy only of his English manufacture and refuse the foreign." Plot also recorded that Dwight "hath caused to be modelled statues or figures (a thing not done elsewhere, for China afford us only imperfect mouldings) which he hath diversified with great variety of colours, making them of the colour of iron, copper, brass, and patty-coloured as some achat stones."

Here then is proof that Dwight modelled figures of outstanding quality at least eight years before applying for a further patent, No. 234, granted in June 1684. The preamble of this more clearly classified the wares and articles for which protection was now petitioned: "Severall New Manufactures of Earthenwares, called by the Names of White Gorges, Marbled Porcelane Vessels, Statues, & Figures, & Fine Stone Gorges and Vessells, never before made in England or Elsewhere; and alsoe discovered the Mistery of Transparent Porcelane, & Opacous Redd, & Darke-coloured Porcelane or China and Persian Wares, & the Mistery of the Cologne or Stone Wares." Gorge was the old name for a pitcher in brown or white stoneware.

In 1693 Dwight began legal proceedings against several potters operating at Burslem, Nottingham and Fulham, charging them with infringement of his patent. This was the first action of its kind to be brought before the Courts. Sir Arthur Church discovered the documents relating to the case in the Public Record Office and published them in the *Burlington Magazine*, 1908. Here it is shown that John

Dwight and "his servants have for several years past made and sold" the stonewares listed in the preamble of the patent. "But having formerly hired one John Chandler of Fulham and employed him in the making . . . thereupon John Elers and David Elers (who are foreigners and by trade silversmiths) together with James Morley of Nottingham and also Aaron Wedgwood, Thomas Wedgwood and Richard Wedgwood of Berslem in the County of Stafford and Matthew Garner . . . did insinuate themselves into the acquaintance of the said John Chandler and inticed him to instruct them and to desert the complainant's service to enter into partnership together with them to make and sell the said wares, but far inferior to them. And the said confederates, the better to colour their said unjust and injurious practises, pretend that the earthenwares made and sold by them are in no way like those invented by the complainant but differ from them in form and figure and have several additions and improvements . . . whereas the truth is they are made in imitation of the complainant's wares."

Garner's answer shows that for eight years from 1680 he was apprenticed to Thomas Harper, Southwark, and that afterwards he invented a method of making salt-glazed brown stoneware pans and mugs. David Elers stated that he learned to make stonewares at Cologne and that in 1690 he and his brother began potting brown mugs and red teapots in England, employing John Chandler. Injunctions were granted on all counts.

These documents shed some light upon the Staffordshire potting industry in the early 1690s. They show that by 1693 red stoneware teapots were already being made there, as well as the fact that by 1690 brown stoneware glazed with salt was being made by the Wedgwoods at Overhouse, and by Garner.

Dwight's chief productions in cheap salt-glaze were hollow, thrown on the wheel, such as bowls, jugs, tankards, mugs and so on, as well as the well-known greybeards or bellarmines then made in their tens of thousands and now assiduously collected. This handled bottle had a spherical body tapering towards a round flat foot, its diameter measuring about that of the belly. The shoulder tapered upward to a narrow neck, its mouth strengthened with an encircling string rim. The narrow base and bulging body ensured that, with careful pouring, the sediment then common to alcoholic liquors was not dispersed through the drink. They were made in four stock sizes: the gallonier of one gallon capacity; the half gallon pottle pot; the pot holding a quart—these are "jugge pottes"—and the little pot containing a pint.

Below the string rim, on the concave curve of neck and shoulder, immediately opposite the handle, was applied the greybeard mask about one-third as long as the vessel itself. Below this, on commissioned work, was a coat of arms, crest, cypher, tavern or inn sign or other motif. Stock types displayed a variety of pseudo-arms, often associated with the monarchy and containing a cypher such as QE, JR or CR.

Many greybeards have elliptical markings or concentric circles or grooves on the base, usually starting at a fixed point near one edge and extending entirely across, caused by the twisted wire or cord used to cut the clay from the potter's wheel while it was slowly revolving after completion of throwing. Many, however, were afterwards thumbed smooth.

Greybeards or bellarmines, according to Chambers' *Book of Days*, 1863, were named after Cardinal Bellarmine (1542–1621) "during the religious feuds that raged in Holland during the sixteenth century. The protestant party originated a design for a drinking jug, in ridicule of Cardinal Bellarmine who had been sent to oppose in person, and by his pen, the progress of the reformed religion." Bellarmine was described as "short and hard featured", and thus he was typified by the corpulent beer jug. To make the resemblance greater, the cardinal's face, with the great square-cut beard then worn by ecclesiastics and known as "the cathedral beard", was placed in front of the jug. The name bellarmine was recorded by William Cartwright in his play, *The Armoury*, 1634:

"Or like a lager jug, that some men call
A Bellarmine . . . with beard episcopal,
Making the vessel look like tyrant Eglon!"

Greybeards were known also as d'Alvas, a name used by Dr. Plot and again by Evelyn in his *Diary*, 1697. Regarding the Duke of Alva (1515–89) he wrote: "there are a Thousand Pictures (not on medals only but on every Jugg-Pott & Tobacco-Box) shows a most malicious, stern aspect, fringed with a prolix and squalid Beard, which draws down his meagre and hollow Cheeks, Emblems of his Disposition." The Duke of Alva was a Spanish general associated with cruelties in endeavouring to secure the Low Countries for Spain. His government in Holland is reported to have put 18,000 citizens to death.

Importations of greybeards continued until the mid-1670s when John Dwight obtained his patent. He possibly licensed his process to provincial potters such as Symon Woolties (senior and junior) of Southampton. After expiry of the patent in 1698 salt-glazed stoneware bellarmines continued in production for more than two hundred years, the late examples having merely an outline of the greybeard impressed on the neck and shoulder or even omitted. Several Scottish potters made them throughout the nineteenth century: examples have been noted in production at a London pottery during recent years.

Surviving productions of Dwight's Fulham pottery are few indeed. Proof of their high technical and artistic excellence was provided by the outstanding examples preserved by the Dwight family as heirlooms until 1862. They were then sold to Mr. C. W. Reynolds, who lent them to the South Kensington Museum, now the Victoria and Albert Museum. In May 1871 they were sold at Christies, the twenty-seven lots including: "A life-size bust of James II [re-named Prince Rupert] with gold collar of the Order of the Garter, £39.18.0; Flowers, £14.0.0; a bust of Charles II, in large wig and lace necktie, £27.0.0; a bust of Lydia Dwight [daughter of the potter] lying on a couch, her head resting on a pillow, a broad lace band over her forehead, in her hands a bouquet of flowers, with an inscription 'Lydia Dwight, dyed March 3, 1672' £150."

The modelling of Dwight's remarkable bust of Prince Rupert, now in the British Museum, has been attributed to Grinling Gibbons. The style of carving, however, more resembles the hand of John Bushnell (1619–82) whose terra cotta bust of Charles II is in the Fitzwilliam Museum. Furthermore, Bushnell in 1675 carved the statue of Lord Mordaunt (*d.* 1675) at Fulham Parish Church, close to Dwight's pottery. Bushnell also carved a bust of Mrs. Pepys for St. Olaves Church, where it still remains: in the British Museum there is a somewhat similar portrait bust by Dwight in salt-glazed stoneware, believed to be Mrs. Pepys. It seems, then, that Bushnell rather than Gibbons modelled for Dwight.

In the Victoria and Albert Museum are two mugs attributed to Dwight and described as "pale buff stoneware with globular body, wide horizontally reeded neck and grooved loop handles. The mouth of each is mounted with a silver collar engraved with the initials 'SS' and the date 1682. Height, 3¾ inches". These jugs are translucent in places, justifying Dwight's claim to have succeeded in imitating the translucency of Chinese porcelain.

After John Dwight's death in 1703 the high standard of craftsmanship at the Fulham Pottery gradually deteriorated. By 1720 little more than heavy, coarse, brown and grey salt-glazed stonewares were made, such as domestic ware and drinking vessels plain or ornamented with sprigged reliefs and their upper parts coloured with a dark brown slip. The factory was operated by Dwight's descendants: first by his widow, then by his son Samuel who died in 1737 and was succeeded by his widow and son-in-law Thomas Warland in partnership. They were unsuccessful and became bankrupt in 1746. The pottery was then acquired by a Mr. White who married Mrs. Warland after the death of her husband. The White family ran the pottery until 1862.

When the Fulham Pottery was being enlarged in 1864 the demolition workmen unearthed a walled-up cellar containing stoneware ale pots, greybeards and so on. Burton described the collection as "most of them in the shape of common ale jugs or wine bottles, and so similar were they in material, shape and decoration to the pieces we know to have been imported from Cologne, that but for this we should have been in doubt if such stoneware was of English or German make. In addition to these were many round-bellied grey jugs, with scratched and stamped ornaments and patches of cobalt blue and manganese purple used as grounds. Several of the latter kind bore the cypher of an English sovereign, below a crown stamped on the front, and this gives us a definite place of origin for¸some of the well-known pieces of this description." Collectors should be warned that during the following ten years or so large quantities of similar salt-glaze ware were potted at Hohr, Germany, for the English market.

Other pottery districts were making salt-glazed stoneware by the end of the seventeenth century. James Morley, who had been indicted by Dwight for infringing his patent, continued its manufacture immediately after the patent expired in 1698. *The Annals of Nottinghamshire*, 1757, refer to this poetry:

> "Mr. Morley was a manufacturer of brown earthenware, carrying on his works in the lower part of Beck Street, and by this business he amassed a considerable fortune. This ware was at one time of great celebrity throughout the whole of the Midland Counties, especially its famous brown mugs for the use of public houses: and the appellation of Nottingham ware is still in many villages attached to the better and more highly finished class of every description of salt-glazed pots."

Nottingham ware quality was not by any means a thing of the past at this time, for a century later the London merchants preferred to market Derby salt-glazed pottery under the term "Nottingham Ware".

The typical salt-glazed stoneware made by the Morleys was in shades of bright russet-brown with a slightly metallic lustre produced by a wash of ferruginous slip, often containing blackish specks of glistening oxide of iron. The ware was potted more thinly than was usual among competing potters, being turned on the wheel after throwing. This turning, followed by a finishing process, was responsible for its unusual smoothness of surface. Morley's salt-glazed stoneware is much less mottled and granular than that of other contemporaneous potters. Decorations included incised designs of formal flowers with inscriptions which might also be carried out in a darker brown or by a "resist" process in which the design appeared in a lighter colour than the ground. Other decorations show use of the roulette; simple stamped designs composed of geometrical motifs; encircling bands roughened with fragments of rough clay; double and triple incised bands; outlines of flowers and foliage; and, more rarely, moulded patterns and applied reliefs. Morley was also responsible for introducing to stoneware a style of decoration cut through the outer layer of a double-walled vessel such as a jug or teapot, by a process known as carving. The carved stoneware was made in two parts consisting of an inner vessel and the more globular envelope which was pierced to give an effect of lightness to the heavy stoneware. In some instances the pattern was hand-carved into the outer surface and not saw-cut. Many remaining pieces of salt-glazed stoneware attributed to Nottingham are dated: some are inscribed "Made at Nottingham" with the day, month and year.

Early in the eighteenth century James Morley issued an engraved trade card illustrating six examples of his salt-glazed stoneware: a cylindrical "Mogg" or mug encircled with wide bands composed of incised lines; a beak-spouted jug named "a Decantor"; an urn-shaped flower pot with square plinth, a pair of snake handles, applied swags of leaves and flowers encircling the upper part, and with the rounded base carved; a globular teapot with carved body and cover; a carved jug; and a "capuchine", that is, a drinking vessel which when inverted suggested the shape of a woman's capuchine cloak and hood. Beneath these sketches an inscription states "Such as have Occation for these Sorts of Pots commonly called Stone-Ware, or for such as are of any other Shape not here Represented may be furnished wth them by the Maker James Morley at ye Pot-House, Nottingham." A copy of this trade card is preserved in the Bodleian Library, Oxford.

James Morley was succeeded as owner of the pottery by Charles Morley, a Sheriff of Nottingham in 1737. Because the staple production consisted of cylindrical mugs, the pottery was known as "the Mug-House" and the address Mug-House Lane. Vendors of Nottingham stoneware sold also large bowls, tobacco jars, puzzle and bear mugs, and would hammer a piece against the counter boards to prove its strength. There were in London several retail shops trading as "Nottingham Warehouses" such as William and David Melvill, Wood Street. Manufacture ceased early in the nineteenth century.

The manufacture of brown salt-glazed stoneware extended in London in the Fulham and Lambeth districts: the white salt-glaze trade established itself almost exclusively in Staffordshire (see Chapter 3). John Rocque's map of London, prepared during the 1740s, marks several pot works along the banks of the Thames. Mortimer's *Director*, 1763, lists "the only potters in or near London" to the number of twelve, including six "brown stone potters" and excluding reference to the porcelain factories operating at Chelsea and Bow. It is emphasised that "the following are the real manufacturers of the blue and white and plain white earthenwares [tin enamelled] except those that are distinguished as Brown Stone Potters who make only jars, jugs, mugs, etc., and do not undertake any part of the white branch." The "brown stone potters" were John Jones, and Henry White, Lambeth; William White, Fulham; Samuel Swabey, and Sanders & Richards, Vauxhall; William Sanders, Mortlake.

Chesterfield brown stoneware, made in Derbyshire since the mid-eighteenth century and extending over the district including Denby and Brampton, is still in production. At first there was little to choose between Chesterfield and other brown stoneware except for the most costly Nottingham ware. A writer passing through Chesterfield in 1772 remarked: "it is a large town, but I saw nothing uncommon but the ugly church; it is old and built of bad stone, but rendered most disgusting by its wooden spire (covered with lead) being so much warped that I discovered its crookedness at three miles distance. In the town is a manufacture of pots." Pilkington, writing in 1789, refers to coarse brown stoneware being made at three potteries employing sixty hands. Forty years later Sir Richard Phillips recorded that the Chesterfield stoneware potteries then employed "about 200 persons at wages from 10/- to 13/- per week, and for better workmen, from 18/- to 25/-. The description of manufacture is exclusively brown ware, except in one instance, which includes black also. The number of potteries is ten."

The quality of Derbyshire salt-glazed stoneware remained unaltered until November 1823 when Joseph Bourne of Denby was granted a patent for an improved stoneware kiln, twice the height of ordinary kilns. The resulting ware was harder, more compact, with a more durable glaze and also much less costly to fire. Bourne was granted a further patent in August 1847 and this entirely revolutionised salt-glaze kiln technique. The specification shows that two kilns were built, one above the other, the "lower one being heated at two levels, at bottom and half way up. Heat from the lower kiln passes into the upper. Instead of five flues as in the old designs there is only a single chimney at the top." Three qualities of brown stoneware could be fired in these kilns. It is possible for experienced collectors to distinguish these qualities from stoneware made under the previous patent, and this from earlier ware.

The variety of wares made in Chesterfield brown stoneware were soon in great demand. Among other things, collectors may find the following: hunting, game, cottage, tulip and other jugs; figured Stilton cheese stands; fruit dishes and trays; tea and coffee pots; tobacco jars, often with goblet and candlestick; Toby jugs; figures of stags and dogs; grotesque and twisted pipes; moulds for puddings, blanc-manges, jellies; puzzle jugs. Many of these are in so-called "antique" forms copying exactly the ware made a century and a half earlier. Only by inspection of the ceramic itself is it possible to attribute the period, unless it is marked.

Puzzle jugs or tavern teasing pitchers were made in forms unaltered from those of the eighteenth century, complete with inscriptions and dates. The problems posed by puzzle jugs were as old as the hills, but the need for skill of hand and eye most entertainingly remained. It must be emphasised that their "puzzle" was familiar to anyone. The problem was to empty the pitcher without removing it from the mouth or spilling a drop of liquor. Many a jug even bears a legend stressing this, but the puzzle theory dies hard.

The most usual design had a bulbous or baluster-shaped body and a long vertical neck decorated with perforations. Circular piercings might be placed to form a date and initials: such vessels, obviously, were made to commission.

The majority, however, were pierced with geometric motifs such as hearts, diamonds, stars, crescents and semi-circles arranged in formal designs or haphazardly. Some were patterned with overlapping circles or vertical pales. Height normally ranged between seven and eight inches, but there were 10-inch giants and 5-inch dwarfs.

The mechanical principle of teasing pitchers was unvarying. Obviously neck perforations made drinking in the normal way impossible. The brim appeared to be strengthened with plain convex moulding, but in fact this was a hollow tube that passed down through the length of the handle and inside the vessel to within half an inch of the base. All liquor drunk from the jug had to be drawn up this tube. The mouthpiece was a horizontal nozzle projecting from the tube at the brim. But this alone would make the task too easy, so the teasing pitcher had at least three projecting nozzles around the brim, one for the drinker's lips and the rest to be sealed by his fingers. As yet another contribution to his discomfiture he also found a hole in the undercurve of the handle and this, too, he had to close. With care he could seal it with the hand that raised the jug, leaving the other hand for closing the unwanted nozzles. In this uncomfortable posture he would suck the liquid through the narrow tube into his mouth. The task was difficult for momentary distraction might cause a finger to loosen and the liquor to spill.

From the 1760s the brim tube with its nozzles began to be placed half an inch or so below the rim proper, but the original type also continued until the 1790s. Early in the nineteenth century this encircling tube was placed about half-way down the neck, with perforations above and below. There was an early Georgian series of teasing pitchers without nozzles from which it was impossible to drink, much to the bewildered victim's chagrin. In another series the problem was made more confusing by fitting as many as eight nozzles, but in fact all but one were sealed at the brim entrance.

The Chesterfield potters made these jugs in their original form, but more meticulously potted in a harder brown stoneware more smoothly salt-glazed under the 1847 patent.

41

The nozzle tube was placed centrally around the neck. The bulbous body might be plain, incised with pseudo-eighteenth-century inscriptions and dates, or ornamented with simple scenes and figures in relief. The makers overlooked the important detail of the nozzles' position on the neck.

Teasing pitchers will also be found in tin-enamelled earthenware, cream-coloured earthenware, pearl ware and terracotta painted with a peculiar mottled effect. Thomas Oldfield of Brampton made them in stoneware dipped in slips of various colours.

Impressed marks found on Chesterfield brown stoneware indicate nineteenth-century origin. Each pottery used several styles, incorporating the proprietor's name and include:—BOURNE, Bourne & Son, Denby; BRIDDON, William Briddon, Brampton; BURTON, William Burton, Codnor Park; KNOWLES, the Welshpool and Payne Potteries, Brampton; OLDFIELD, John Oldfield & Co, Brampton.

Salt-glazed brown stoneware appears to have been made in Bristol as early as 1735 by John Townsend, a mug-maker of Tucker Street. The dense clouds of dark vapour emitted by his kiln when firing were considered a nuisance and the Corporation, owners of the land, ordered him to cease potting in December 1738. The kiln had cost him £130 and he demanded compensation from the Corporation.

Brown stoneware was again in production during the third quarter of the eighteenth century, the chief manufactures being public house mugs and jugs made to measure (see page 44) and domestic ware. The impressed mark PATIENCE is probably that of Thomas Patience (*d.* 1785) of Temple Street, and ALSOP might be James Alsop senior, Temple Street, or James Alsop junior, Thomas Street. Antony Amatt made strong salt-glazed stoneware of the public house variety early in the nineteenth century. His bill heading for 1813 describes him as "Iron Stoneware Manufacturer, Crew's Hole, Bristol".

Bristol salt-glazed stoneware achieved no widespread repute although the quality of ceramic was extremely hard and durable. Complaints were frequent regarding imperfections of glazing, such as incompletely fused salt tainting the contents of vessels. Inspection of the interior of a broken vessel will disclose innumerable tiny flaws and possibly some fire cracks. In one recently excavated specimen a single fire crack extended $\frac{1}{32}$-inch into a $\frac{1}{2}$-inch section and measured 1 inch in length, obvious harbourage for dirt and germs.

William Powell of Temple Gate Pottery experimented with new methods and in February 1835 he invented a leadless glaze impervious to the action of any liquid likely to come in contact with it. The appearance of the ware was also greatly improved, surfaces now being even of texture, uniform in colour and easier to clean. From 1835 Powell's entry in the *Bristol Directory* reads "Powell, W^m, Temple Gate. Inventor and sole manufacturer of stoneware which is glazed inside and out with a glaze warranted to resist acids, and not to absorb." The green stoneware was double slip glazed, that is, the upper part of the unfired vessel was dipped into a liquid glaze which matured to a rich creamy or brown colour when fired: then, when dry enough for handling, the lower part was dipped into another glaze which fired to a creamy yellow. Variations of tint could be obtained. The dippers were skilful in making the two glazes overlap exactly the right amount, but collectors will notice from time to time an unglazed space between them. The firing matured the colours and in that process the ochre or brown flowed over the yellow. The heat of the kiln produced a rich glaze over the slips.

Stoneware glazed in this way became known to the trade as "Bristol Ware". The recipe remained a secret and stoneware potters in other districts, such as Henry Doulton and James Stiff of Lambeth, were compelled to buy "Bristol Stoneware Glaze" from Joseph and James White of Bristol. According to J. F. Blacker, Henry Doulton did not produce a comparable glaze until 1866.

Bristol glazed stoneware tobacco jars have been noted impressed with the name POWELLS BRISTOL and the registration symbol for 6th March 1849. The surface of such a vessel was encircled with subjects in high relief made lifelike by painting in full colour. These often depicted a scene of huntsmen and hounds chasing their quarry, with other relief subjects of trees, windmills, beehives, men seated smoking or drinking, or in groups walking. This appears to have been the first successful use of colour on brown stoneware.

Although Bristol glaze largely superseded ordinary salt-glaze for domestic ware, the old brown stoneware continued in production. J. & C. Price & Brothers, for instance, issued a range of productions resembling those of Chesterfield (see page 40) including the so-called "antique" patterns.

Brown stoneware drinking mugs and serving jugs for use in taverns, inns and ale houses were in great demand, being difficult to fracture. Customers assumed them to be of correct capacity when filled to the brim: liquors were rarely sold from a separate measure. This led to abuses at which the stoneware potters connived by making short-measure mugs. The account books kept during the early 1780s by Joseph Ring of Bristol who advertised in 1785 that "The Brown Stone Manufactory is carried on as usual", show that pint mugs were usually ordered to be made "two tablespoons under the full"—hence the potters' term of "made to measure" or "Birmingham measure". There are numerous records of such short-measure requests, such as that by a Shrewsbury innkeeper who wanted "4 dozen quart cider mugs to hold three half-pints each when full". So that the deficit should not at once be apparent such mugs were made with a recess beneath. In 1824, however, an Act of Parliament brought into operation the imperial system of weights and measures.

Chapter Three

ORIENTAL porcelains, massed in colourful display, were very much to the liking of late seventeenth-century Englishmen, already fascinated by Far Eastern splendours. William III and his Dutch supporters, accustomed to flamboyant ornament, found an enthusiast in Mary II, who set the seal of royal approval upon the collection of blue and white wares; and when Daniel Marot was appointed court architect in the 1690s he designed rooms to be dominated by costly porcelain bowls, vases, bottles, figures, cups and saucers. Vases were displayed on ledges above doorways and along cornices; walls were hung with carved and gilded brackets supporting more vessels and figures; chimney pieces were virtually concealed behind shelves and brackets magnificent with these wares. One of Marot's drawings represents a "Chinese cabinet" in which three hundred porcelain vases and plates decorate the chimney piece, hearth and door ledges. The craze eventually became a mania, and the china-sellers' warehouses in London were likened to Eastern bazaars.

English potters were jealous of this success and used their limited resources to produce less expensive ceramics of comparable quality. In this they were entirely unsuccessful until the mid-eighteenth century when the Bow, Chelsea, Derby and Worcester porcelain factories were operating.

Meanwhile, however, the Staffordshire potters developed white salt-glazed stoneware. This was the first refined earthenware evolved in England and was potted principally in Burslem: it was never made successfully abroad and vast quantities were exported. Its fine texture permitted a vigorous design and clear-cut relief ornament well calculated to appeal to a public long dominated by the silversmith. Manufacture continued uninterruptedly until the early 1780s.

The early English salt-glazed stoneware was either grey or drab, and was known to its Staffordshire potters as crouch ware. Several unconvincing reasons for this name have been inferred, but in fact at Kreussen, in the Cologne district of Germany, tall jugs in grey salt-glazed stoneware with applied relief decorations were known as "cruches" and imported into England under this name. When similar jugs were made in Staffordshire the dialect converted the German cruche into "crouch", and when other articles were made of the same material they became known under the generic term of crouch ware.

A hitherto unnoticed definition of crouch ware was published in 1846 by William Evans in *The Art & History of the Pottery Business*. Here Evans declared that crouch ware was "a kind of ware made in Burslem by mixing the marl, where the coal bussets or crops out, with the finely pulverised millstone grit of the moorland ridge. This is the *Crouch Ware*, which when glazed with salt appears compact, clean and durable; and at this day [the 1840s] the thin pieces, by vitrescence rendered semi-transparent, excite surprise that they failed to suggest the manufacture of porcelain." Professor Church in 1884 expressed the opinion that crouch ware would have ranked as porcelain "if a little alkali had entered into its composition: in chemical nature and physical texture alike it would have been a veritable hard porcelain."

The progressive improvements of the grey crouch ware to white salt-glazed stoneware have been traditionally credited to Robert Astbury, Shelton (1678–1743). Josiah Wedgwood compiled a list of forty-three potters operating in Burslem between 1710 and 1715: five of these were potting stoneware, probably grey crouch ware. This he described as "glazing our common clay with salt, which produced Pot'd Grey or Stone Ware". Robert Astbury probably established himself as a master potter between 1715 and 1718. In an endeavour to whiten the crouch ware he covered its surface with an engobe or dip made of fine white pipe clay from Bideford in Devonshire, in much the same way that tin enamel concealed the coarse body of delft ware.

In about 1720 he hardened the body by incorporating white sand from near-by Baddeley Edge and Mow Cop. At some time during the early 1720s he made the important discovery that by substituting pulverised calcined flints he both hardened and whitened the ware throughout its texture and greatly reduced warping hazards in the kiln. This stoneware, in a dull tint known to collectors as "drab", was so translucent when thin that it was sold by many china dealers as porcelain.

Flint-grinding had been established as an industrial process as early as the 1680s in connection with the flint-glass trade in London, South Staffordshire and Tyneside, where earthenware potters were already established. The quantity needed by the glassmen had prompted John Tyzacke of Brierley Hill, Staffordshire, to patent in 1691 a horse-powered flint-grinding mill. The cost of a patent at that time exceeded £300, proof that demand was large. This mill consisted of two stones moving upon a marble bottom edged with sloping boards to retain the flint powder. This was sifted to flour-fineness through a buckram bag shaped like a sleeve. John Houghton in *A Collection of Letters for the Improvement of Husbandry and Trade*, 1696, described the sifting of the powder as "convenient for the workman, 'tis done in a close bin, with only two holes for him to put his arms in and shake the bag about: what-so-ever material is not small enough to sift through is brought again to the mill to be new ground." With the discovery in the late 1690s of suitable sand for flint-glass at Maidstone and the Isle of Wight, the glass-men gradually abandoned the more costly calcined flint.

The flint-grinding trade continued, however, and it seems reasonable to assume that one of the grinders, perhaps Tyzacke, brought this silica to the notice of potters. Josiah Wedgwood, writing in 1777, attributed the introduction of calcined flint to Thomas Heath of Shelton. James Brindley, the celebrated engineer, was commissioned by

John Wedgwood to design and erect a windmill for grinding calcined flints. The cost may have seemed prodigious to the potters in comparison with sand, and experiments appear to have been delayed until the early 1720s.

An improved flint-grinding mill was patented in 1732 by Thomas Benson, indicating increased demand. This flint-mill has survived to the present day. A vertical shaft causes four radiating arms to revolve in a circular pan with a hard stone bottom of chert. This pan contains water and blocks of chert which are pushed around by the arms and grind the flint to a cream. Flint-grinding gradually became a well-established industry with many mills operating in Staffordshire. The proportion of ground flint used in stoneware amounted to about 25 per cent of the formula.

Drab coloured salt-glazed stoneware shaped on the potter's wheel might be decorated with pads of white pipe clay impressed with relief ornament by means of gunmetal stamps. By 1730 this white relief ornament, known as sprigging, also took the form of encircling sprays of vine, the leaves being shaped by stamping, and the stems and tendrils hand-coiled from strips of clay. The potters who applied this ornament were known as "viners", a specialist branch of the Staffordshire pottery industry. The hiring and account books of Thomas Whieldon for 1749 shows that on 4th February he engaged Thomas Dutton as a viner for 6s. 6d. a week, and on 20th February he "hired Wm Cope for handleing and vining cast ware" for 7s. weekly.

Astbury's final improvement was made in the early 1730s, producing stoneware with a whiter body: this discovery gave half a century of high prosperity to about eighty Staffordshire master potters. He discarded local marl in favour of Devonshire pipe clay, thus obtaining increased plasticity and improved vitreous properties, particularly when weathered for a few months before use. This clay was eventually transported to the Potteries in the form of balls—hence the familiar term of ball clay.

Transport difficulties were the subject of a petition sent to the Government by the Staffordshire potters, in which the condition of the industry was outlined in 1762. Here it was stated that:

2. Staffordshire earthenware (left to right): jug with sprigged decoration, height 4 inches; greyhound figure, height 4 inches; tobacco pipe, length 6½ inches; teapot decorated with mingled colour glazes, height 4 inches, about 1750; sugar basin and cover in agate ware, height 4¾ inches, about 1745.

2a. Tin enamelled earthenware: (left) blue dash charger painted in colours and dated 1676, diameter 12¾ inches; (right) white serving bottle inscribed in cobalt blue "CLARIT 1647" height 4⅝ inches.

"In Burslem and its neighbourhood are near 500 separate potteries for making various kinds of stone and earthenware, which find constant employment and support for near 7,000 people. The ware of these potteries is exported in vast quantities from Liverpool, Bristol, Hull etc., to our several colonies in America and the West Indies, as well as almost every port in Europe. Great quantities of flint stones are used in making some of the ware, which are brought by sea from various parts of the coast to Liverpool and Hull; and the clay for making the white ware is brought from Devonshire and Cornwall chiefly to London, the materials from whence are brought by water up the rivers Mersey and Weaver to Winsford in Cheshire; those from Hull up the Trent to Willington; and from Winsford and Willington the whole are brought by land carriage to Burslem. The ware, when made, is conveyed to Liverpool and Hull in the same manner.

"Many thousand tons of shipping are employed in carrying materials for the Burslem ware; and as much salt is consumed in glazing one species of it as pays annually near £5,000 duty to Government. Add to these considerations the prodigious quantity of coal used in the Pottery . . . and it will appear that the trade flourishes so much as to have increased two-thirds within the last 14 years."

The hard, translucent non-porous salt glaze was imposed over the surface of stoneware by the action of sodium chloride (common salt) upon the red-hot surface of the clay. The salt glaze formed better and more thickly upon clay rich in silica—hence the improved glazing that followed the introduction of calcined flints. The shaped ware was enclosed in clay saggars perforated with large holes, piled one upon the other in a specially designed kiln. When the ware was red hot the draught was reduced and salt thrown through fire holes on to the glowing fuel. It was suddenly introduced at the moment of peak temperature, immediately before full vitrification occurred. This was done several times at half hourly intervals: two pounds of salt glazed one ton of stoneware. The perforations in the saggars permitted the fumes from the volatilised salt to reach the stoneware when chemical changes occurred, causing a fine coating of silicate of soda and alumina to be deposited over the surface of the ware. When cold this appeared as a thin, intensely hard film of soda glass fused to the stoneware.

Brilliant when new and of long durability, salt glaze is characterised by its "orange skin" surface, minute pinholes or granulations giving a roughness unsuited to the everyday use of cups, plates and dishes. Wide variations of "grain" are found, even on different parts of a single piece. These could be avoided from the 1750s by smearing the stoneware with red lead before introducing the ware into the oven. This glaze was softer, but thicker and smoother, and could be used for drinking vessels.

White salt-glazed stoneware tea ware was being made by the 1740s, thin, light and translucent, comparing favourably in hardness with Chinese porcelain. Although making no pretence to reach the high standard of the far more costly oriental productions, it appealed to the not-so-rich.

Stoneware might be shaped on the potter's wheel or by hand-pressing or by moulding or casting. Crouch ware was thrown on the old type of potter's wheel outmoded in the 1730s by a Burslem workman named Alsager, whose invention greatly speeded production. In the old type the stoneware vessel was cut from the circular table by a coarse twisted wire or cord passed beneath, while slowly revolving. This caused the series of grooved concentric circles covering the base, their axis usually near one edge. Such marks are present on early Staffordshire salt-glazed stoneware.

The thrown ware in white salt-glaze was marketed for the most part without ornament: in other cases pads hand-stamped with relief ornament were applied.

The walls of white salt-glazed stoneware in certain small sizes could be made as thin and delicate as porcelain by hand-pressing. A thin bat of plastic clay was placed over a well-oiled brass or copper mould, plain or sunk with an intaglio design. An upper mould of similar shape but without a pattern was placed over this and the two moulds squeezed sharply together. The clay was shaped and decorated by a single blow. In this way vast numbers of small objects such as jelly moulds, trays, sweetmeat and pickle saucers, plates, cups and spoons were made as thin as porcelain and almost as white, but with ornament in sharper relief. In the Hanley Museum is a brass mould used for a cup bowl together with a white salt-glazed cup made from the mould. This is about 25 per cent smaller than the mould, demonstrating the great contraction that occurred during firing in the kiln.

A more vigorous method of shaping and decorating than by throwing on the wheel, followed by laborious sprigging and vining or by hand-pressing, was evolved in the 1730s by carving a master mould from a block of alabaster, a soft type of gypsum plentiful in Derbyshire. Moulds, known to the Staffordshire potters as blocks, consisted of several pieces: oval vessels were made in two sections; round hollow-ware in three; square in four sections for the sides with extra moulds for base, top and lid. Intaglio patterns successfully cut in these moulds covered a limited range, most of them adapted from contemporary domestic silver such as scallop shells, foliage, flutings, volutes, diapers and frets. Instead of being concealed the section joints were incorporated into the designs, for example forming borders to the panels composing the design.

These sections were joined and from them was made a further mould in porous clay or terra cotta pressed into the alabaster block, dried and fired: this was known as the pitcher. Worn pitchers could be replaced from the alabaster blocks as often as required.

Probably the most highly skilled block cutters were the brothers Ralph and Aaron Wood of Burslem, whose work was in great demand by all the leading potters of white glazed stoneware. In the Victoria and Albert Museum are stored moulds intended for white stoneware, some of them from the private museum of Aaron's son Enoch Wood. Among these is a sharply cut cup mould with a cup taken from it. A cream jug mould is incised with the initials of Ralph Wood and the date 1749 on three flat spaces where they would be concealed by the addition of tripod feet. This suggests that in the fabric of some white salt-glaze ware may be hidden the date of the mould, the earliest year in which the piece would have been made. The ware could be either pressed by hand or cast in the pitcher which was, of course, slightly smaller than the original model, but otherwise identical, with the relief ornament sharply moulded.

The final step in casting dates from the mid-1740s when Ralph Daniel of Cobridge introduced from France, where he had been working, the use of plaster of paris moulds and wax models which quickly replaced block and pitcher.

Notching ensured that the various parts of the plaster moulds locked into each other. Slip or liquid clay was poured into the dry mould until it was filled. The slip included a percentage of grog, that is, finely ground earthenware wasters which lessened the shrinkage of the body in the forms.

The mould immediately began absorbing moisture from the slip. After standing for a few minutes a sufficient thickness of clay adhered to the mould interior. Surplus slip was then poured away leaving behind a clay shell. This was set aside to dry. In drying the clay contracted, permitting the shaped piece to be lifted out, carefully cleaned, the seam marks smoothed and relief ornament tooled where required. After every fifty castings the plaster moulds required scraping to remove a deposit which formed on the casting surface. Impressions from plaster moulds were less sharp than those from pitcher moulds as continuous use blunted the relief work.

There was a considerable production of teapots in shapes resembling animals, favourites being camel, squirrel, bear and cat. A long series represented houses, and their wide range of patterns forms a collector's byway. They were all in white and never enamelled, although made until the 1780s. They are almost square or oblong on plan with rounded corners.

These teapots are usually made with two different façades and are double-fronted, suggesting three-storeyed dwellings with six windows on each side of the doorway. Others suggest two storeys on one side and three on the other. The spout may be in the form of an animal's or bird's neck and head, with a human arm and hand clasping it on the upper surface and masks and dolphins below. In other instances the spout has a raised female figure riding astride. The head on the spout is matched on the knob of the lid. Handles are of four types: plain, crabstock, snake and lizard.

Early Staffordshire salt-glazed stoneware, shaped on the potter's wheel, might be given additional interest with colour. Patterns, the majority flowers and foliage with inscriptions, names and dates, were cut into green ware with a sharp point operated by a woman known as a "flowerer".

These lines were accentuated with cobalt-stained clay slip, or by powdered zaffre dusted into the incisions before firing. When stoneware emerged from the salt-glaze oven the incisions showed dark blue fading off into a lighter blue, the remainder of the surface being drab or white. The rims of hollow-ware might be encircled with bands of rough cross hatching in blue. The result was crude but greatly in demand, being advertised as late as the early 1760s. To collectors this decoration is known as "scratch blue".

A handsome and now rare type of decoration on white salt-glazed stoneware was evolved by William Littler of Longton during the late 1740s and continued in production during his period of porcelain manufacture until about 1760. This was a coating of rich brilliant blue. The green ware was dipped into a carefully lawned slip coloured blue with costly smalt. This improved the smoothness of the surface and when salt-glazed the slip matured to a deep opaque blue. Simeon Shaw misinterpreted the process used, indicating that the blue slip was in fact a glaze. On the strength of this various authorities have wrongly attributed to Littler the introduction of liquid glaze.

This blue slip was also used on some relief work from which it acquired additional beauty through tint variations. Although the blue usually remained unadorned, examples are known enriched with designs such as peony flowers and foliage in oil gilding, and others enamelled in black and opaque white.

Two Dutch enamellers, William Horlogius and Anthony George Van De Schalk (d. 1778), in about 1750 established the first independent enamelling workshop for decorating white salt-glazed stoneware in bright colours in the manner of oriental porcelain. The site selected for their workshops was at Hot Lane, now Cobridge, remote from any pottery and where they thought to work in secrecy. Here they founded what became an important branch of the Staffordshire pottery industry. Enamelled salt-glaze incorporating a slaty blue colour has been ascribed to the Dutchmen.

The first Staffordshire potter to compete was Ralph Daniel who eventually attracted a few experienced porcelain decorators from Chelsea, Derby and Worcester. The enamelling processes could not long be kept secret and gradually Hot Lane became the centre of a prosperous decorating industry. John and Ann Warburton were among the most successful of the Hot Lane enamellers and decorated for Josiah Wedgwood during his early years at Ivy House, Burslem. The enamellers' craft soon spread, for in 1760 Robinson and Rhodes, Leeds, advertised that they enamelled "stoneware which they sell as cheap as in Staffordshire".

The on-glaze enamels contained a large proportion of flux, so that after painting the ware needed only to be raised to a clear red heat in the muffle kiln to fuse the colours firmly upon the salt glaze. When they were thickly applied the granulated surface of the salt-glaze enhanced their brilliance by a mass of added reflections. In some instances the greater part of the salt-glaze was covered with a single ground colour, either red, turquoise or gold-purple. Reserves were left for patterns such as posies in red, yellow and various shades of green, all maturing at a single firing. Examples have been noted in which the palette has been enlarged by the use of colours requiring additional firings in the muffle kiln. Colours were less gaudy than on Chinese porcelain, but entirely suited for inexpensive wares. Relief work was skilfully decorated with fine lines of red and blue, sometimes enhanced with touches of other colours. As the Staffordshire enamellers became more accomplished they used less and less of the costly enamels by laying them on more thinly.

Salt-glazed figures, until the introduction of casting, were modelled in various anatomical sections by rolling, cutting and pinching the clay. For instance, above the waist a woman was shaped from an almost plain solid cylinder formed by rolling clay between the palms of the hands. The upper end was shaped into a neck and a ball of clay rolled and modelled into a head. Arms were then attached, their flattened ends tooled to represent hands and fingers. This figure was then dressed, the garments being cut from clay rolled into flat sheets which eventually fired to about $\frac{1}{16}$-inch thick. Black ruffs were wrapped around forearms and wrists to give the illusion of sleeves. No legs were hidden beneath the billowing skirt, composed of alternating strips of black and white clay, the surfaces of the white stripes being decorated with milled lines. Over this elaborate skirt was placed a long, plain white apron, then high fashion wear. The potter completed the ensemble by fitting a pleated cap. Eyes, necklace and other dots were of black or dark brown slip.

Men were more completely modelled than the women, their dress enveloping them less thoroughly. Clothing was fitted over a skeleton core in the same way as the woman's. Boldly curved ringlets of narrow strips of clay were attached to the head which might wear a tricorn hat. Stained clay was used for the hat, neck ribbons, cuffs and shoes, whilst the edges of the hat brim and shoe buckles remained white. The man might hold a musical instrument such as bag-pipes or fiddle. Such figures fashioned singly are usually attributed to the 1730s, but technical details show many to belong to the 1740s.

Salt-glazed figures of this type are found in the so-called pew groups, the solid, high-backed settle forming a convenient background for the seated figures, consisting of one or two men and a woman. The settles sometimes resemble church pews, but no religious significance is to be inferred. Themes vary, love and music being the most frequent. The back of the settle might be decorated with a simple cut-out design composed of spades, circles and a heart. Solon in his *Art of the English Potter* states that these cut-out motifs imitated a German style of decoration in brown salt-glazed stoneware, and were popular in England during the second quarter of the eighteenth century. The backs of some pew groups were decorated with a design in scratch blue: none has been noted decorated with enamels.

Collectors expect to find in Staffordshire salt-glazed stoneware figurines such as the Dog of Foo, hawks and monkeys and tiny manikins adapted from Chinese porcelain, as well as a variety of birds, such as peacocks and barnyard fowls. Other models included such domestic animals as horses, dogs, cows, swans, sheep, rabbits with eyes and other details in brown or blue. Small arbour groups may be noted, and figures depicting craftsmen, huntsmen and the equestrian pieces known to collectors as mounted hussars.

In the Marian Wood collection of Staffordshire figures in the Hanley Museum are two mounted hussars, one in white salt-glazed stoneware, the other in lead-glazed earthenware, so nearly alike that they both must have been issued by the same potter. Further evidence of such a practice was discovered when wasters of both types were found among the potsherds excavated from the site of Thomas Whieldon's pottery two centuries after its establishment in 1740.

White salt-glazed stoneware figures from 1750 might be painted in enamel colours. These were sometimes adapted from Meissen porcelain such as "The Turk and Companion" modelled in 1745 by J. J. Kändler from an engraving by M. de Ferriol, Paris, 1714. The Staffordshire adaptations, enamelled in brilliant green, blue and yellow, have been attributed to William Littler. Figure makers became more ambitious as the century progressed and in about 1780 appeared the $18\frac{1}{2}$-inch figure of Shakespeare after the Peter Scheemakers statue executed for Westminster Abbey in 1740. An earthenware figure from the same model, painted in enamels, is attributed to Enoch Wood, 1790.

The collector will rarely find white salt-glaze ware decorated with transfer printing: existing specimens are essentially of poor quality owing to the granulated surface. A set of eight octagonal plates in the Victoria and Albert Museum have rims moulded in trellis pattern and enamelled in turquoise blue. The centre of each displays an Aesop Fable printed in brick red.

Rarely was Georgian white salt-glazed stoneware impressed with the potter's name or trade mark. The major makers were, according to Simeon Shaw: Thomas and John Wedgwood, Burslem; R. and J. Baddeley, Shelton; Thomas and Joseph Johnson, Lane End; R. Banks and John Turner, Stoke-upon-Trent; John Barker and Robert Garner, Fenton; John Adams and John Prince, Lane Delph. Many other potters produced poor quality work: it has been recorded that in Burslem more than sixty salt-glazed potters operated between 1725 and 1775.

In the third quarter of the nineteenth century there was a revival of ornamental salt-glazed stoneware for displaying in cabinets. This, sold under the name of "Elizabethan

Ware", was not intended to deceive, but the marks with which it was impressed have since been removed and prices enhanced. The number of salt-glazed teapots in mint condition that have come to light during the past forty years has reached significant proportions. Plain ware of Georgian manufacture has been enamelled within recent years to increase its value.

Chapter Four

VARIEGATED EARTHENWARES: MARBLED, AGATE AND
TORTOISESHELL

———

AS early as the sixteenth century English potters decorated earthenware with a crude form of surface marbling, combining two clay slips that were of equal consistency but would mature to contrasting colours in the kiln. Existing examples of Elizabethan marbling display reddish veins clouded with a dull yellow or grey. By the mid-seventeenth century oxides of iron and manganese were in use to tint clay slips throughout their texture. Thin washes of these light coloured slips were applied in lines and splashes to the shaped earthenware when it was dried to leather hardness but before firing. The usual contrasts were red, drab, buff and brown, light red and buff, red and brown. Marbling was difficult on a curved surface: the slip had to be so moistened that a light touch would move it over the smooth body of the earthenware.

The process of slip marbling was recorded by Dr. Plot in his *Natural History of Staffordshire*, 1686, following his visit to Burslem in 1677. Whilst fairly moist the slips were worked singly or mingled together over the surface of the ware with a leather, wire or horn comb and a sponge, using the paper marbler's technique. The resulting patterns were as varied and unrepetitive as the veins on coloured marble. The collection of early eighteenth-century owl jugs in the British Museum demonstrates the great skill eventually acquired in this work. By the 1750s almost pure white slip had been evolved and was associated with other colours in three or four tints. Slip marbling continued until the end of the eighteenth century and is found on mugs, jugs, porringers, caudle cups, loving cups and other earthenware. The process was revived during the third quarter of the nineteenth century in recognised "antique forms" intended for collectors' cabinets.

When William Duesbury, potter of Derby and Chelsea, opened London showrooms at No. 1 Bedford Street, Covent Garden, his trade card of 1770 announced "a great variety of useful and ornamental articles and a fine assortment of biscuit group and singles: also a curious selection of Derbyshire fluors, Alabasters, Marbles, &c." By such displays he influenced a fashion in decoration. Every family of distinction endeavoured to garnish the drawing room mantelshelf with a set of three or five massive blue john or marble vases turned from the solid stone quarried in Derbyshire. These vases or urns were in a fascinating colour range with translucent crystalline formations. The blue john mines at Castleton were owned by Duesbury who later sold them to the potter Champion of Bristol in whose family they remained until recently. John Singleton Copley's painting of the Sitwell children at Renishaw, Derbyshire, shows one of what was evidently a garniture of three blue john vases on the mantelshelf.

This ornament constituted a challenge to Josiah Wedgwood, who thereupon introduced much less costly ornaments simulating quarried marbles, by evolving the technique of slip glazing the surface of thrown and turned vases in cream-coloured earthenware.

Four standard types of variegated glazes became fashionable: marbled, granite or mottled, porphyry, agate. Passable effects of variegated marbles were achieved by laying on lines and splashes of colour oxides mixed in the substantial slip glaze. This was then combed. When the ware was fired, the mingling of the colours produced variegated effects. Granite effects were produced with a grey or bluish mottled glaze, and porphyry by sprinkling green glaze with cream-coloured glaze. Vases resembling agate were made by covering the creamware biscuit with a mixture of coloured glazes in various hues of brown, grey, blue, green and fawn. The handles, of scroll or snake form, rims and applied relief ornament such as husks, were then gilded. The round feet might stand upon square plinths of black basaltes or white jasper. Other Staffordshire potters were soon competing with Wedgwood, notably Henry Neale & Co., and John Turner.

Painted marbling decorated cream-coloured earthenware and pearl ware from about 1815 until the late 1830s. Streaks and curls in yellow, reddish brown and chocolate coloured enamels covered the body in the manner of the freer type of paper marbling. Some hollow-ware, such as bowls, mugs and cans, might be encircled with moulding around brim and foot, thinly coated with a bright green glaze. Painted marble ware was made in Staffordshire, at the Don Pottery in Yorkshire, at Swansea and in Scotland. Rarely is an example of surface marbling found impressed with a mark.

Earthenware variegated throughout its texture with markings superficially resembling those of agate and similar gem stones was termed agate ware by the Staffordshire potters. Dr. Thomas Wedgwood (1695–1733) probably introduced the process to Staffordshire in about 1730, although it had been known to Britons in the days of Imperial Rome.

In the early 1740s Thomas Whieldon (1719–95) of Fenton Low improved on the existing agate ware, substituting attractive striations for the wide layers of contrasting clay. He used white burning clay stained with metallic oxides, obtaining, for example, brown from manganese, green from copper, and blue from cobalt. Flat bats of differently coloured clays were piled one upon the other and beaten to drive out enclosed air and make the separate clays adhere to each other. The mass was then transversely cut into slices with wires. This laborious process of laying, beating and slicing was repeated again and again, care being taken to preserve the run of the grain. The fine wavy lines of coloured clays were disposed in countless folds with an irregularity of striations just sufficient to secure a picturesque effect while avoiding violent contrast between the darker and lighter lines. As potters became more skilled in this work, the striations became thinner and extremely attractive effects were obtained.

This mass of vari-coloured clays became almost non-plastic and inclined to split if shaped by throwing on the wheel. The difficulty was overcome by squeezing the bats of striped clay into smooth-surfaced moulds, thus retaining the veining without distortion. A teapot, for instance, might be so assembled that the veins of colour appeared unbroken across the seam. In the spout the veining was usually broken. Until about 1750 the shaped ware was glazed by sprinkling the dried clay with galena glaze. This fired to a rich yellow hue toning down the colours of the striations. A more pleasing finish was possible from about 1750, following the introduction of transparent liquid glaze. The biscuit ware was dipped into this after hand polishing. By 1760 the glaze was faintly tinged with cobalt, the result more nearly resembling natural agate.

Collectors chiefly associate early agate ware with Whieldon's galena glazed snuff-boxes and knife hafts which set him on the road to prosperity. The boxes were bought by Birmingham chapmen who fitted gilded brass mounts with hinges and fasteners. The knife and fork hafts were sent to Sheffield and London merchants. Hafts dipped in transparent lead glaze proved even more popular and production continued until the 1790s. Coffee-pots, cups and saucers, dishes, cans, sauce-boats, pickle leaves, candlesticks, and well-shaped toy teasets were made. Manufacture declined, however, from the early 1790s and had ceased by about 1820.

Agate ware potters included Thomas Astbury, Daniel Bird, Ralph Wood, Josiah Spode. Some exceptionally beautiful work came from Ralph Brown, Caughley Hall, Shropshire, during the 1750s. Catalogues of the Leeds Pottery published in the 1780s announced its manufacture. Josiah Wedgwood during his partnership with John Harrison (1752–54) and Whieldon (1754–59), and later on his own account at Burslem and Etruria, made excellent agate ware. Handles on late examples might be oil gilded or the whole surface might be veined and spangled with gilding properly burnt in. Imitations were made in France by the firm of Castellet & Apt, Vaucluse.

Georgian agate ware is rarely found in mint condition, although fine examples are to be discovered where their interest as antiques has been unappreciated. For instance, three authenticated teapots came to light in different parts of the country during August 1957 following a magazine reference to agate ware.

Few marked examples are known. A vase in the Wedgwood Museum, impressed WEDGWOOD & BENTLEY, is attributed to 1778. A set of three pale brown and greyish white jugs in graduated sizes, now in the Liverpool Museum, are impressed HERCULANEUM and are of early nineteenth-century manufacture. Modern copies of Georgian agate ware have been made.

A considerable amount of agate ware was made late in the nineteenth century, particularly at the Britannia Pottery, Glasgow. The method of preparing the clay differed from that formerly used, enabling it to be thrown on the wheel. When leather hard it was turned on the lathe with a sharp tool, removing the outer crust and more effectively displaying the agate-like striations. It was then hand polished and glazed. Imitation horn tumblers were also made in Scotland at this period, but it was a tedious process costing more than real horn.

Buff or whitish earthenware coloured with variegated mottled manganese-brown glazes and mingled colour glazes displaying no definite pattern was known to Georgians as tortoiseshell ware. Because the improvements that led to its popularity were introduced by Whieldon, tortoiseshell ware has come to be known by collectors under the generic term of Whieldon ware although it was a standard product of many other Staffordshire potters, and made also at Liverpool and Leeds. This effect was secured at first by sprinkling the leather-hard unfired ware with powdered lead oxide and calcined flint mixed with a trace of manganese oxide. When fired a glaze with a highly lustrous mottled effect was produced.

Immediately after the introduction of transparent liquid glaze in about 1750 Whieldon observed that this moved freely and smoothly over the surface of his earthenware. He then produced mingled colour glazes by tinting the surface of the biscuit with metallic oxides and then coating it with the liquid transparent lead glaze. These blended during firing into a range of variegated colourings. The limited palette consisted of green, yellow, slate-blue, dark brown and mottled grey. The more frequent combinations were mottled green and brownish grey; brown, green and slate-blue; mottled grey, green, slate-blue and yellow. Diluted manganese oxide produced a passable flesh tint for figures. This was Whieldon's first important contribution to the pottery trade.

Advertisements invariably used the term "tortoiseshell ware". An advertisement inserted in the *New York Gazette*, 3rd August 1762, by Keeling & Morris, included "Tortois Table Plates and Dishes of the Neatest Patterns, Tea-Pots, Milk-Pots, Bowls, Cups and Saucers". Ten years later the same firm announced "Tortois Shell and Agate Ware, viz. Tea pots, coffee pots, milk pots, sugar dishes, bowls, mugs, salts, mustard pots, cups and saucers".

Professor Church in 1884 declared that:

"Whieldon's perforated double teapots of rich tortoiseshell ware, with his beautiful octagonal plates, displaying the same rich glaze, have never been surpassed: the latter are now rarely met with, though inferior pieces, with one colour only, or with two or three colours rather roughly and mechanically mottled are not uncommon. But the deep soft glaze of the best sort is at once the admiration of modern [1880s] collectors and the despair of modern potters. Good plates and dishes of this quality exist chiefly in private cabinets: they measure 13¾ and 8¾ inches in diameter. They may be distinguished from the later inferior pieces by their flatness and by the breadth of their horizontal rims which are always bordered by applied strips with transverse grooves. Four-fifths of the surface is covered with a flooded mass of rich manganese brown colour. There is usually an irregular V-shaped pattern of a light hue resembling raw sienna, and about this and elsewhere on the surface there are soft splashes of copper-green and cobalt blue, the latter being sparingly introduced, and of a soft indigo-like tint. The lead glaze is finely crackled or crazed. . . . The finest collection of tortoiseshell glazes perished in the Alexandra Palace fire of 1873, including pickle and sweetmeat trays, milk jugs, cornucopia and baskets: also a pigeon house with many birds about it."

A similar pigeon house, formerly in the collection of Enoch Wood, is in the Hanley Museum.

By the early 1780s the popularity of tortoiseshell ware had become overshadowed by brilliantly enamelled Queen's ware. None of the eighty major potters entered in *Tunnicliffe's*

Directory, 1787, is referred to as making tortoiseshell ware. Whieldon made no effort to compete by developing new ceramics and retired a rich man, so that production gradually ceased.

Chapter Five

RED AND CANE-COLOURED STONEWARES

TEAPOTS of unglazed red stoneware were ideal vessels for early-eighteenth-century tea-making. The tea itself was thought to retain its aroma unspoilt if made in these tiny teapots, never exceeding four inches in height; and they were preferred to silver except on highly formal occasions. A conversation piece by Quinkhardt painted in the 1730s shows a tripod table set out for tea. Here are to be seen blue painted porcelain cups and saucers, a huge slop basin, dishes piled with lumps of sugar royal, a large silver tea kettle with spirit lamp, a tea trunk containing three canisters, and a small hexagonal teapot of red porcelain. The miniature size of the teapot is in harmony with the early Georgian fashion for the hostess to make tea individually to suit each person's taste, hence the necessity for a slop basin.

The first of these teapots were imported during the last quarter of the seventeenth century from Yi-Hsing, near Soochow, by the Great Lake of China. The London china sellers introduced them as red porcelain; by the 1740s they were known as red china ware, a term that continued until the 1820s, when the name red stoneware was preferred. These teapots of dense, vitreous stoneware were impervious to liquids, thus obviating the necessity for glaze, and they possessed the important advantage over ordinary earthenware and porcelain of enduring boiling water without fracture.

English potters inevitably tried to copy this red stoneware. First to succeed was John Dwight (1633–1703) of Fulham, who was granted a patent on 12th June 1684 for several ceramic inventions and among them included two types of "red porcelain". His notebook for 1691 recorded recipes for "red porcelane clay" of two qualities. The finer of these he termed "a bright red clay wth Staffordshire red cley." This required "sifted Staffordshire cley thirty pounds. Ffine dark cley twenty pounds. Mingle and tread." A lesser quality contained "red cley sifted twenty pounds. Ffine dark Earth fifteen pounds. White p. Cyprus five pounds. Mingle and tread." This compares with the nineteenth-century formula quoted by William Evans in *Art and History of the Potting Business*, 1846: "Bradwell Wood Clay 25; yellow brick clay 50; flint 25."

No example of Dwight's "red porcelain" has been identified, but the records of the law suit heard in 1693 regarding infringement of Dwight's patent prove manufacture of "brown muggs and [red] thea-potts . . . his servants for many years past having used the said invention and sold them."

The several defendant potters included David Elers (1656–1742) and John Philip Elers (1644–1738), who had formerly worked in Cheapside as silversmiths. It is continually and wrongly stated that the brothers were of Dutch origin and arrived in London with the entourage of William III in 1688. An entry in the *London Gazette*, 1686, disproves this by referring to "Mr. David Elers, Silversmith, London". The brothers were grandsons of Admiral Elers who commanded the German fleet at Hamburg and married a princess of the royal house of Baden. John Philip was a godson of the Elector of Mentz, after whom he was named. No doubt whilst trading as silversmiths the Elers became aware of the great preference for red stoneware teapots to the disadvantage of silver.

The manuscript report of the court action, preserved in the Public Records Office, reveals that David Elers had established a stoneware pottery at Vauxhall and by 1690 was selling teapots of "red porcelain", the red clay being carried from Bradwell Wood, Staffordshire: this was doubtless the source, too, of Dwight's Staffordshire clay. The excellence of their productions is confirmed in minutes of the Corporation of Newcastle-under-Lyme, 1691, which record that "a present be made to my Lord Chiefe Justice Holt at his coming to the Burrough from Lancaster Assizes of some of Mr. David Elers' earthenware to the value of three pounds or thereabouts." (*Evening Sentinel*, February 1944.) It is evident that Staffordshire at this time could not compete with London for quality goods, although already on the way to monopolising the potting of everyday earthenware.

Dr. Martin Lister, writing in *Philosophical Transactions*, 1693, emphasised the importance of Elers' red stoneware: "the *teapots* now sold at the Potters in the *Poultry* in *Cheapside*, which is not only for art, but for beautiful colour, too, are far beyond any we have from *China*; these are made from the English Haematites in Staffordshire, by two Dutchmen [?] incomparable artists." Elers' red teapots were costly, selling at 12*s*. to 25*s*. each: that is, at prices ranging from ten to twenty guineas in present-day currency. Obviously they were only for the well-to-do, then paying as much as 20*s*. for a pound of tea. The Elers are also credited with the manufacture of cups and saucers, bowls and cans.

Although an injunction was granted in John Dwight's favour, the Elers continued the manufacture of red stoneware teapots which were sold openly at their retail shop in the City of London. Obviously, then, they must have been licensed by Dwight to continue manufacture until his patent expired in 1698.

So successful were Dwight and the Elers with their re teapots that by 1694 John Houghton in his *Collection* d *Letters for the Improvement of Husbandry and Trade* could report that no more than ten teapots had been imported during the previous year, adding that "those made in Faux-Hall being as good as any from abroad." He had already noticed that the Elers potted on a site at Vauxhall containing red clay suitable for teapots.

The Elers had established a red stoneware pottery in Staffordshire by 1695 at Bradwell Wood under Red Street, Woolstanton. The red clay which gave the district its name (some authorities prefer to believe that the name commemorates the site of a battle between Saxons and Danes in which much blood was shed) formed the basis of their finest red stoneware. The clays were sifted, cleansed by washing, made homogeneous by treading for many hours with bare feet, and then potted on the wheel. When air-dried to leather hardness and still unfired the thrown ware was turned in the lathe until thin of section and notably light in weight: this was a Chinese process introduced by the Elers. The ware was then fired. Its red colour, due to the presence of iron oxide in the clay, varied from brown to vermilion, rich reddish brown being considered ideal. Kiln temperatures at that time could not easily be controlled: overfiring resulted in a dark brown hue; pieces placed in positions of lowest temperature emerged from the kiln bright red. When Enoch Wood examined the ruins of the Elers' kilns in 1813 he was of the opinion that they could have been used only to fire stoneware.

The Elers' outstanding craftsmanship was the direct result of their training as silversmiths. Their red tea ware was made in shapes adapted from contemporaneous silver plate. So far as teapots were concerned the silversmiths copied the graceful, smooth-surfaced Chinese teapots with domed lids and highly placed spouts. Until the early 1720s red stoneware teapots were made in a wide range of shapes from the plainly globular to the inward sloping polygonal: thereafter they followed the basic shapes and sizes made fashionable by the silversmiths. Decoration in relief by sprigging is thought to have been used at this period on the evidence of certain brass stamps excavated from the site of Dwight's pottery: proof is lacking, however, that they were in fact made during Dwight's lifetime. Remaining examples of Elers' teapots are few indeed, but apparently many copies exist for when a paragraph illustrated by a museum specimen was printed in 1959 more than twenty readers reported recent acquisition of identical pieces.

It has been assumed that the Elers potted simultaneously at Vauxhall and Bradwell Wood until 1710, work ceasing only when the clay ran out. This is inaccurate, for supplies of red clay for stoneware were dug continuously until Victorian days. The brothers described "late of Foxhall in Surrey, Potmakers", became bankrupt in December 1700.

John Philip, with the financial assistance of Lady Barrington, became a glass and china seller in Dublin: David is believed to have continued as a merchant at their shop in the Poultry, London.

The manufacture of red stoneware naturally increased after the expiration of Dwight's patent in 1698, for red teapots continued fashionable and imports remained negligible. Josiah Wedgwood, M.P., in *Staffordshire Earthenware*, 1947, states that red stoneware became a staple product of the Burslem district. There is, however, no reference to this branch of potting in Josiah Wedgwood's list, prepared in 1765, of forty potters and the kind of ware they produced at Burslem between the years 1710 and 1715.

Among the several known imitators of Elers' red stoneware were Joshua Twyford and John Astbury, both of Shelton. Astbury established his pottery in the mid-1720s and during the early 1730s he tried to emulate the new fashion for embossed ornament on silver teapots by decorating his red stoneware with relief work in a contrasting colour. These motifs consisted of small, flat pads of white clay applied to the red ware in its green state. These were impressed with designs in relief such as figures, birds, animals, flowers and trees, by means of brass stamps sharply cut in intaglio. The whole was then glazed by sprinkling the surface with lead oxide which, in the course of firing, matured to a transparent glaze with a yellowish tinge.

This method of sprigging was the forerunner of vining, by which trailing plants, notably the fruiting vine, meandered over the surface of the teapot. The flowering prunus, called the tea plant by eighteenth-century potters, was frequent, with scrollwork threads and connecting lines. These were hand-shaped from thin, flat sheets of white clay and pressed sparsely on the red ground. These specialist decorators were known as viners (see p. 48), a branch of the trade that continued into the nineteenth century.

Experiments in red stoneware had been financed early in the century by Augustus the Strong. In 1709 his chemist, J. F. Böttger, evolved a red stoneware so hard that it was capable of taking a high polish on the lapidary's wheel, in fact it could be cut and polished in facets on a glass-cutter's wheel. Not until 1729 was a comparable red stoneware potted in England. In that year Samuel Bell, Lower Street, Newcastle-under-Lyme, invented and patented what the specification describes as "red marble stoneware, [made] with mineral earth found within this kingdom, which being firmly united by fire will make it capable of receiving a gloss so beautiful as to imitate, if not to compare with the rubie. That stoneware may be formed into vessels for any necessary use." It is to be feared that Samuel Bell had no close acquaintance with rubies, for this was merely a red stoneware, but harder and more finely grained than any formerly made in England. This intense hardness was brought about by adding calcined flint crushed to flour fineness to the red clay of Bradwell Wood and brick clay, making the stoneware appreciably harder than the red stonewares of Dwight, Elers and others. Friction gave to its surface a brilliant polish.

Bell naturally entered the red teapot trade and so great became the demand that by 1734 he was prosperous enough to be placed upon the voters' list and when he died twenty years later he was a rich man. Several examples of his teapots are preserved in the museum at Newcastle-under-Lyme. It must be conceded, then, that red stoneware containing flint in its composition cannot be dated earlier than about 1730. The harder material may be recognised by the smooth fracture of chips.

Bell's hard stoneware was capable of being shaped into sharply defined intricate patterns. These were pressed upon thin pads of clay which were then attached to the shaped leather-hard ware. Finishing was carried out by hand tooling and surplus background scraped away, leaving the ornament in delicate relief. Close examination of such a piece will betray evidence of scraping. This relief decoration simulated, as far as possible with a ceramic, the rococo embossments on fashionable silver tea ware.

A globular teapot with crabstock handle and spout in the Victoria and Albert Museum is decorated in this way. On each side are shown identical figures of George III and Queen Charlotte holding hands, with the initials G R and two cupids below scrolled ornament. This is flanked by reliefs of Chinese women with a parrot and cage and parrot and hoop. On the cover are relief sprays and scrollwork. The body and cover are encircled with bands of wavy lines impressed by means of a roulette. This teapot is commemorative of the royal marriage in 1761. Red stoneware teapots were now of slightly larger capacity than formerly, measuring about five inches in height.

When Josiah Wedgwood was experimenting in the manufacture of dry or unglazed stoneware bodies during the early 1770s, he evolved a hard red stoneware which he named *rosso antico*, supplies of ferruginous clay being obtained from Bradwell Wood. Although Wedgwood's *rosso antico* was considered superior in colour to that of any other potter, he was never enamoured of red china. On 3rd March 1776 he wrote to his partner Bentley: "My objection to it is the extreme vulgarity of red wares . . . we shall never be able to make *Rosso Antico* otherwise than to put you in mind of a red Pot-Teapot."

Wedgwood's *rosso antico* is of two types. Much was thrown on the wheel, turned on the lathe and ornamented with engine-turning. The remainder was shaped by pressing into moulds sunk with stereotyped fashionable patterns in relief: its section was appreciably thicker than thrown and turned red china. Both methods were in continual use by the Wedgwood firm until the 1820s.

During the final quarter of the eighteenth century, when *rosso antico* was decorated with dry stonewares in contrasting colours, it was highly valued: in reverse it might form the relief ornament on black basaltes. In addition to teapots, hot water jugs, coffee pots, mugs and vases have been noted impressed WEDGWOOD.

There has long been a belief that early red stoneware teapots, sold originally in imitation of the Chinese, were impressed with square seals in the pseudo-Chinese style in which English letters may be detected. This is merely wishful thinking, for none has been noted on flintless red stoneware, and it is difficult to attribute such marks to earlier than the 1760s. So far the potter has not been positively identified.

China-sellers' advertisements in the late eighteenth

century make frequent references to "red china teapots", showing production to have been considerable. Bailey's *Western Directory*, 1784, lists but two makers of red china ware in the Potteries: Forrester & Meredith, Lane End; and Thomas Holland, Burslem, described also as a gilder. It was possibly he who issued the hexagonal teapots with panels of relief work, the backgrounds gilded to accentuate the red design: cover finials were also gilded. Careful inspection of late eighteenth-century red stoneware teapots has occasionally revealed evidence of all-over gilding, apparently with lightly fired gold leaf to which the red ground gave a fiery brilliance.

Other Staffordshire potters known to have made red stoneware at this period are Enoch Wood, Josiah Spode, Samuel Hollins, noted for the lustrous surface of his teapots, and Robert Wilson, whose red stoneware ornamented with figures in black basaltes is highly valued. Red stoneware was potted also at Liverpool and Bristol. The inventory of the stock-in-trade of Richard Franks, Bristol, taken in 1784, contains the entry "Red china Ware, £3.16.2."

These potters of "red china" for the most part made pressed teapots, and by the end of the century pictorial work had become popular. Canopic teapots, decorated with Egyptian motifs such as sphinx, crocodile, lotus and pyramids, became fashionable after Nelson's victory on the Nile in 1798. Early in the nineteenth century texture and definition coarsened.

Although competing with Egyptian black teapots, in the first half of the nineteenth century red stoneware held its own in inexpensive versions until displaced by the more popular teapots in granite ware. Marked examples include the work of James Dudson, Hanley, established 1835, who made tea and coffee pots with several registered designs in relief known as fern, barley, wheatsheaf and pineapple; G. R. Booth & Co., Hanley, who, between the 1830s and 1860s, issued teapots and jugs decorated with wreaths, medallions and other relief work; Thomas Till, Sytch Pottery, Hanley, who enriched his red teapots with enamels and gilding and made hot water jugs with Britannia metal swing lids.

3. (left to right) Staffordshire salt-glazed stoneware teapot with shell and other ornament moulded in relief and painted with enamels, height 5¼ inches, about 1750; flask in Nottingham brown stoneware inscribed "Joseph Poyne 1723", height 4½ inches; Staffordshire salt-glazed tea canister with scratch-blue decoration and inscribed "Bohea", "Elizabeth Lamble 1768", height 5 inches, about 1740.

Early in the 1820s red stoneware was found to be the most suitable base for copper lustre. Given a high polish, it reflected brilliance into the film of metallic oxide.

Among the unglazed earthenwares, known to potters as dry bodies, is a fine-grained tan-coloured stoneware capable of enduring the stresses and strains of boiling water without cracking. It was derived from the light buff-brown stonewares popular in the 1750s made by several of the Staffordshire potters. Among these was the firm of Banks and Turner, Stoke-upon-Trent. When John Turner withdrew from the partnership in 1762 he was succeeded as manager by Josiah Spode who, in 1770, became proprietor. Moulds used at this period are preserved in the Spode-Copeland Museum.

During the late 1770s a finer body was evolved by adding a proportion of Cornish stone to refined local fireclay marls dug from beneath the coal measures which cropped out in many districts. Careful preparation resulted in a fine-textured body ranging in tint from light cream to buff. It is believed that Josiah Wedgwood was responsible for this improvement: the 1787 edition of his catalogue refers to this fine stoneware as "*Bamboo*, or cane-coloured bisque porcelain".

Cane-coloured stoneware began to be potted on an extensive scale in the 1780s at the expense of red stoneware. Wedgwood put this new body into artistic use, with the same methods and moulds as for his red stoneware and black basaltes. Sprigged ornament was usual, such as foliage in lighter or darker shades of tan and green. A frequent pattern bearing the Wedgwood mark consisted of encircling vertical fern leaves with small star-like paterae: according to tradition Wedgwood designed this for his son-in-law, Dr. Erasmus Darwin. It is known to collectors as the Darwin pattern.

Cane ware is known decorated with Wedgwood's encaustic paints, but more usually was enriched with touches of brilliant blue and green enamels. This startling colour combination, later joined by red, was used because these enamels could be matured by a single firing in the muffle kiln. The honey pot and cover is an interesting piece moulded in the form of a straw beehive skip and attached to a saucer-shaped stand. These are glazed inside. Caneware was also made to imitate bamboo in forms such as teapots, hot water jugs and bulb pots for plants and flowers, the shape and modelling suggesting short lengths of bamboo lashed together with thin cane.

Cane ware was potted into realistic representations of piecrusts. These dishes, with lids representing elaborately fashioned cooked pastry, appear to have been evolved in times of flour scarcity. The food was cooked in saucepans and served from the piecrust dishes. The *Life of George Brummell* by Captain Jeffs, 1844, records that "the scarcity two years after Brummell's retirement in 1800, was so great that the consumption of flour for pastry was prohibited in the Royal Household, rice being used instead. The distillers left off malting; hackney coach fares were raised 25 per cent, and Wedgwood made dishes to represent piecrust."

Cane-coloured stoneware was made by other eminent Staffordshire potters. John Turner became celebrated for his skilful imitations of piecrust ware, making it to such a pitch of perfection that it became almost a deception. According to Simeon Shaw, Turner dug his clay at Green Dock, Longton: "from where he obtained all his supplies for manufacturing *Stone Ware Pottery* of a cane colour . . . some of them representing different kinds of pastry." Burton states that he mixed this with china clay and china stone, the result being cane colour stoneware of exceptionally fine grain and close vitreous fracture, ranging from light cream to piecrust brown.

A series of Turner's cane ware jugs are in a design with a cylindrical neck encircled by incised lines, and a spherical body, the lower part gadrooned and the space between containing bas relief figures, sporting subjects, ships, trees and drinking scenes. The neck and upper part of the handle are generally coated with a dark chocolate coloured glaze, occasionally a greyish black or blue. The lower part of the handle has a double attachment. Turner's cane ware included bowls, dishes, wine coolers, monteiths, bulb pots, inkstands, busts and statuettes.

Burton tells of a tradition handed down in Longton,

"that as a *tour de force* of imitative skill Turner made in stoneware a group of vessels shaped and coloured like the astral roasts of one of the homely county feasts of the day. A baron of beef, a roast leg of mutton, a sucking pig, goose, turkey, and many other pieces completed this queer assemblage, which on completion was exhibited at one of the inns at Lane End, where it made a nine-day wonder for the country-side." In the Mayer Collection at Liverpool are four or five such pieces with Turner's name impressed: they are triumphs of technical skill.

When Josiah Spode was operating his own pottery from 1770, he produced excellent cane ware, including a most attractive series of teapots. In these the body surface was divided into compartments containing classic figures in relief, each compartment framed with relief cartouches enriched with green and blue enamels. The cover was surmounted by a reclining female figure. Spode decorated cane ware with engine-turning. Jewitt attributed the first use of this incised ornament on cane ware to William Baddeley of Longton.

Foremost among the specialist dry body potters was Samuel Hollins (1748–1820), Cauldon Canal, Vale Pleasant, Shelton, Staffordshire. He began business in the late 1770s and retired in 1815 a rich man. His unglazed fine stonewares—dark red, cane colour, buff, chocolate, and costly olive green and maroon—were of exceptional quality and potted with outstanding skill. The colours, except for red, were derived by the addition of ochreous earths or oxides to the clay. Hollins appears to have concentrated on teapots and coffee pots, services, and hot water jugs, in shapes mostly adapted from those of Georgian silversmiths.

The major part of his productions were in red, hard fired from Bradwell Wood clays. Authenticated specimens show that his chocolate coloured ware had a surface almost as lustrous as that obtained by Josiah Wedgwood on his black basaltes.

Decoration in relief, such as figures, flowers, foliage, animals and scrollwork, was sprigged to the body in clay of the same colour and formula as the basic ware. In his later bas relief decoration in red and chocolate colour, the

75

ornament was in contrast, usually black. Some of his productions were decorated with inlay of Egyptian black, and further enrichment might be secured by sprigging blue and white jasper relief work or by inlay. These date from the late 1780s.

The lids of many of Hollins' teapots and coffee pots, as with those of so many of his competitors such as Wedgwood, Mayer and Turner, displayed the well-known widow knob. These date from the 1760s and are believed to have been designed by William Greatbach (see page 109). The original model was a young woman wearing a shawl; in the second version she wore a flat-brimmed hat; the third was an older woman with folded arms and her head covered with a shawl arranged as a cowl, the fourth was a younger woman not entirely hidden by a shawl. Details differ in individual potters' widow knobs.

A cane-coloured coffee-pot recently discovered is in Queen Anne silver shape with a highly domed fluted lid and a double scroll handle. The lower half of the pear-shaped body is fluted, the upper half encircled with sprigged ornament in the Flaxman manner: it is inscribed S. HOLLINS beneath. A bowl and a teapot in the British Museum are similarly marked. Samuel Hollins was also a partner in the firm of Hollins, Warburton, Daniel and Co., New Hall China Factory, Shelton, where hard porcelain was made under the Champion patent (page 110).

Few of the potters' entries in Bailey's *Western Directory*, 1784, are accompanied by more than the word "Potter" as their trade. Of Enoch and Ralph Wood, Burslem, however, it is stated that this firm "Manufactures all kinds of useful and ornamental earthenware. Egyptian Black, Cane, and various other colours; also black figures, seals and cyphers." Thomas Woolf, Stoke-upon-Trent, is shown as a "Manufacturer of Queen's ware in general, blue printed, and Egyptian Black, Cane, etc."

Elijah Mayer, Hanley, although entered only as "enameller", was soon to become one of the foremost potters of his day, manufacturing, among other earthenwares, Queen's ware, simple line ware, black basaltes and handsome cane-coloured stoneware. His output included vases festooned with cleverly modelled flowers in high relief; tea and coffee ware including the celebrated services commemorating Nelson's victories of the Nile and Trafalgar, and piecrust ware. In 1805 he was joined by his son Joseph and they traded as E. Mayer & Son. The impressed marks were E. MAYER and E. MAYER & SON. It was reported a century ago that Elijah Mayer's cane ware was already rare.

Joseph and John Mayer were potting at Longport in the early 1840s. *The Art Union*, 1845, illustrates a cane-coloured stoneware jug adapted from Rossi's collection of antique vases. By about 1850 they were joined by Thomas Mayer and moved to Dale Hall (formerly Dole Hall), Burslem. Here, in cane ware, they made some exceptionally skilfully potted serving jugs, notably the "oak" pattern, in which the body of the jug resembles a section of an oak trunk entwined with ivy and coloured green. Several examples have been noted during the 1950s impressed MAYER BROS. The Mayers potted the first successful tea urns in earthenware, using cane-coloured stoneware, capable of withstanding the essential variations of temperature. Jewitt illustrates two very highly ornate examples.

Collectors will find a long series of dry body ware marked S & G and W S & S, marks attributed by most reference books to the Isleworth Pottery, operated by Shore and Goulding in the early nineteenth century. The composition of the body is buff colour in various tones with a slip decoration in red, chocolate, brown or black with a glossy surface. Some pieces are lustred. W. B. Honey has shown these not to be of English origin, but the productions of Bohemian potters "Schiller and Gerbing of Bodenbach; the similar wares marked W S & S come from Wilhelm Schiller und Sohn of the same place, or Wilhelm Sattler und Sohn of Anspach, near Kissinggen". These were imported during the third quarter of the nineteenth century.

Outstanding among the many Victorian cane ware potters were John and William Ridgway, who evolved, probably in the mid-1830s, a cane-coloured stoneware with a translucent body which enhanced the definition of the relief work. A series of cleverly-designed matching teapots, hot water jugs and cream jugs are marked "Published by / W. Ridgway & Co / Hanley / October 1st 1835" and serving jugs marked "Published by / W. Ridgway, Son & Co / Hanley / September 1st 1841." These dates are those on which the designs were registered at Stationers' Hall, thus securing copyright protection against industrial piracy. Charles Meigh, later to be incorporated into the firm of William Ridgway & Son, made comparable cane ware. Perhaps best known are his octagonal hot-water jugs, each of the eight panels depicting a church dignitary and with a Britannia metal lid stamped T. BOOTH, HANLEY. The jugs are marked with "a royal coat of arms / March 11 1842 / Charles Meigh / Hanley."

Evans recorded in 1846 that cane-coloured stoneware was at that time in great demand for "dishes resembling baked pastry", thus showing piecrust ware to have had more than half a century of popularity. He published six formulas, all consisting of black marl, Cornish stone and brown or blue clay in varying proportions such as 56, 22 and 22 parts by weight.

Ironstone cane ware, possessing the important characteristics of strength and capacity for heat endurance, was evolved at about this time by the Derbyshire potters who sold it primarily potted into the form of inexpensive fireproof baking dishes, the first ever to have been made. Piecrust dishes were also made, cheaper than formerly, as well as teapots, coffee pots, hot-water jugs, serving jugs, mugs and other household ware. Hunting jugs similar to those in salt-glazed stoneware were also made.

Much of this ware was potted at Woodville, or Wooden Box, Derbyshire. Jewitt gives the reason for this curious name: the original name rose from an old wooden "box" or hut which formerly stood on the toll-house site, where a man used to collect toll, but was afterwards burned down. The original "box", it may be added, "was an old port-wine butt, from Drakelow Hall, and in this the collector, Diogenes-like, spent his days." There were only two houses in the neighbourhood, one, strangely enough, being Butt House, the home of Lord Stamford.

The ironstone cane ware potters who impressed their names upon their better quality productions included: Woodville Pottery, Woodville Potteries, Hartshorn Pottery,

Rawden Pottery, and the Wooden Box Pottery. These potters were all established as manufacturers of salt-glazed stoneware early in the nineteenth century. Sharpe Brothers & Co., Swadlincote, made similar ironstone cane ware.

Chapter Six

STONEWARE coloured black throughout its texture was a Staffordshire production of the Georgian and Victorian periods. This unglazed stoneware, unlike earthenware of the early eighteenth century, was inexpensive, yet it would stand up to continual use with boiling water without danger of fracture: hence its long vogue for tea ware. Cups could be made of thin section and its surface was smoother than that of the period's salt-glazed stoneware, which was inclined to chafe the lips.

The collector will find three kinds of black stoneware, each in varying qualities:

1. Egyptian black stoneware stained with iron oxide, dating between about 1720 and the mid-1760s.

2. Basaltes, a fine hard stoneware stained with manganese dioxide, made from the mid-1760s.

3. Egyptian black stoneware of improved quality, stained with manganese dioxide, from the mid-1760s to 1890s.

The earliest authenticated specimens of Egyptian black to be noted are two tiny teapots given by Enoch Wood to the Hanley Museum more than a century ago and stated by him to have been made by Thomas Twyford of Shelton. These have a dull black surface and they follow the shapes of rare William and Mary teapots, one having a porringer-shaped body and flat lid, but with a crabstock handle and spout of a later period.

This early Egyptian black was stoneware stained black with oxide of iron. Stoneware is ordinary earthenware fired at a temperature high enough partially to vitrify the ingredients and make the ware impervious to liquids. Iron-stained Egyptian black continued in production until the 1760s. Keeling and Morris advertised in the *New York Gazette*, 1762, that they had received from London a consignment of "Egyptian black Teapots, Milk-pots, Mugs and Tea-bowls of all sizes". There is no authentic confirmation that any other type of ware was then made in Egyptian black stoneware.

When Josiah Wedgwood established himself as an independent potter in 1759, operating at Ivy House, Burslem, until 1764, Egyptian black stoneware was among the many ceramics he improved, thus evolving his first ornamental ceramic, a fine quality black stoneware. This was composed of refined Staffordshire ball clay, calcined ochre, and glassy slag from puddled ironstone, with the addition of ten per cent of manganese dioxide to stain these constituents black.

The resulting stoneware was intensely hard, its texture uniformly dense and finely grained. The black biscuit emerged from the kiln without the slightest undulation of surface and was given a permanent gloss by a coating of potter's varnish and re-firing to a red heat. After removal from the kiln and whilst slightly warm, it was rubbed vigorously with a soft rag dipped in skim milk. This double firing produced an ultra-hard stoneware capable of taking a high polish at the lapidary's wheel. Plinths for figures and busts could be polished to a brilliant reflecting surface.

Wedgwood differentiated his fine stoneware from the earlier and later Egyptian black by naming it basaltes and defining it in his catalogue of 1787 as "a black porcelain biscuit of nearly the same properties as the natural stone: striking fire with steel, receiving a high polish, serving as a touchstone for metals, resisting all the acids, and bearing without injury a strong fire: stronger, indeed, than the basaltes itself."

Not until Wedgwood had moved to the more convenient Bell Works, Burslem, in 1764, did he put basaltes into commercial production in the form of thrown vases. The smooth black ground was ideal for colourful ornament applied directly to the body with no intervening glaze. By

1769 he had devised a series of encaustic paints in eight colours and bronze: these matured to a matt surface when fired in the muffle kiln. Vases treated with these colours he catalogued as "painted Etruscan" and "bronze Etruscan". He applied for a patent in March 1769 and this was granted, No. 939, in the following November for "the Purpose of Ornamenting Earthen and Porcelaine Ware with Encaustic Gold Bronze, together with a peculiar species of Encaustic Painting in Various Colours in Imitation of the Antient and Roman Earthenware." The patent names the ingredients and describes the preparation of the colours: red, green, blue, orange, yellow, white, shining black and dry black. The demand for basaltes enriched with colour became so great that in 1770 Wedgwood established decorating workshops primarily for encaustic painting, although these were used also for enamelling finer queen's ware.

Gold bronze became a fashionable all-over decoration, being painted over the basaltes and so tooled that the finished article might be mistaken for a costly ornament in solid bronze. The bronze powder was prepared by dissolving one ounce of pure gold in *aqua regia*, precipitating it with copper. The precipitate was then freed from acid by repeated washings in hot water, and then dried. This was ground in oil of turpentine and applied by sponge or pencil brush over the unfired green ware, if the basaltes were substantial; over lead-glazed biscuit in the case of delicate vessels or figures. Finally the gold bronze was burnished. Parcel bronzing of relief ornament was very frequent from the late 1770s. Aaron Steele was Wedgwood's principal bronzer from 1784 to 1845, proof of the long period during which such ornament was used. Silvering and coppering have been recorded, probably from about 1815 when silver bronze was invented. Specimens come to light with the gold bronze in perfect condition; encaustic bronze was unable to withstand intensive cleaning, and careful inspection of an apparently black example sometimes reveals traces of gold bronze in crevices. A festooned vase impressed with the mark WEDGWOOD & BENTLEY was recently found to have been bronzed originally. Humphrey Palmer also decorated basaltes with encaustic painting and gold bronze.

Wedgwood had further improved his black stoneware by 1770 and was soon to term it in his catalogue "black porcelain", thus ensuring differentiation between his fine stoneware and an improved Egyptian black now being potted. When bats of black clay were pressed into alabaster moulds the improved stoneware displayed well-defined decoration in relief. Thrown vases were now sprigged with low relief ornament. Five more years elapsed before profitable results could be achieved by pressing ornament on a piece with curved surfaces. Vibration whilst pressing the ornament was the prime difficulty. Pressing actually meant a lengthy hammering of the plastic clay with a wooden mallet to ensure that every detail carved in the mould was sharply accentuated. This problem was solved eventually, as far as Wedgwood was concerned, by inserting in the ground an oak-tree trunk, the root end, cut flat, upwards. This passed through the ground floor room's ceiling, providing a steady bench in the room above. The invoice for the tree trunk still exists.

Among the great variety of Wedgwood basaltes catalogued in 1777 were vases with bas reliefs "from three to four inches high to more than two feet, the prices from 7s. 6d. a piece to three or four guineas, exclusive of the very large ones, and those which consist of several parts. The sets of five, for chimney pieces, are from two guineas to six or eight guineas a set . . . lamps and candelabra; busts and small statues, boys and girls; heads of illustrious Romans and moderns; flower pots and root pots; vases and tripods; inkstands; tea and coffee services including chocolate pots, sugar dishes, cream ewers, cabinet cups and saucers, plain and enriched; intaglio and medallions in wide variety."

Other potters who made fine black stoneware or basaltes numbered no more than half a dozen. Humphrey Palmer, Hanley, was perhaps the most formidable. By 1770 he was producing ornamental groups such as were only in the experimental stage at the Bell Works. Two of the finest basaltes figure groups in existence are signed "F Voyez Sculpt 1769" and impressed "MADE BY H PALMER HANLEY STAFFORDSHIRE". It was Palmer who challenged the validity of Wedgwood's patent by persistent infringement. An injunction was served upon him by Wedgwood, but a compromise was reached and the two men shared the patent rights until 1783, when their processes of encaustic painting and bronzing became free to all.

Palmer failed in 1778 and he took James Neale into partnership. The manufacture of basaltes continued, however, on a necessarily less lavish scale, with a body more compact of texture and brilliantly black. Neale introduced more fashionable and less complicated patterns. Of his vases, M. H. Grant writes: "nearly all have square shoulders, sometimes terraced or duplicated; the festoons hung between masks, scrolls, or long-necked heads of birds or beasts; the embossed rosette, or the suspended cameo." Basaltes, including tea ware of high merit, was made until about the early 1790s, when its manufacture was discontinued in favour of poor quality Egyptian black.

The Turners of Lane End made limited quantities of excellent basaltes capably modelled from 1762 to 1803. William Turner's basaltes may be distinguished from that of Josiah Wedgwood by a faintly silvery tinge on the body and the slightest sensation of roughness to the touch. Domestic ware and vases are of thinner section and show little evidence of lathing inside and beneath, their roughness being in marked contrast to the exterior surface. After Turner's sons succeeded in 1786 their basaltes was faintly tinged with green and its modelling lacked individuality. Until 1780 the mark was TURNER; then, during his partnership with Abbott until 1786, TURNER & Co. After Turner's death in 1786 and the departure of Abbott in the same year, the mark reverted to TURNER. In some examples of the late 1780s there is a blur showing where & Co was removed from the die.

The *Topographical Survey*, 1786, entered Enoch Wood and Ralph Wood as "Manufacturers of all kinds of useful and ornamental earthenware, Egyptian black, Cane and various other colours, also Black Figures, seals and cyphers." This clearly differentiates between the two types of black stoneware—basaltes and Egyptian black. Few other potters made basaltes. Josiah Wedgwood & Sons Ltd. and Adams of

Tunstall have both made excellent reproductions of old forms.

The improved Egyptian black evolved during the 1760s, stained with manganese dioxide, is invariably mistaken for basaltes. Tea ware cast in moulds was much less costly to manufacture than the harder basaltes thrown on the wheel or pressed, and required but one firing and little surface finishing apart from lathing. Cast work is simple to recognise: details of relief work are not accentuated and for the most part it displays a dull, dead-black unfired appearance. It might also be decorated with engine-turning or painted with encaustic colours.

Josiah Wedgwood is usually credited with the invention of the engine-turning lathe in the early 1760s: its invention has also been attributed to William Baddeley of Eastwood. One or other of these potters no doubt adapted the lathe tools to make clear, incised lines in black stoneware. The engine-turning lathe itself was used in the seventeenth century and was fully described and illustrated in *L'Art de Tourner*, by Charles Plumier, 1701. Wedgwood made his own engine-turning lathes, used at first for decorating red stoneware, and Baddeley established workshops for their manufacture. The engine-turning lathe rotated the black stoneware to be decorated with an eccentric oscillating movement whilst the cutting stone remained still. This could be adjusted to engrave a great variety of designs composed of complicated chevrons, chequers, zig-zags, dice, as well as to cut flutes on black stoneware in the unfired or green state. This did not pull against the tools and took shallow clear-cut incisions, impossible with ordinary earthenware.

An immense demand for tea- and coffee-ware in this long-lasting ceramic was created on the continent and America, some exporters such as William Mellor of Hanley distributing his entire output in this way. From the exporters' and foreign merchants' point of view Egyptian black was excellent, because its toughness enabled it to travel long distances by packhorse with a negligible proportion of breakages. The more friable earthenware might arrive with more than one-third of a consignment cracked or broken.

The existence of an inordinately large number of Egyptian black teapots and coffee pots was the result of their capacity to withstand boiling liquids. This prompted a large sale of single pots for everyday use in association with the more fragile lead-glazed earthenware tea-cups; porcelain and, in the nineteenth century, bone china, stone china and so on, were preferred, but these were costly.

Seven types of Egyptian black teapots sold in the late eighteenth century are recorded in an invoice issued by John Twemlow, Shelton, in 1797, and formerly in the possession of L. Jewitt. These were "E Black Teapots, Capt, fest^d, and fig^d [Egyptian black teapots, capped or galleried around the opening, mouldcd in relief with festoons and figures]; ditto upright [cylindrical], fest^d and fig^d; Oval E Black Teapots; ditto prest [sprigged] leaf, scollop top, fest^d and fig^d and banded; ditto, prest leaf and fest^d and fig^d and banded a'tip; ditto creams to match; ditto fluted; ditto coffee pots; octagon teapots with scollop top, and creams to match; oval plain teapots." These were all of small capacity and about four inches in height. From about 1815 teapots were made with progressively larger capacity.

Only a small proportion of Egyptian black was marked. Variations in weight, texture, hardness, and colour show that each potter evolved a formula to suit his personal circumstances, such as the capabilities of plant, the quality of the ware to be made and its price.

Characteristic features of marked examples are given below, taken from personal observation and from *The Makers of Black Basaltes*, by E. H. Grant.

BADDELEY, William Eastwood (1790s–1825) was entered in *Holden's Directory*, 1805, as "Egyptian black manufacturer". His ware was appreciably lighter in weight than that of most of his competitors. The teapot lid finial of a swan with a reversed neck is characteristic. EASTWOOD is stamped on the lower front edge of a piece—on teapots immediately below the spout.

BARKERS of Lane End produced this ware in the late eighteenth century and until 1810. The firm consisted of three brothers and a partner named Robert Garner. Their ware was of cottage quality, heavily built and carelessly finished. Teapot bodies shaped as sharp-pointed ovals were favoured. The curve might be interrupted by projecting buttresses, converting the piece into a hexagon. A gallery, scalloped or wavy edged, encircled the opening and was so deep that it concealed all but the finial of the lid. In some instances lids were hinged. Low relief ornament included curiously scrolled and swelling columns. The name BARKER was impressed beneath.

BIRCH, Edmund John, Hanley (1790–1810), had an immense output, the jet black body being closely compact and the potting of high standard. Narrow engine-turned ribbing is characteristic, and broad, flat fluting less frequent. Teapot and coffee-pot lid finials were invariably of the widow pattern, the figure sitting cross-legged with a flat cake in the right hand and a two-handled covered cruse in the left. Galleried rims were scalloped. Bases were carefully lathe-finished and polished. Modellers might impress their cypher at the handle-base, PM and RD being most common. The name BIRCH is impressed in capitals or lower case letters in several sizes, or EIB.

BRADLEY & CO., Coalport, at work in the early nineteenth century were originally makers of clay pipes. Their teapots in Egyptian black are in a rough, poorly coloured body with casting details badly blurred. The projecting columns suggest adaptation from the pattern associated with the Barker firm of Lane End, and the lion finial on lids is adapted from the colossal lion of Cnidos in the British Museum. The mark is BRADLEY COALPORT.

CASTLEFORD, Yorkshire (1790–1820) made the ware with a deep bright black body faintly tinged with green and so hard that it was highly polished despite its inherent roughness of texture. Moulded details are poor. Mark, DD & Co CASTLEFORD.

CLEWS, J. & R., Cobridge (c. 1814–36) made a brittle body of poor quality with a high gloss and decorated it with engine turning. Mark CLEWS.

HACKWOOD, W. & Son, Hanley (1842–56) followed

the patterns of Wedgwood's basaltes but in a coarse grey, gritty body disfigured with flaws and blisters and impossible to bring to a polish. Engine turning is poorly defined. This curiously enough was in great demand in some continental countries and was impressed HACKWOOD. In 1856 the pottery was acquired by Cookson & Harding, the same poor black being manufactured until 1862, impressed C & H LATE HACKWOOD.

HERCULANEUM POTTERY, Liverpool (1793–1841) is of interest as the recipe book kept by the manager, B. Tomkinson, records the formula of Egyptian black: blue clay 100, calcined ochre 60, manganese dioxide 40, iron scales 20. The resulting body tended to display a greyish hue, and was rough and gritty. In addition to the ever-popular tea ware attempts at good modelling in the Wedgwood taste exist, but the quality and processing of the black stoneware were too poor for success. Vases were made with plinths of white stoneware. The impressed marks were HERCULANEUM and HERCULANEUM POTTERY inside the lips of vases.

KEELING, Anthony, Tunstall (late eighteenth century) is entered in the *Topographical Survey*, 1786, as "manufacturer of Egyptian Black", but no marked examples are known.

KEELING, Joseph, Hanley, was at work in the early nineteenth century. Two recently discovered specimens show his Egyptian black to have been of coarse body with a tendency towards a greyish tint, poorly potted and badly designed. These were impressed JOSEPH KEELING: the name in full distinguished him from his relative James Keeling.

LAKIN AND POOL, Burslem (early 1780s–95) may be noted for the very compact texture of their ware, jet black with glossy surface. Excellent figures were made in imitation of Wedgwood's basaltes, but quality was, of course, inferior to that of the finer stoneware. Tea ware and vases are characterised by borders of interlaced circles. Marks, LAKIN; LAKIN & POOL; POOL LAKIN & Co.

LEEDS POTTERY, Yorkshire introduced basaltes and Egyptian black to their manufactures in about 1800. Their basaltes were densely compact and intensely hard with a faintly bluish hue on the black, which takes on a high polish at the wheel, the undersurfaces being turned and finished with equal brilliance. The impressed mark, always including the name LEEDS, is clear and distinct, showing it to have been impressed deeply and carefully before turning.

Leeds Egyptian black was rarely marked. Jewitt's investigations show that up to 1815 between ninety and a hundred patterns and sizes of teapots were placed on the market, oval, cylindrical, octagonal and twelve-sided, with a comparable array of cream jugs and sugar basins. Decorations included flowers, fruit, festoons, geometrical borders, trophies, medallions, groups of figures and other ornament moulded in relief, and engine turning, checkered and fluted patterns predominating.

Borders were frequently composed of interlacing rings traversed by a cable and a jagged frieze resembling wheat stalks without their corn. Lids included all types then fashionable, inward and outward fitting, sliding, and hinged: their finials were mainly lions, swans, flowers and the widow.

MAYER, Elijah, Hanley (1775-1813) produced a dense-textured fabric displaying a soft bluish tint. Details of moulded decoration are usually indistinct. Teapots and coffee-pots were exceptionally substantial, and from about 1790 were accompanied by cups of porcelain thinness. These features probably made Elijah Mayer's Egyptian black the most popular on the market, for more remaining specimens bear his mark than that of any other potter, Wedgwood and Birch being runners-up. In the early nineteenth century hollow-ware rims were encircled with the Greek key pattern, and there might be a medallion in moulded relief on each side of the body, often of commemorative interest. This may provide a clue to the date of first production, such as the Nelson teapot which displays trophies of Trafalgar and the Nile. The hinged lid was made by this firm. A mark is usually present: E MAYER or M, impressed on the encircling foot rim, thus preventing removal on the lathe, or, if no foot rim is present, in microscopic letters on the extreme edge of the piece and very difficult to discover. The initial M has been noted beneath the handle and inside the rim.

MAYER, Joseph & Co., Hanley (1813–30) were successors to Elijah Mayer, and produced similar black ware marked MAYER & CO.

MOSELEY, John, Burslem (early nineteenth century) made a dense black, close textured smooth body, with an excellent polish. It is appreciably lighter in weight than most Egyptian black. The mark is MOSELEY.

MYATT, Joseph, Lane Delph (1790–1825) produced a body closely resembling Mayer's Egyptian black, with a faintly bluish tinge, but cups and saucers are more substantially potted. The ware is marked in bold capitals MYATT within an impressed rectangle.

SHORTHOSE & HEATH, Hanley (c. 1780–1823) made three-piece tea sets of fine quality jet black body, decorated with engine turning and moulded ornament. The marks are SHORTHOSE; SHORTHOSE & HEATH; and then SHORTHOSE & CO. from 1805 to 1820.

SPODE, Josiah I and II, and COPELAND, Stoke-upon-Trent (1780s–1880s) marked work in which the body approaches the quality of basaltes, with comparable sheen and smoothness. An engine-turned teapot with cylindrical body recently found in the works was marked SPODE. Manufacture continued into the Copeland period from 1829, when Etruscan shaped vases were made, decorated with encaustic paints more brilliant than those of Wedgwood.

TAYLOR, George, Hanley (1802–30) made Egyptian black that was light in weight and finished with a smear glaze. Teapots are sometimes duplicates of those made by the Barkers from whom possibly he acquired the moulds in 1810. Mark, GEO TAYLOR and G TAYLOR.

WEDGWOOD & CO., Knottingley, Yorks (1792–1826) made a close imitation of Josiah Wedgwood's tea table basaltes, but this is to be recognised at once by inferior craftsmanship. Mark, WEDGWOOD & CO.

Dozens of Staffordshire potters made second-rate Egyptian black during the late Georgian and early Victorian periods, but little of this was marked. The majority was exported. That demand continued is shown by the fact that Henry Venables established a pottery at Hanley in 1860 as a specialist in this ware. Again, in 1880, H. Aynesley & Co., Longton, began manufacture from moulds formerly used by Robinson & Chatham who ceased manufacture in 1870.

Basaltes and Egyptian black require careful treatment from the collector. E. H. Grant advises that "this ware *should never be washed*. Its beauty depends upon its 'bloom' and this can be instantly and for long destroyed by the use of water. Should a piece be acquired dingy and dusty, friction with a soft cloth will soon restore the polish, and every rubbing will add to its beauty . . . if, as is too often the case, the article has been recently washed, a little oil, walnut for choice, will at least remove the objectionable deadness of the surface, though the artificial sheen will never equal the velvet overlaid by one or two centuries of time upon the original lathe polish of the potter."

The collector will meet with a series of excellently potted Georgian teapots in earthenware displaying the outward appearance of Egyptian black but known to the pottery trade as "Egyptian". These are in a hardish but coarse red or brown ceramic, midway between earthenware and stoneware, coated with black encaustic paint. These inexpensive vessels were cast with relief ornament, but could not be engine-turned as this would reveal the clay beneath.

One early potter of this deceptive ware was Joseph Cyples, who operated at Longton 1780 to 1800. In the *Topographical Survey*, 1786, he is entered as a "manufacturer of Egyptian and Pottery in general". Characteristically, the body of a teapot, dark brown in colour, might be encircled with a band of moulded relief work against a ground of stippling. This would be impressed CYPLES on the base. John and Richard Riley, who potted in Burslem 1800 to 1827, made similar black ware possessing a lightweight base, covered with encaustic paint which fired to a dull gloss and feels soapy to the touch. This ware is impressed RILEY.

Chapter Seven

JASPER

TO most people Josiah Wedgwood's name is associated first and foremost with immensely decorative classical or semi-classical figures and their festoons and arabesques, clear-cut as carved gem-stone cameos and gleaming white against the matt, subdued opacity of their coloured backgrounds. This is as it should be, for these creations in his celebrated jasper were Wedgwood's great original contribution to English pottery: other ceramics he improved and adapted, sometimes almost out of all recognition, but here alone he evolved something entirely new as well as lastingly appealing.

Wedgwood's success with basaltes prompted him to continue with experiments that culminated in the production of fine white stoneware. Jasper is basically a white hard, close-textured stoneware made to suggest porcelain by the addition of barium sulphate. Its smooth non-porous surface required no glaze, and when spread thinly it was translucent. No reference to jasper was made in the first edition of Wedgwood and Bentley's 60-page catalogue published in London during 1773. In the second edition, however, issued a year later, it was listed as "a fine white *terra cotta*, of great beauty and delicacy, proper for cameos, portraits and bas-reliefs." At first the bas-reliefs were off-white, but two years later a perfectly white stoneware was in production, enabling Wedgwood to write triumphantly to his partner, "We are now absolute with Jasper". This name was given because its density permitted it to be given a high polish on the lapidary's wheel in the same way as natural stone.

Wedgwood's experiment book still exists detailing the

results of the many hundreds of trials. It proved impossible, however, for Wedgwood or any other Staffordshire potter to evolve a pure white fine stoneware without Cornish stone. This ingredient in its purified form was held under a patent monopoly until 1775, when its free use for earthenware products was obtained through the strenuous efforts of Wedgwood and his fellow potters. Wedgwood immediately secured an interest in a china clay mine at St. Austell, Cornwall, operating it until his death under the name of Wedgwood and Carthew and supplying other potters at reasonable prices. Searle gives one formula for pure white jasper as: barium sulphate 48, Cornish stone 16, blue ball clay 14, flint 10, a little gypsum. After about 1820 potters might use barium sulphate 59, china clay 59, flint 10, barium carbonate 2.

Although it was so hard and vitrified, jasper could be stained throughout its substance by any of seven colours that would serve as a background for the applied embossments in white to stand out clearly in high relief: dark blue, lavender, a bluish pink known to collectors as lilac, sage green, olive green, black and, rarely, an attractive yellow. These varied in tone for technical reasons then difficult to overcome, such as impurities in the materials and difficulties in controlling firing temperatures.

These mineral oxides did not stain the pure white decorations applied in relief. Blue was secured by adding 0.5 per cent cobalt oxide to the white body; chromic acid produced sage and olive green; refined manganese coloured lilac, but owing to the uncertainty of the tint it was seldom used. The yellow tint was given by adding Naples yellow, and black by a mixture of calcined ochre and manganese dioxide.

The early panels for plaques, medallions and so on coloured throughout their body were known as solid jasper. Three main difficulties were met with during potting: the panels could not be made perfectly flat, they had almost imperceptible undulations, and warping resulted in a large percentage of wasters; many of the applied reliefs in white became spotted or coloured in firing; and hollow-ware was unprofitable.

By 1785 Wedgwood had overcome these and other problems

by evolving a solution of coloured jasper into which white jasper could be dipped before firing, so that the ware was covered in a film of colour, uniform in thickness and tint. White jasper panels were ground flat on front and sides by the same method as mirror glass, since abrasion marks were concealed beneath the dip. Hollowware could now be finished by turning and still, when dipped, possess an impeccable finish. On 21st November 1785, Josiah Wedgwood wrote: "The new jasper, white within, will be the only sort made in future: but as the workmanship is nearly double, the price must be raised. I think it must be about 20 per cent . . . as these are my latest, I hope they will be found to be my most approved works." Apart from tiny medallions for setting in jewellery and the like, solid jasper, it appears, was discontinued after the death of Wedgwood until 1858, when it was revived following technical progress that had made possible the manufacture of perfectly flat panels. A dark blue dip might then cover panels of solid pale blue.

In the sixth edition of the catalogue, dated 1787, no reference is made to the new jasper dip, although jasper is described by name and more fully than formerly, as "a white porcelain *bisque* of exquisite beauty and delicacy, possessing the general quality of the basaltes, together with that of receiving colours through its whole substance, in a manner which no other *body*, ancient or modern, has been known to do. This renders it particularly fit for cameos, portraits, and all subjects in bas-relief, as the ground may be made of any colour throughout, without paint or enamel, and the raised figures of a pure white." The same catalogue, however, is illustrated with an aquatint print in colours of a cup in jasper dip of two colours and described as "thrown and turned and lapidary polished within like the natural stone, ornamented with bas reliefs and very highly finished." Approaching porcelain in its translucency, this cup was touched with gilding.

Laminated jasper was made for a short period in the late eighteenth century, confined to bas-reliefs on blue grounds. In these an extra layer of a darker blue was introduced at the bevelled edges. This might be carried right across the field and is visible in the fire holes cut in the back to prevent warping during firing. This, when polished on the bevelled edge, gives all the effects of a two-strata or three-strata cameo.

Original models for the white relief work applied in jasper were carved in wax. From these intaglio moulds were prepared of plaster of paris or fire clay. The potter pressed the moist white jasper into these moulds with his thumb until every line and crevice was filled. Superfluous clay was then scraped off level with the face of the mould. A few minutes later the pattern in relief was extracted skilfully from the mould, dipped in water and applied by hand to the coloured panel by a process known as sprigging. The plastic relief was then finished by hand-tooling, shadows being sharpened by undercutting the edges. The subsequent firing was a technical triumph resulting from long and patient experiment and requiring considerable skill on the part of the operator concerned. Special, lightly covered saggers were used, correct placement in the kiln being important to prevent the warping of panels which rarely exceeded one-quarter inch in thickness.

When Wedgwood began to issue bas relief medallions and cameos a vogue was set for collecting them as "cabinet pictures". Like portraits, each was sold in a paper wrapper printed with the name of the subject, its source, and Wedgwood's catalogue number. In July 1774 Thomas Bentley wrote to Wedgwood that he had "very great Satisfaction in setting out all the Medallions, Bas-reliefs, &c. before me at once, a Sight I could never gratify myself with before. They can now be seen by customers . . . . . and I think must considerably promote the Sale of them." By 1777 more than 1700 different specimens were on view in the display cases in the London show-rooms, Greek Street, Soho.

Cabinet makers enriched furniture such as bookcases and writing tables with Wedgwood's jasper; architects demanded sets of five or seven for insertion in marble mantelpieces; and continental coach builders set them in coach panels.

A considerable trade was carried on in the manufacture of jasper portraits to private commission, no order being accepted for fewer than ten copies. The catalogue instructed clients to take to the London show-rooms a profile portrait in wax carved by one of the many wax portraitists then in business: this would cost three to five guineas. Wedgwood himself recommended Joachim Smith as a portraitist conversant with his requirements. The wax model was required to be one-fifth larger than the completed portrait in jasper. The catalogue notice regarding personal portraiture read:

" . . . if gentlemen or ladies choose to have models of themselves, families or friends, made in wax, or cut in stones of proper sizes for seals, rings, lockets or bracelets, they may have as many durable copies of these models as they please, either in cameo or intaglio, for any of the above purposes, at a moderate expense. . . . A model of a portrait in wax, when it is of a proper size for a seal, ring or bracelet will cost about *three* guineas, and a portrait from three to six inches in diameter *three*, *four*, or *five guineas*. Any number of *portraits* in the same material, from three to six inches in diameter, not fewer than ten at 10s 6d each."

In early portrait medallions there is a circular hole at the back covered by the solid modelling of the head: this prevented warping and cracking during firing.

Jewellers and toymen mounted bas-reliefs in ormolu frames which might be delicately chased, double gilded, and parcel burnished: the more ornate were given elaborate crestings. Frames have been noted, too, in gilded silver, designed with bows and scrollwork or cast with floral sprays and birds. Wedgwood wrote of his bas-relief cameos: "these are set in gold and cut-steel mountings for rings, lockets, bracelets, snuff-boxes, watch-keys, and chains, and a number of other trinkets which have lately been much worn by the nobility." Miss Meteyard listed some thirty other articles into which they were set, such as chatelaines, hair pins, belt buckles, brooches, pendants, ear-rings and coat buttons.

Boulton and Fothergill, Soho, near Birmingham, manufactured mounts for jasper jewellery, specialising in cut-steel. Facets cut as diamonds, highly burnished and so treated as to be rust resistant, reflect light as brilliantly today as when they were taken from the wheel. Such a mounting might be enriched with an inner fillet of gold and the addition of polished jasper beads. Reversible cameos were made for pendants and ear-drops with figures on both sides.

There appears to be no evidence that vases were made in jasper until the mid-1780s. Of these Wedgwood wrote to Sir William Hamilton in June 1786: "They have been the object of very much labour and time, every ornament and leaf being made in a separate mould and then laid upon the vase with great care and accuracy, and afterwards wrought over again on the vase itself by an artist equal to the work." Some of these vases are miracles of patient tooling, such as the Bacchanalia and grapes adapted by potters for a century to come.

John Coward was appointed manager of Etruria's ornamental department at its establishment in 1769, his salary being £200 a year. At the same time William Hackwood, an engraver of transfer prints for the painted enamel trade at Bilston, joined Wedgwood and became his chief staff modeller in bas-relief. In 1774 Wedgwood wrote: "Hackwood is of the greatest value and consequence in finishing fine small work. We want half-a-dozen more Hackwoods." He remained with the firm until 1832. Some of Hackwood's plaques equal in every way those designed and modelled for Wedgwood by eminent sculptors of the period. In January 1776 Wedgwood recorded that "The Birth of Bacchus", modelled by Hackwood from Michelangelo's seal, was then the largest jasper plaque that had been produced. It measured 27 inches across by 12 inches high and sold for thirty shillings. "The Trumpet of Bacchus" made immediately afterwards was larger.

Hackwood's excellent profile portraits include those of George III, Queen Charlotte, Josiah Wedgwood, David Garrick, all modelled in 1777, Admiral Keppel, Dr. Priestley, Louis XVI, and an old bricklayer Edward Bourne, employed on the Etruria pottery kilns. This portrait of Bourne and the profile of Wedgwood are signed W.H in script, the only instances of a modeller's mark to be found on the surface of any jasper bas-relief.

More than seventy independent designers and modellers were employed by Wedgwood during the next quarter of a century. Among the earliest was John Flaxman, later a Royal Academician. His first Wedgwood commission was in 1775 when he was twenty, the great potter becoming a welcome source of revenue for the next twelve years. He made many excellent profile portraits in wax including the complete series of George III and his family, the Duchess of Devonshire, Captain Cook, and Doctor Johnson, at prices ranging from two to three guineas. Included in Flaxman's account for 1784 was the still existing model "A bas relief in Wax of Veturia and Voluminia entreating Coriolanus, £9–9–0"; in 1787, "a wax model of Mercury uniting the Hands of England and France, £13–13–0"; and "a bas relief of Hercules in the Hesperian Garden, £23–0–0", in modern currency approximating £250. This celebrated group was the last he did for Wedgwood, for shortly afterwards he left for Italy for the purpose of study and as director to a group of Italian freelance modellers employed in copying from museums classical designs considered suitable for bas-relief work on jasper hollow-ware. These were Angelini, Dalmazzo, Fratoddi, Mangiarotti, Manzolini and Pacetti.

Coward had been succeeded by Henry Webber as ornamental manager at Etruria in 1782. Six years later he was sent to Rome as technical adviser to the Italian modellers of whom Pacetti was the most important. Among his works were "Priam Begging the body of Hector", "The Sacrifice of Iphigenia", "The Nine Muses", "Apotheosis of Faustina", and "Endymion Sleeping on the Rock Latmos". In addition John Dadaere worked in Flaxman's studio on a salary basis until 1794. Here he modelled the large Borghese vase and pedestal, eventually succeeding Webber as head of the ornamental department at Etruria.

Collectors sometimes specialise in the work of a single designer or modeller such as Flaxman, Hackwood, Louis François Roubillac, Lady Diana Beauclerk or Lady Templetown. The story of Lady Templetown's designs for Wedgwood's jasper is typical. The daughter of Sir William Shuckworth Broughton, Poston Court, Hereford, at the age of twenty she married Clotworthy Upton, clerk-comptroller to the Dowager Princess of Wales. Seven years later, in 1776, her husband was elevated to the peerage with the title Baron Templetown of Templetown in the County of Antrim. Lady Templetown's name is often mis-spelled:

Josiah Wedgwood himself invariably wrote "Templetoun" and some authorities have preferred "Templeton".

Like most educated women of her period Lady Templetown devoted considerable time and energy to a hobby. Her enthusiasm was the study of art, at which she showed more then average ability, as is indicated by a landscape drawing in the Victoria and Albert Museum. During the early 1780s there was a vogue for decorative cut-outs or shadow pictures—the work now better known as silhouettes. Lady Templetown delighted in the craft, cutting the paper without the aid of preliminary drawings, and it was in the form of cut-outs that much of her work was accepted by Wedgwood. It has been suggested that an interest in modelling and sculpture prompted him to consider designs for his bas-reliefs. No such work by her has been recorded, however, and it must be remembered that other talented amateurs were applying their cut paper work to decorative purposes. Mrs. Delany, wife of the Dean of Down, was reputed to have decorated innumerable mantelpieces long before Wedgwood's jasper panels were used for this purpose.

Records in the Wedgwood Museum show that Lady Templetown's first cut-outs were received by Wedgwood on 21st June 1785. These were "The Bourbonnaise Shepherd" and "Maria and her Dog", both based on scenes from Laurence Sterne's then popular book *A Sentimental Journey*. An opera-glass with a single telescopic glass mounted in ivory and ormolu and ornamented with "Maria and her Dog" in jasper, white on blue, was made for Queen Charlotte. The cut-outs were handed to William Hackwood, who gave them form in relief.

The original of "Domestic Employment", depicting a series of homely incidents in classical style including a graceful woman with a distaff, was drawn late in 1783 and modelled in the same year. After being used as a plaque, this design was divided into sections and, with "Maria and her Dog", was used to decorate an early morning tea-set of jasper in white on blue. "The Sacrifice to Peace", one of the largest reliefs from Lady Templetown's designs, was supplied by her as a drawing.

Another plaque, "Maternal Affection", designed in 1783

and modelled by Hackwood in the same year, was so finely executed that she wrote congratulating Wedgwood on the masterly result. Designs for medallions bought by Wedgwood in 1793 included "Sportive Love", "The Young Seamstress', and "Young Girl Reading", all modelled by Hackwood. Various cupids such as "Cupids' Parade" and "Cupids at Play" were designed in 1784 and issued as plaques two years later, at once achieving considerable popularity. Among other designs were "Charlotte at the Tomb of Werther"; "An Offering to Ceres", of which the model was made in December 1787; and "Friendship Consoling Affliction". Some of Lady Templetown's plaques were catalogued in pairs, such as "Contemplation and Companion", "Genii and Companion", "Family School and Companion", "Study and Companion".

Samuel Smiles in his *Life of Wedgwood* wrote: "had Lady Templetown been a poorer woman she might have made a fortune by her wonderful gifts." She does not appear to have continued this work after her husband's death in 1785 when she took over the management of his extensive estate.

Until early in the nineteenth century the surface of Wedgwood's jasper continued to suggest satin to the touch, in the manner associated only with the firm's finest jasper. Until the 1820s texture remained fine and uniform of grain. During the second quarter of the nineteenth century there was little demand for jasper and in examples noted the relief work has had a chalky appearance. In 1846 Robert Brown joined Francis Wedgwood as partner. Jewitt describes Brown as "a man of great experience and wonderful business talents. He realised a handsome fortune entirely by his own industry and exertions and possessed a refined taste." The firm responded to his influence and by 1851 the Jury of the Great Exhibition was able to record that the Wedgwood exhibits "consist chiefly of a faithful revival of the forms originated by the enterprise of the elder Wedgwood, some of the most remarkable of which were suggested by the genius of Flaxman. The classic beauty of some of these designs in jasper and fine stoneware have never since been surpassed or equalled." The firm was awarded a prize medal.

The jasper entries in the Official Catalogue are a useful

reference guide, preventing confusion with eighteenth-century designs:

"Blue jasper, with white bas-reliefs from the antique:—Vase, 25 inches high, with pedestal 10 inches high, 'Sacrifice to Cupid'. Vase, 27½ inches high, 'Apotheosis of a Poet'. Vase, with pedestal, 19½ inches, 'Ulysses discovering Achilles'. Another to match, 'Infancy of Achilles.' Vases and pedestals, 21 inches, 'Muses'. Vases, 12 inches, 'Hunting and Hawking', and 'The Arts and Sciences'. Various other vases of different sizes, plain and ornamented, including 'Hercules at the Garden of the Hesperides' [designed as a panel by Flaxman in August 1787 at a charge of £23-0-0]. Bacchanalian subjects, rivers and arabesque designs. Cameos of various colours, with white bas-reliefs from the antique. Set of chess-men; thirty-four pieces by Flaxman [who in 1784 charged six guineas for designing them]."

The Art-Journal Illustrated Catalogue, 1851, gives the name of the firm as Wedgwood and Brown, and states that "the ground of each article is of a lavender tint, the figures and ornaments in pure white clay in relief upon the surface, have the delicate and beautiful shades of the tint faintly appearing through the more delicate parts": nineteen examples are illustrated. Solid jasper was re-introduced in 1856. Robert Brown died in 1859. Jasper continued to be the great speciality of the works. J. F. Blacker, writing in 1910, illustrated fourteen jasper vases and fifty-five plaques then in current production.

Wedgwood's jasper from 1772 was impressed with the name of the firm: in that year he wrote to Bentley, "Going on a plan to mark the whole." Until Bentley's death in 1780 the mark was WEDGWOOD & BENTLEY impressed in four sizes. Intaglios also had the catalogue number impressed beneath the name of the subject title. In 1774 Bentley complained to the works that "many of the Heads have been number'd and marked wrong". From 1790 the name WEDGWOOD or Wedgwood in six varying sizes of type was impressed. The word ENGLAND has been impressed beneath the name from 1891. Occasionally in recent years an unscrupulous dealer has converted the word *England* into *Bentley*, preceded by &, presumably by the use of an electric tool. But the alert collector will recognise such conversions, which are illegal. Symbols consisting of three capital letters indicating date of manufacture have been impressed since 1860.

The number of potters capable of producing jasper ware was severely limited owing to the costly technical difficulties involved. William Adams, a favoured pupil of Josiah Wedgwood, left his master in 1789 to establish a pottery at Greengates, Tunstall, where he produced some of the most successful imitations of Wedgwood's jasper bas-reliefs, using the processes he had learned at Etruria. After his death in 1805 manufacture of jasper was abandoned until the 1880s, when his successors used exactly the same methods. J. F. Blacker commenting on this noted that "it is worthy of remark that the jasper designs used by the old potters only resembled each other when similar casts were bought from independent designers."

Humphrey Neale of Hanley claimed to have been earlier in the field of jasper bas-reliefs than Wedgwood himself. But for the marks it would be difficult to distinguish between the work of the two potters. The firm of Palmer and Neale made a series of exceptionally large medallions from 1776.

John Turner and his son, of Lane End, produced bas-reliefs in an excellent, fine-textured jasper, either slaty-blue, green or black. He was a formidable competitor of the Wedgwoods from about 1790. This fine jasper ware, marked TURNER impressed, must not be confused with ware marked TURNER JASPER WARE. This was made during the 1860s and 1870s by Bates, Walker and Company, Burslem, who possessed Turner's original moulds. These were used for reproducing Turner's jasper in a terra-cotta body covered with slip coloured green, blue, chocolate, buff or maroon, to which jasper bas-reliefs in white were applied. The vitreous terra-cotta, however, lacks the fineness and hardness of real jasper.

Jasper has been noted impressed with the names of the following Staffordshire potters: Elijah Mayer, E. J. Birch, Humphrey Palmer, and T. & J. Lockett.

It is stated frequently that only English potters could manufacture jasper. Several German potters, however, adopted Wedgwood's methods in the 1790s. For instance, Louis Victor Gerverot was employed at Etruria from about 1786 to 1795: he then moved to Fürstenburg as manager, remaining there until 1814. During this period he introduced the manufacture of jasper vases and bas-reliefs, direct imitations of Wedgwood's forms and patterns. These are still reproduced from the original models. The mark is a script capital F with or without a crown above.

The Ilmenau pottery in Thuringia also copied Wedgwood's jasper from about 1792 under Christian Nonne, who became proprietor in 1808. There was an extensive production of vases, portrait cameos and medallions between 1800 and 1815, marked N & R from 1808.

Chapter Eight

CREAM-COLOURED EARTHENWARE

THOMAS ASTBURY of Shelton, early in the reign of
George I, made a ceramic discovery destined to revolu-
tionise the pottery of Staffordshire. By mixing ball clay from
the West Country with light burning marls from near-by
Fenton Calvert and adding calcined flints he produced a
hard white stoneware suitable for salt-glazing. This same
body, fired at a lower temperature, produced a whitish
earthenware from which eventually was derived cream-
coloured earthenware. This was glazed by applying to the
surface finely powdered and sifted natural sulphide of lead,
known to Georgian potters as smithum and to collectors as
galena. The shaped and decorated leather-hard ware,
sprinkled with smithum, was fired only once, at a moderate
temperature, baking and whitening the clay and melting the
lead in one operation. The smithum spread into a film
covering the surface with a rich yellowish or brownish
glaze, the tint being caused by the presence of iron in either
the clay or the smithum. A colourless glaze of higher gloss
was secured more expensively by using calcined lead ground
to a flour-like powder. This glaze penetrated further into
the body than did that prepared from smithum. A range of
purples and browns was obtained by blending the colourless
glaze with manganese—known to the old potters as magnus
—and greens by adding copper oxide.

A quarter of a century later Enoch Booth established
Tunstall's first large pottery and set out to improve the
earthenware evolved by Astbury. In this he succeeded far
beyond his expectations. By carefully washing local clay,
mixing it with clays from Devonshire and Dorset, and

adding calcined flint he produced a deep cream-coloured earthenware.

Booth is usually credited with the invention of liquid glaze in about 1750. Liquid glaze had been invented earlier, however, by Thomas Frye, who was granted a patent (No. 649) on 11th November 1749. The process, therefore, was Frye's monopoly until 1763: Booth must have been a licensee. This invention enabled the plastic clay to be fired to a porous or biscuit state until sufficiently firm to be handled and dipped into liquid lead glaze, composed of calcined lead ground with calcined flint, clay and water. The glazed biscuit was given a second firing which converted the biscuit into earthenware and fused the glaze to its surface. The resulting glaze was highly lustrous and of uniform thickness and tint. For the first time every piece in a matching service could be glazed exactly alike. This combination of flint glaze and double firing completely revolutionised the pottery industry. From its tint and glaze this ceramic became known as cream-coloured earthenware. This was quickly copied and improved by other Staffordshire potters and was the base from which Wedgwood developed his celebrated Queen's ware.

Josiah Wedgwood (1730–95) was only eleven when he began work as a thrower for his eldest brother Thomas, and this was but a preliminary to the five-year apprenticeship begun in 1744 to learn "the Art, Mystery, Occupation, or Imployment of Thrower and Handleing". When he left his brother at the age of twenty-two he was already a practical potter with an all-round knowledge of his craft and eager for greater responsibility. His first venture was a partnership with John Harrison, working a pottery formerly operated by John Alders at Stoke-upon-Trent. Here they made agate, tortoiseshell, black and salt-glazed wares, but this partnership was a period of frustration to the energetic Josiah anxious to extend their scope of production, and the agreement was cancelled early in 1754.

Wedgwood then entered into a five-year partnership with Thomas Whieldon of Fenton Low, who was then extending his productions to include tortoiseshell ware. This was a deep cream-coloured earthenware of the Astbury type decorated with a mottled lead glaze stained green, greyish-black, brown, blue and yellow. Correspondence exists showing that Wedgwood was at liberty to experiment on his own account without obligation to reveal formulas or results to his partner. That he was already a technician of unusual ability is proved by the progressive improvement in Whieldon's earthenware and glaze at this time, during which he evolved the now celebrated green glaze and cauliflower ware.

Six months before his partnership with Whieldon ended in 1759 Wedgwood was preparing the ground for independent action. An agreement dated 30th December 1758 exists to prove that he then engaged his cousin Thomas Wedgwood, "Journeyman potter now liveing at the City of Worcester", to work for him as a journeyman potter from 5th May 1759 to 11th December 1765 at a wage of "twenty-two Pounds of lawfull money for every years service." It is to be assumed that Thomas was employed at the Worcester Tonquin Manufactory where he had every opportunity of observing the organisation of a prosperous porcelain factory employing a large number of people, in contrast to the master potters of Staffordshire. This experience he was later to find invaluable: in the event he became works manager at Ivy House and after expiry of the agreement Josiah took him into partnership.

Thus it was as a practical potter with some managerial and research experience, and already looking beyond the tradition-bound methods of his immediate competitors, that Wedgwood took the plunge and for ten pounds a year rented Ivy House, a small pottery with a thatched living cottage in the centre of Burslem. His period as a potter was no more than five years, but it proved revolutionary in its ultimate effects upon the national pottery trade.

To begin with Wedgwood potted the staple manufactures of the Burslem district, using local clays, speed of production being his first consideration. Craftsmanship was leisurely and crude and his plant primitive, comprising little more than potters' wheels, common turning lathes, and a few cutting tools and knives. Tool marks distinguish the early Ivy House productions. Wedgwood, eager to produce finer wares than his competitors, gradually abandoned old-fashioned methods. For example, each teapot in its pattern group had to be exactly alike, without any of the minor decorations which now delight collectors of early Staffordshire ware. Although in poor health he supervised every process in the pottery, instructing each man individually, designing and making new tools, designing and building more efficient kilns and drying pans.

Ivy House productions at first reflected the Whieldon style: it is difficult to distinguish between them. Wedgwood immediately set to work to lighten the deep cream-coloured earthenware by handwashing the unpurified Devonshire and Cornwall clays carried by packhorse from Northwich Docks to Ivy House. This success was matched by his introduction, in April 1760, of a hard, brilliant yellow glaze, recorded in his notebook as "Experiment 100". This transformed the earthenware, concealing blemishes, rendering it impermeable to liquids, and producing a smoother, harder surface better suited to withstand spoons and cutlery than any earlier lead glaze.

Josiah C. Wedgwood in *Staffordshire Pottery and its History*, 1925, states that Wedgwood's original cream-coloured earthenware consisted of cleansed plastic clay 75–85 per cent, and calcined flint or sand 15–25 per cent. The glaze was composed of flint or sand 30–40 per cent, carbonate of soda 15–20 per cent, and nitre, fritted together. To the frit was added 35–45 per cent of red lead ground to a creamy consistency in water. The glaze was made available by Wedgwood to the entire industry.

Mr. Mankowitz reports that "in early items [of Wedgwood creamware] the glaze often shows an oily, iridescent or rainbow effect when held at an angle to the light; the body is light in weight; there is no crackle; items with border decorations are usually 'impress marked in upper case, while earlier freelance and transfer decorated items carry the lower case mark: workmen's tool marks are commonly found in all items in the range."

Caudle parties at this time were fashionable events to celebrate births, and it was customary to present mothers with sets of caudle cups, stands and covers as congratulatory gifts. This was a conceit even more popular after the birth of the Prince of Wales in August 1762. Josiah Wedgwood, sensing valuable publicity, took advantage of this custom and presented Queen Charlotte with a combined caudle and breakfast service, probably seventy-three pieces in all, made from his improved glazed creamware.

Its yellow glaze was applied over raised sprigs of jessamine and other flowers, which were then painted in natural colours by Thomas Daniel and Daniel Steel, with lavish gilding fixed and burnished under Wedgwood's direct supervision. The Queen was so delighted that she later ordered a table service of the same material. Wedgwood submitted several pieces which, Llewellyn Jewitt has recorded, "were approved with the exception of the plate which was the common barleycorn pattern, then being made by the salt-glaze potters. Her Majesty disliked the roughness—the barleycorn work as it was called—and therefore this part was made smooth: on the edge was left only the bands marking the compartments and being approved by Her Majesty, the pattern was called Queen's Pattern." When George III saw the service he commissioned one for the dinner table without bands or ribs and suggested other alterations. The revised version was marked on the back of each piece, "The Royal Pattern" in gold. Thereafter Wedgwood always made his domestic ware with a smooth surface. In appreciation of these royal favours Wedgwood named his improved cream-coloured earthenware "Queen's ware".

At Ivy House and later, Wedgwood made innumerable globular teapots. Some were decorated with landscapes in relief, others ornamented with sprigged work or covered with a mass of impressed dots. This shape otherwise followed the Staffordshire rustic style with crabstock, twisted and notched handles. Many were covered with tortoiseshell glaze, but in 1760 he introduced improved green glaze and issued teapots and other vessels cast in the form of cauliflowers and pineapples, their lower portions being encircled with appropriate leaves rising from the base. These are to be distinguished from those of his competitors by their more detailed modelling and finer finish. They might be enriched with gilding.

Wedgwood now designed and made complete tea services in which the vessels were cast and coloured to represent various fruits and vegetables such as apples, melons, pears, lemons, quinces, cucumbers and so on, for which there proved to be an immense sale. Nearly a decade earlier the porcelain potters had developed the idea from Meissen originals: Wedgwood's productions had the advantage of being immeasurably cheaper, although his profits were high.

Soon after he had established Ivy House, Wedgwood began buying ware from William Greatbach of Lane Delph, Fenton, who was considered by Wedgwood to be one of the three outstanding modellers operating in Staffordshire. Greatbach supplied cream-coloured ware in the biscuit which, at Ivy House, was glazed and decorated by Wedgwood's secret formulas. A glimpse of the output is offered in a letter written by Greatbach to Wedgwood in May 1764: "There are now ready two of the crates of the Pine Apple ware, and a large quantity of Plates—about a gross, & 1–2 of Light Couler teapots & a good quantity of China tpts the same as Mr. Whieldon & other sorts."

The creamware supplied by Greatbach was unmarked. Wedgwood himself was already impressing his name upon his productions. The letters of his name in lower case were irregularly placed, the first "d" sloping to the left, the second to the right.

Wedgwood was the first Staffordshire potter to foresee the immense potentialities of transfer-printed decoration which eventually brought increased prosperity to the Potteries. The process, evolved at the Battersea enamel factory in the early 1750s, was adopted by Sadler & Green of Liverpool who, by 1760, were acknowledged as specialists in transfer-printing on locally-made delftware tiles and porcelain. An account dated 1764 shows that a considerable trade was already being carried on between Wedgwood and Sadler & Green in the decoration of creamware. The pictures, printed in black and red over the glaze, were skilfully engraved but not always well placed.

The success of the new creamware astonished even Wedgwood himself. In 1767 he wrote to his friend Thomas Bentley:

"The demand for the S^d Cream-colour, alias Queen's Ware, alias Ivory, still increases. It is really amazing how rapidly the use has spread allmost over the whole globe, & how universally it is liked [and it must be remembered that it was not yet perfected]. How much of this general use and estimation is owing to the mode of its intro- duction, & how much to its real utility and beauty, are questions in which we may be a good deal interested for the Government of our future conduct. . . . I had with me yesterday an East Indian Captain, & another Gent^m & Lady from those parts, who ordered a good deal of my ware, some of it printed and gilt, to take with them for presents to their fr^{ds}, & for their own use. They told me that it was allready in use there, & in much higher estimation than the present Porcellain, the Captⁿ said he had dined off a very complete service just before he left India."

Ivy House had already proved too small for Josiah's enthusiasms, and late in 1765 he removed to more extensive premises at near-by Brick House. He had married, on 25th January 1764, his cousin seven times removed, Sarah, daughter of Richard Wedgwood, tanner, of Spen Green, Cheshire. Sarah was heiress to a fortune estimated at £20,000, approximating half a million in current values. This was an incalculable asset to an energetic rising potter. Brick House in its turn proved too small, and in 1769 Wedgwood was building the Etruria Works at Stoke- upon-Trent.

Not until the end of 1775 could Wedgwood make his final improvement to his Queen's ware by incorporating Cornish china-clay and china-stone into the body, for until then their use in ceramics was a monopoly protected by patent No. 898 granted to William Cookworthy of Ply- mouth on 17th March 1768, in connection with his hard porcelain enterprise. The only known method of purifying these minerals was covered by this patent, for which an extension until 1796 was being asked for by Richard Cham- pion of Bristol. Months of costly wrangling in the Com- mons and finally in the Lords resulted in a compromise in September 1775, when the Cornish ingredients were made available to makers of earthenware.

In the "Case of the Manufacturers of Earthenware in Staffordshire" submitted to Parliament early in 1775, Wedgwood had stated that "Queen's Ware has already several of the properties of porcelain, but is yet capable of receiving many essential improvements. The public have for some time required and expected them. . . . One person is petitioning the legislature, in effect, to stop all improvements in earthenware and porcelain in this kingdom but his own." Earlier Wedgwood had declared on oath that he had "discovered the art of making Queen's Ware, which employs ten times more people than all the china [porcelain] in the kingdom and did not ask for a patent for this important discovery. A patent would greatly have limited its public utility. Instead of *one hundred manufactories* [Wedgwood's italics] of Queen's Ware, there would have been *one*; and instead of an exportation to all parts of the world, a few pretty things would have been made for the amusement of the people of fashion in England."

It is shown here that cream-coloured earthenware was an invention rather than an improvement, so that its origin should be dated no earlier than Wedgwood's partnership with Whieldon. Wedgwood's vigorous protest effectively prevented the extension of Cookworthy's patent to 1796 so far as earthenware was concerned, enabling all master potters to incorporate Cornish china clay and Cornish stone into their cream-coloured earthenware. The use of Cornish stone reduced shrinkage in the kiln owing to the smaller clay content required, and the percentage of wasters was lessened. The quality of the earthenware was improved and surface flaws virtually eliminated, thus permitting the use of a transparent glaze when required.

Wedgwood availed himself of the fruits of his opposition by immediately entering into partnership with Carthew of St. Austell, Cornwall, for the working of china clay and Cornish stone, and operating a purifying plant. He supplied the cleansed minerals to potters in England and on the Continent. The firm, Wedgwood & Carthew, was operating at the time of his death in 1795 when an existing quotation said: "The clay will be four guineas per ton in London, Bristol, or Liverpool, the casks included. Weight 112 lb to the cwt. in 4 casks of 5 cwt each. The stone 30*s* per ton in the same places—120 lb to the cwt."

Wedgwood's Queen's ware containing the new ingredients was far stronger than the old type, possessed improved manipulative properties and was lighter in weight than any other earthenware that had preceded it. This was an important point, for much was to be exported to the Continent, where ceramic excise duty was payable according to weight. Wedgwood exported Queen's ware to France, Holland, Spain, Russia, Germany, East and West Indies and North America. In common with other potters he made every endeavour to produce a light-weight ware, and in this he and Leeds were notably successful. A globular teapot, painted blue in the Chinese manner, weighed 12½ ounces: a teapot of similar shape and capacity of early nineteenth-century bone china weighed exactly double.

The title page of Wedgwood's pattern book issued from time to time from 1774 reads: "*A Catalogue of the Different Articles of Queen's Ware, which may be had either plain, gilt, or embellished with Enamel Painting, Manufactured by Josiah Wedgwood, Potter to Her Majesty.*" In later editions was added, "and to his Royal Highness the Duke of York and Albany." The wholesale price at Etruria of "A Service of Queen's Ware, of a middling size" consisting of 146 pieces of twelve types, was £3 17s. 0d. plain, and ranged from 19-inch meat dishes to mustard pots. Additional dining-table ware included pickle stands, ice pails, oil and vinegar stands, bread baskets, pudding cups and monteiths.

Productions covered every conceivable piece of ware used on the Georgian table. The dessert range, for instance, included plates, compotiers in various shapes, patterns and sizes; fruit bowls with covers; cream and sugar bowls; sweetmeat baskets; croquants or sweetmeat dishes; glaciers consisting of cover, ice container, and basin to contain the ice-creams; ice-cream cups and covers; ice-cream bowls; strawberry dishes and stands; custard cups of different forms; tartlets; dessert spoons.

As with his ornamental wares, Wedgwood commissioned patterns for domestic pottery from celebrated artists, his Queen's ware for the most part being attributed to the sculptor John Flaxman. Efficiently strong, yet elegant, clean and pleasant to handle, this was for the most part sold undecorated. Enamelling at this time was costly: the Imperial Russian Service of 952 pieces, for instance, cost £51 8s. 4d.

PLATE 1

(Top left) Pitchers of buff earthenware with horizontal wheel markings, partly covered with green glaze: (left) height 18¼ inches, fourteenth century, (right) height 14 inches, fourteenth century. (Top right) jug of light red earthenware with foliage ornament painted in white slip under glaze. Height 10 inches. Fourteenth century. (Lower left) pitcher of red earthenware decorated in applied relief with rosettes of red and white clays, and with strips of clay impressed with a small diaper pattern and coloured green; yellowish glaze. Height 12¾ inches. Fourteenth century. (Lower right) jug of red earthenware, with vertical ribs applied under a green glaze; thumbed base. Height 9¼ inches. Fourteenth century.

PLATE 2

(Above left) honey pot of dark red earthenware decorated with white slip over a dark brown ground. Late seventeenth or early eighteenth century. (Above centre) double-handled posset pot in slip ware with marbled decoration. Height 5⅝ inches. Dated 1682. (Above right) tyg of Wrotham slip ware with four double scroll handles modelled in relief in a brown and cream-coloured glaze. Dated 1649. (Left) Staffordshire slip ware cradle decorated with white earthenware fiddler and six modelled busts. Second quarter of the eighteenth century.

PLATE 3

Delft ware tiles: (Top) nine tiles painted in blue with incidents illustrating the history of the Titus Oates plot of 1678, copied from a pack of engraved playing cards. Lambeth. Each tile is 5 inches square and $\frac{5}{16}$-inch thick. About 1680. (Below) panel painted in blue with a sea view showing a coalburning lighthouse in the foreground. Bristol. 38 inches by $8\frac{1}{2}$ inches. About 1750.

PLATE 4

Liverpool wall tiles decorated with transfer-prints in black: (top left) signed "J. Sadler, Liverpool"; (top right) signed "Sadler Liverpool"; (left centre) signed "J. Sadler, Liverpl"; (right centre) signed "Green"; (lower left and right) from Green's set of celebrated actors and actresses first issued in the 1770s.

PLATE 5

Liverpool punch bowls in contrasting porcelain and tin enamelled earthenware. The porcelain is enamelled in colour with the fully rigged sailing ship "The Swallow" and the earthenware example is painted in cobalt blue with a caricature coat of arms. (Lower left) Bristol pictorial wall plaque in tin enamelled earthenware painted in cobalt blue. (Lower right) punch bowl and cover in Bristol tin enamelled earthenware decorated with the Carpenters' Arms in underglaze blue and polychrome flower panels over the glaze. Dated 1709.

PLATE 6

(Upper left) tankard of Fulham salt-glazed stoneware decorated with horizontal mouldings and applied moulded reliefs, with silver rim. On the front is a bust of Queen Anne between two Beefeaters, above an encircling pattern of huntsman, hounds and hare. Height 9 inches. 1720s. (Upper right) tankard of Fulham salt-glazed stoneware decorated with a hare-hunting scene. Incised "Southwell for Ever CWM 1739." Beneath the base is incised "John Harwell." Height 10 inches. (Lower left) punch bowl of Nottingham grey stoneware coloured brown. Decoration hand-incised and wheel impressed. About 1750. (Lower right) wine bottle or bellarmine of Fulham salt-glazed stoneware. About 1680. This was found in a walled-up chamber of the Fulham Pottery in 1862.

PLATE 7

Brown salt-glazed stoneware: (Top left) spirit flasks modelled after Lord Brougham and William IV and issued as election propaganda at the time of the dissolution of Parliament in 1831 following the rejection of the first Reform Bill. Made by Joseph Bourne, Denby, in the early 1830s. (Top right) tobacco jar with applied relief decoration in a design adapted from the mezzotint "Old Toby Fillpot" published in the 1760s. Height 7 inches. Impressed DOULTON & WATTS LAMBETH POTTERY LONDON. About 1840. (Below) l. and r. Spirit flasks modelled after Lord Brougham (14½ inches high) and Lord John Russell, impressed LAMBETH POTTERY DOULTON & WATTS 15 HIGH STREET LAMBETH. Jug encircled with boar and stag hunting figures in relief. Height 9¼ inches. Impressed DOULTON LAMBETH. Nelson jug made in 1837. Height 7½ inches. Impressed DOULTON & WATTS LAMBETH POTTERY LONDON.

PLATE 8

(Top left) swan and cygnet in salt-glazed stoneware painted in enamels. Height 5½ inches, Staffordshire. 1750s. (Top right) basket dish in salt-glazed stoneware with applied ornament on rim and painted centre. Diameter 10 inches. Staffordshire. About 1760. (Below) early English pottery. (Left to right) Lambeth wine bottle, inscribed in blue "Whit Wine 1641"; stoneware mineral water bottle, Fulham, mid-eighteenth century; Lambeth earthenware jug inscribed with the date 1628; brown salt-glazed stoneware bowl, Nottingham, dated 1726; stoneware mug, Fulham, with silver mount hall-marked 1682.

PLATE 9

Staffordshire salt-glazed stoneware teapots: (Top left) lozenge-shape on plan with contracted moulded foot, shaped by casting in moulds, the pattern on each side consisting of a small sunken shell set in a ground incised with birds and formal flowers and foliage on winding stems. Height 5½ inches. About 1740. (Top right) heart-shaped on plan with wavy shoulder and base; loop handle; spout with snake-head terminal and moulded in low relief on the upper surface with a human arm and on the lower with snakes and masks; on the body fruiting vines. Remains of oil gilding are visible. Height 5 inches. About 1745. (Below) moulded in relief and painted in pink, yellow, green and red. On each side in a panel surrounded by foliate scrolls, partly coloured green, are George III and Queen Charlotte seated before an altar with two cherubs and an angel holding a laurel wreath above. Height 4½ inches. About 1761.

PLATE 10

White salt-glazed stoneware: (Top left) jug enamelled with musicians in a landscape inscribed "Success to Mr. John Calverly of Leeds", probably issued at the time of the parliamentary election of April 1763. (Top right) pear-shaped jug with beak spout, decorated in the style of Chinese *famille rose*, with coat of arms beneath the spout. (Below) Staffordshire salt-glazed stoneware, about 1740: (l. and r.) teapots with drab-coloured bodies decorated with applied stamped reliefs in white clay; white crabstock handles and spouts and traces of oil gilding; (centre) milk jug with unpainted white body bearing applied stamped relief decoration, pear-shaped with loop handle and acorn knob on lid, height 6½ inches.

PLATE 11

(Top) teapot in agate ware. Height 4 inches. About 1740. (Left centre) posset pot in dark red earthenware with marbling in white. Height 6⅜ inches. About 1740. (Right centre) marbled slip ware dish. Diameter 13¾ inches. Late seventeenth or early eighteenth century. (Bottom) teapot in agate ware, the highly ornamental effect achieved by mixing blue, white and brown clays: the lid handle in the form of a Chinese lion. Height 4¾ inches. About 1745.

PLATE 12

Whieldon figures: (Left to right) an actor wearing a turban, coloured in green, manganese and yellow, height 5¾ inches, about 1745; sportsman with dog retrieving a partridge, height 8 inches, about 1740; pair of lovers in cream and green glazes on a brown splashed base, height 4½ inches, about 1745; Falstaff represented by Quinn the actor, from a print dated 1742, in grey, brown, green and yellow glazes, height 8¼ inches, about 1745. Joseph and Mary and the Christ Child in cream earthenware with typical Whieldon glazes, height 6 inches.

An all-white pew group in salt-glazed stoneware showing Adam and Eve standing before a settle and an espalier apple tree.

PLATE 13

Three early equestrian figures of soldiers: (Top) by John Astbury, wearing a three-cornered brown hat with cream binding, brown tunic with cream decorations and cream breeches, and with gun hanging at his side, seated on a light brown horse, with cream harness, on an oblong splashed plinth; about 1750. (Left) by Ralph Wood, with casque and cape. Believed to represent George II at the Battle of Dettingen, 1743, the last occasion when a British monarch led his troops in battle. White earthenware splashed with light blue, the cape in blue, edged with yellow, on a high shaped and splashed base. The letters GR incised on the holster. Height 10¾ inches. About 1745. (Right) by Thomas Whieldon in cream earthenware splashed with brown manganese glaze and traces of blue glaze, on a rectangular plinth. Height 8¾ inches. About 1745.

PLATE 14

Staffordshire pottery figures of the late eighteenth century. The bird second from right in the third row is a whistle.

PLATE 15

Group of Ralph Wood figures: (Top row) "The Lost Piece of Silver" from the New Testament, in delicate glazes of white, light brown and yellow. Height 8¼ inches. "Apollo" draped in rich green, the lyre in yellow. The rebus mark of a group of trees on the side of the base is the "Wood" mark. Height 8¼ inches. (Middle row) "Roman Charity" in light colour glazes of green, blue and brown: one of the few Ralph Wood pieces with four figures. Height 8 inches. "Jupiter", holding in his upraised right hand a bundle of thunderbolts, his cloak in beautiful cream glaze, lined in blue. Height 10 inches. (Bottom row) "Minerva", with robe in manganese brown, lined olive; Dutch gardener boy and girl on square plinths, in fawn, green, brown and blue glazes.

PLATE 16

Three Ralph Wood figures in white earthenware with clear glaze. Hamlet, with details in green and brown, and touches of gilding, height 13 inches. Piper with coat and bag-pipes in thin brown glaze, cap and breeches with slight green glaze. Probably modelled by Aaron Wood. Height 8 inches. Ophelia, pair to Hamlet, standing against a tree trunk with designs of flowers, on a shaped base with shell design, white glazes with light brown and green decorations. Height 13½ inches.

PLATE 17

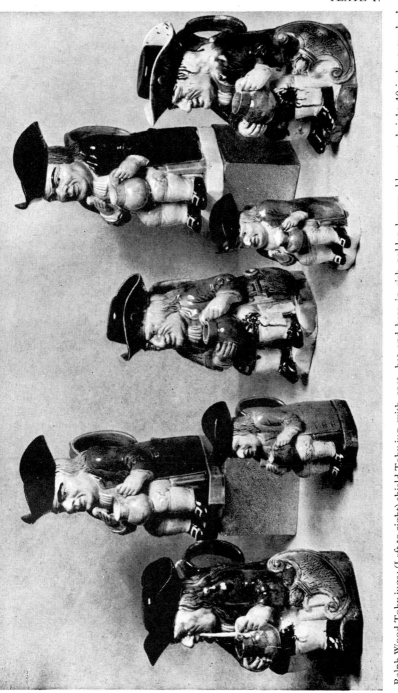

Ralph Wood Toby jugs: (Left to right) shield Toby jug with coat, hat and base in rich golden brown, blue vest, height 10 inches; standard figure in grey-green coat, yellow breeches, black hat and shoes, brown base, heavily marked eyebrows and eyes, height 11 inches; miniature model in Littler blue coat, yellow breeches, jug and hair brown, hat and shoes black, vest white, height 7 inches; shield Toby with green coat and base, waistcoat blue, breeches, shoes and jug and cover to hat dark brown, height 10 inches; miniature model with light grey coat, yellow breeches, hat and shoes dark brown, height 7 inches; standard figure in Littler blue coat, yellow breeches, black shoes and hat, height 11 inches; shield Toby with coat, hat and base in rich golden yellow, blue vest, height 10 inches.

PLATE 18

Wedgwood cream coloured earthenware with green glaze: (Top) dessert centrepiece in vine leaf pattern modelled by William Hackwood. Late 18th century. (Centre) cauliflower ware teapot, a design illustrated in Josiah Wedgwood's pattern book for 1759. The piece at the side is the original model for the cover. (Lower left) plate with embossed pattern made in about 1850. (Lower right) Soup plate modelled to represent a cauliflower, *c.* 1770.

PLATE 19

Busts and figures in black basaltes by Wedgwood: (Top) busts of Sir James Prior and Sir William Congreve, each impressed with name at back. Height 7 inches. About 1810. On ebonised stands. (Below) figures of Rousseau and Voltaire with names impressed. Height 10¾ inches. About 1810.

PLATE 20

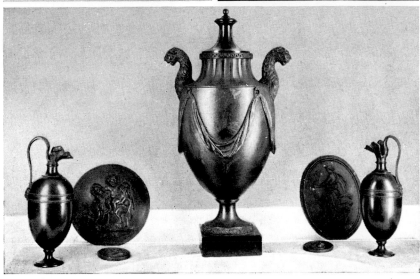

Black basaltes impressed with the name WEDGWOOD. (Top left) three-burner lamp known as "the Michael Angelo Vase" and adapted from one of his sculptures. Applied arabesque decoration on font. Height 14 inches. 1783. (Top right) "Sacred to Neptune", a water vase decorated with gilded copper. About 1800. (Below) a collection of ornamental basaltes impressed "Wedgwood and Bentley". 1770s.

PLATE 21

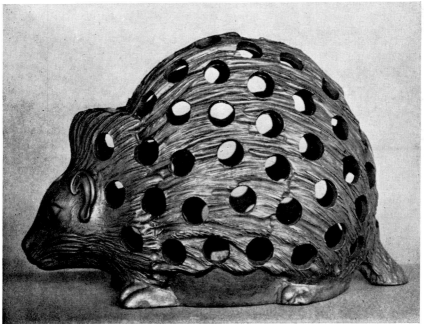

(Top) black basaltes. Cup and asucer decorated in red and white encaustic colours. Height
2½ inches. 1778. Teapot thrown and engine-turned with cupped rim, lion finial on cover.
Impressed WEDGWOOD. Height 4½ inches. 1780. (Below) Wedgwood black basaltes bulb
pot in the form of a porcupine. Late eighteenth century.

PLATE 22

(Top left) lozenge-shaped teapot in cane-coloured stoneware painted in red, blue and green to emphasise the bamboo motif; and with glazed interior: by Josiah Spode. 1790s. (Top right) bowl of cane-coloured stoneware resembling bamboo: Wedgwood, late eighteenth century. (Centre left) oval teapot in black basaltes, surface decorated with engine-turning: by Josiah Spode, 1790s. (Centre right) bulb pot in unglazed red stoneware decorated in black and with glazed interior: Wedgwood, 1770s. (Lower left) fruit basket in white earthenware, its base moulded in relief: Newcastle-upon-Tyne, first half of nineteenth century. (Lower right) punch pot and cover with brazier, in red stoneware, unglazed: Wedgwood, about 1765.

PLATE 23

Wedgwood jasper ware: (Top) designed in 1783 by Lady Templetown and modelled by William Hackwood, white on blue; (left to right) teapot decorated with "Charlotte at the Tomb of Werther" and "Sportive Love", 1790, marked "Wedgwood"; jug decorated with "Domestic Employment", 1783, (height 8 inches); teapot, thrown and turned, and with applied ornaments on a rough ground, white handle and spout, 1785. (Below, left to right) cup and saucer, lilac dip, thrown and engine-turned, and with applied Cupid decoration designed by Lady Templetown and Lady Diana Beauclerk, lapidary polished inside (height 2½ inches), 1785; coffee cup and saucer, lilac dip, diced pattern, applied green quatrefoils (height 2½ inches), 1790; teacup and saucer, white on grey-blue, engine-turned, lapidary polished inside (height 2½ inches), 1785.

PLATE 24

(Top left) Quintal flower horn in cream-coloured earthenware, decorated with polychrome painting. Leeds. Height 7⅜ inches. (Top right) tea kettle with stand for spirit lamp in cream-coloured earthenware printed and painted in black. The pierced stand is decorated in black. Leeds. (Below) chestnut basket in cream-coloured earthenware moulded in relief. About 1780.

PLATE 25

Plate 7 from Josiah Wedgwood's pattern sheets engraved by William Blake in 1816. The tureen and stand, No. 146, and the covered dish, No. 347, are seen on Plate 26.

PLATE 26

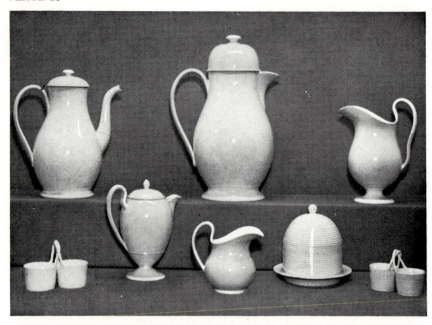

Queen's ware in the white designed for Josiah Wedgwood, F.S.A., by John Flaxman, R.A., in the late 1770s and engraved by William Blake in 1816 for the firm's new pattern book.

PLATE 27

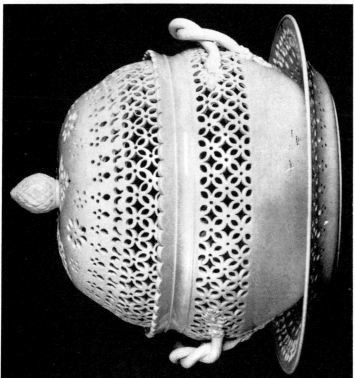

(Left) Leeds cream-coloured earthenware in the pierced patterns particularly associated with this famous firm. This covered chestnut basket has the double intertwined handles also typical of the firm. Late eighteenth century. (Right) drum-shaped cruet in Newcastle cream-coloured earthenware. The larger vessels are replacements but indicate the style of work. First half of the nineteenth century.

PLATE 28

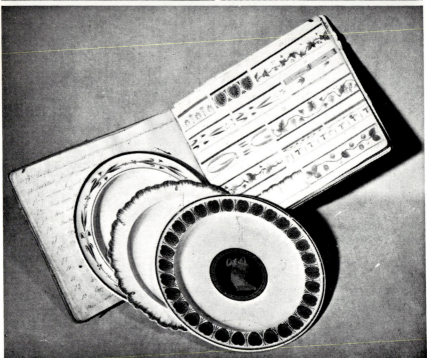

(Top left) Queen's ware jug made for the Staffordshire Regiment, hand-painted with multicolour designs. Height 8 inches. Marked WEDGWOOD. 1786. (Top right) Two dishes in Wedgwood's queen's ware, decorated with number 384 design from Josiah Wedgwood's pattern book of 1770. Impressed WEDGWOOD. 1798. (Below) a page in Josiah Wedgwood's original pattern book of 1770 showing borders and plate designs for early cream-coloured ware. The three 10-inch plates with borders taken from the pattern book are: (back) hand-painted blue border and centre, Pattern No. 74. 1788; (centre) black and green shell edge, hand-painted, No. 83 in the original pattern book. 1772; (front hand-painted red and black lotus border and Etruscan centre, with border pattern No. 72 in the pattern book of 1770. 1780.

PLATE 29

Bedside food warmers and night light holders in cream-coloured earthenware, early nineteenth century: (Left) impressed WEDGWOOD. Height 9⅞ inches. (Right) impressed DAVENPORT. Height 10 inches. Satyr and Bacchus jugs: (Left) small, the front forming a mask, on a shaped base, the lip and handle forming a fish, in green and light manganese colours; height 5 inches. (Centre) large, the head crowned with grapes and vine leaves on a shaped base, the top part forming the lip shaped with a laughing mask of Bacchus, and the handle formed of youth with bottle. The whole is in delicate shades of green, blue, manganese and purple; height 8½ inches. (Right) classical figure formed as a jug with a lion's skin over his shoulder, seated on a wine barrel which is decorated with vines and fruits. The handle is in the form of a monkey, and there is a figure of Pan on the reverse site of the dolphin-spout. The whole is in delicate manganese brown, green and blue. Modelled by Voyez; height 13½ inches.

PLATE 30

Part of a tea service in bone china decorated with a bold design in silver resist lustre. Early nineteenth century.

A group of late Georgian serving jugs in silver resist lustre.

PLATE 31

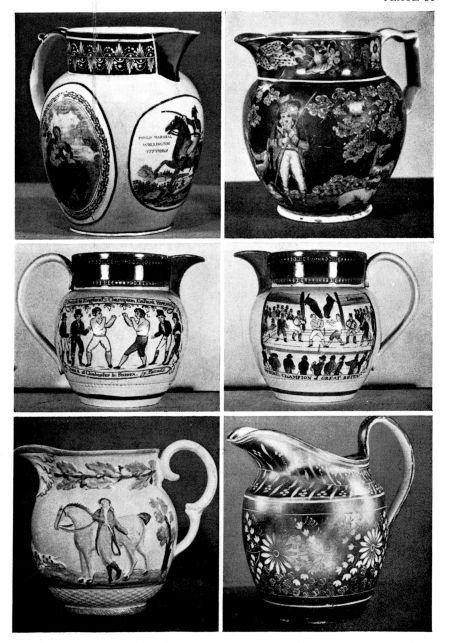

Lustre ware jugs: (Top left) With canary yellow ground, handle, spout, and neck in silver resist lustre: the three oval transfer-printed panels in colour show an equestrian portrait of Wellington, a classical figure, and Lord Nelson's bier. (Top right) Serving jug with a sporting scene in blue transfer printing against a silver lustre ground. (Centre) Both sides of a sporting ale jug, lustred and coloured, commemorating the fight between Spring and Langan at Chichester. (Bottom left) Ale jug encircled with stag hunting scene moulded in relief, with a basketry pattern below and oak leaves above, touched with lustre. Newcastle, about 1820. (Bottom right) Toilet ewer of pearl ware decorated with silver resist lustre.

PLATE 32

Sunderland pottery: (Top) the three figures from the set of Seasons and the pink lustre watch stand are impressed DIXON AUSTIN & CO, a mark used between 1820 and 1826. The carpet bowls were made after about 1850. (Below) lustre-decorated animals probably made by the Garrison Pottery: two cow cream jugs and a cat decorated with pink lustre and other colours; hull in dark copper lustre, and comforter dogs spotted with copper lustre.

PLATE 33

(Top) earthenware jugs and plate decorated with painted and speckled pink lustre: possibly made at the Sunderland Pottery which issued tea-sets in this style. (Lower) Wedgwood jasper portrait medallions in white against blue blackgrounds: dating between 1776 and 1788. (Top left and lower right) Louis XVI modelled by William Hackwood and Marie Antoinette modelled by J. B. Nini. 2½ inches wide. In carved and gilt frames. (Top centre) Dr. Solander modelled by John Flaxman: impressed WEDGWOOD & BENTLEY. 2 inches wide. (Top right) Sappho. (Lower left) Aesculapius. (Lower centre) John Locke.

PLATE 34

Loving cups: (Top left) in Leeds cream-coloured earthenware showing characteristic double intertwined flat handles reeded on their upper surfaces and with their terminals fixed by pads moulded in relief. Painted in cobalt blue under the glaze. Late eighteenth century. (Top right) in Leeds cream-coloured earthenware painted in blue under the glaze. 1780—1800. (Lower left and right) front and reverse of three dated examples: (left) white earthenware exceptionally light in weight and hand-painted in cobalt blue, dated 1796; (centre) reddish-brown earthenware coated with white engobe, painted with medium-hued cobalt blue, dated 1784; (right) cream-coloured earthenware decorated with blue transfer-printed portraits of George III and Queen Charlotte, issued in 1809.

PLATE 35

Loving cups: (Upper left) decorated with transfer printing under the glaze; cover with candle-socket for lighting spills. (Upper right) ovoid bowl encircled with shallow flutes coloured tan; scrolled handles. Rim and foot decorated in blue. About 1800. (Below) two views of a loving cup in hard white earthenware decorated with black transfer designs associated with the Manchester Unity of the Independent Order of Odd-fellows, overpainted with transparent green and yellow. The handles are cast with ornamental busts on their outer curves and their upper terminals join the bowl with short struts. Height 7 inches.

PLATE 36

(Top left) cream-coloured earthenware mug with flat loop handle, transfer-printed in black with a medallion inscribed "A French Family" showing a man, his wife and three children dancing in a room to music played by a fiddler on one side, and a man with a pipe and tabour and dancing dogs on the other side: after a caricature by Thomas Rowlandson. Made and printed in Staffordshire. About 1800. (Top right) a handled vase of reddish-brown earthenware covered with lustrous black glaze over white engobe and enriched with a band of gilding over the glaze. Jackfield type, but made in Staffordshire. (Lower left) Liverpool Herculaneum Pottery double-handled mug in pearl ware decorated with "The Farmers' Arms" in black transfer over-painted in colours. 1820s. (Right) pair of greyhounds in Jackfield ware enriched with gilded splashes and collars. 1820s.

PLATE 37

Wedgwood terra cotta: (Left to right) vase with Egyptian hieroglyphics in black, about 1810; jug with engine-turned decoration and applied festoons in black, about 1810; vase with engine-turned decoration, dipped in black and scraped, applied hieroglyphics in red, 1810; early trial vase, pressed, dipped and scraped fluting in white, about 1775; teapot in red terra cotta with runner border in brown and white. About 1865. (Below) Wedgwood terra cotta: the tea ware is ornamented with japanned reliefs in white: the inkstand with hieroglyphics in white, about 1820.

PLATE 38

Mason's patent ironstone china: (Top) teapot and plate decorated with blue underglaze transfer-printing; tea cup (height 2 inches) and octagonal jug (height 6½ inches) enamelled in colours. (Below) the two sauce tureens and stands are transfer-printed and enamelled: marked in black "Masons" above a crown (height 6¾ inches); the jug is decorated in the red and black bandana style; the grape tray bears a crest (length 11 inches).

PLATE 39

Staffordshire blue underglaze transfer-printed ware: (Top left) earthenware plate printed with an Anglicised version of a Chinese design in zaffre blue — Spode's "Temple" pattern. About 1815. (Top centre) Spode's "Italian" pattern, produced early in the nineteenth century, illustrating the development of strong, three-dimensional effects with clouds and water. Marked SPODE impressed. (Top right) stone china scalloped-edged plate printed in lilac with "William Penn's Treaty", with wide, intricate geometric border. By Thomas Godwin, Burslem Wharf. Diameter 10½ inches. About 1835. Its marks are: "Tho' Godwin, Burslem, Stone China", and a small house and tower in line and stipple with a scroll beneath containing the title of the picture and the initials T.G. (Lower left) dish with openwork rim and an early Anglo-Chinese design by John Davenport, Longport. About 1800. Impressed DAVENPORT. (Lower centre and right) an early example of Spode printing together with pulls from the original copper plate on tissue paper preparatory to transferring to the biscuit.

PLATE 40

Table ware decorated with blue transfer-printed willow pattern designs: (Top left) sauce boat marked COPELAND & GARRETT in blue: late 1830s. (Top right) dish impressed LEEDS. (Centre left) plate with perforated rim, marked SPODE II impressed and SPODE printed in blue. (Centre right) soup tureen, impressed DAVENPORT, early nineteenth century. (Bottom) the centre dish is in light weight cream-coloured earthenware, impressed LEEDS and 18. The inner plates are in stone china and impressed IEB, mark of Hicks, Meigh & Johnson, Shelton. The end plates are unmarked specimens bought in 1871.

PLATE 41

(Upper left) "Seahorse", a statuette in brown salt-glazed stoneware modelled by Mark V. Marshall for Doulton & Co., 1880s. (Upper right) early Victorian tobacco jar in terra cotta inlaid with mosaic designs in colours. (Lower left) "The Potter" statuette in terra cotta modelled in 1883 by John Broad for Doulton & Co. A vase is shown being thrown on an early type of kick wheel. (Lower right) mantelpiece in Mason's patent ironstone china with moulded decoration in the Chinese style painted in colours on a yellow ground. Height 3 ft. 8 inches.

PLATE 42

Soldiers of the Napoleonic wars in Staffordshire pottery decorated with high temperature colours. The royal coat of arms of George IV was a coronation souvenir issued in 1821. In the centre is the royal arms in full colours and on top a representation of the Crown of State in gold and crimson.

PLATE 43

Architectural ornaments in earthenware painted over the glaze: (Top left) Stanfield Hall, scene of the murder of Mr. Jeremy by James Rush. Height 8½ inches. Staffordshire. 1848. (Top right) model of a church with tower. Height 8¾ inches, About 1790. (Lower left) Westminster Abbey. Height 7 inches. About 1800. (Lower right) pastille burner in the form of a thatched cottage. Height 4 inches. 1820s.

(Left) dish painted in ultramarine blue under the glaze. Diameter 10½ inches. By Hilditch & Son, Lane End, Staffordshire. 1822—1850. (Right) Middlesbrough pottery with bluish-grey ground patterned in a lively deepish blue, tinted with copper lustre. Diameter 14 inches. Mark LONDON with a foul anchor below.

PLATE 44

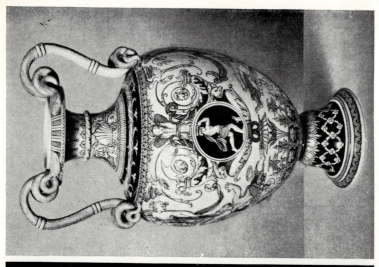

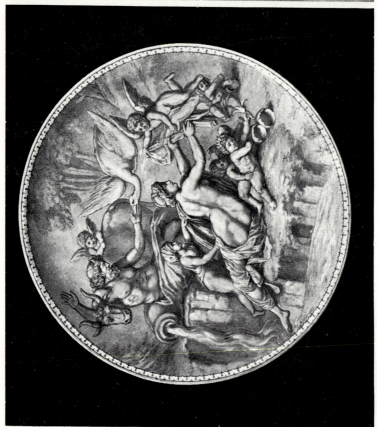

(Left) tazza in imitation majolica painted in light brown with an allegorical subject. Exhibited at the International Exhibition, 1862, by Minton & Co. (Right) vase of enamelled earthenware hand-painted in black and yellow with gilt scroll handles of two serpents in full relief. Designed by Alfred Stevens. Marked "Minton 1864".

PLATE 45

(Top left) rack plate in Portobello pottery with portrait of George IV and flower and foliage decoration in relief. Painted in colours under the glaze. Mid-1820s. (Top right) Staffordshire earthenware figure of Dick Turpin painted in colours and gilt. About 1820. Height 11½ inches. (Lower left) Portobello Toby jug in cream-coloured earthenware painted in polychrome beneath the glaze: early nineteenth century. (Lower right) dark brown Portobello jug with printed design in underglaze yellow: Scott Brothers, late eighteenth century.

PLATE 46

Portobello pottery figures, early nineteenth century. (Upper left) fishwife with creel, painted in colours under the glaze. By Thomas Rathbone & Co. (Upper right) Highlander playing bagpipes, in colours painted under the glaze. (Lower left) cat in brown and yellow slipware. (Lower right) allegorical figure of *Winter* on a square plinth. Painted in colours under the glaze. By Thomas Rathbone & Co.

in its undecorated state: when finished the cost to Wedgwood exceeded £3000.

Josiah Wedgwood II, immediately after the close of the Napoleonic wars in June 1815, realised the potentialities that lay in the long-closed Continental market. He made arrangements for the preparation of pattern books, including one to illustrate the complete range of Queen's ware. Each engraved plate, displaying several articles of domestic ware, was to be faced with a descriptive price list printed in the language of the country it was intended to serve.

It was decided to continue the Flaxman designs, which have never been out of production. John Flaxman was consulted on the choice of engraver: he recommended his friend William Blake, from whom they were commissioned in July 1815, after Blake had submitted a preliminary drawing to Wedgwood at Etruria. Correspondence exists showing that Blake worked from actual pieces of Queen's ware designed by Flaxman long years before. The Wedgwood records suggest that Blake had supplied all the drawings by the end of the year. Each piece was drawn separately, passed as accurate by Josiah Wedgwood, who arranged them to form appropriate pattern book pages before Blake copied them in engraving on the copper plates that would print the catalogues. Twelve of the existing proofs are annotated and corrected in pencil, probably in the hand of Josiah Wedgwood II. These instructions required erasement of certain articles, and replacement ware was sent to London. The 185 drawings prepared and engraved on eighteen copper plates were no doubt costly.

By the end of 1816 only half the work had been completed and Wedgwood called upon his cousin John Rayler Wedgwood to finish the commission. He was a leading engraver of the day, and in 1816 was appointed "Engraver to H.R.H. the Princess Charlotte and to Prince Leopold of Saxe Coburg".[1] A complete set of Blake's eighteen engravings may be seen in the print room of the British Museum, the folder labelled *Book of Designs (after Flaxman) for Potting by J. Wedgwood*. Eight of Blake's original plates still remain in

[1] These copper plates were fully discussed in my article "Blake's Commission by Wedgwood", "Country Life", 1959.

the Wedgwood Museum, but unfortunately all possess alterations made during a catalogue reissue of about 1840.

Under the influence of Robert Brown, who became a partner in 1846, Wedgwood's plant was modernised and more efficient methods were introduced for cleansing and preparing the clay for the potter. The firm's Queen's ware visibly improved, the body becoming whiter, the glaze harder, enamelling clearer, and many new designs were evolved to the virtual exclusion of the old Flaxman forms. From the accession of Queen Victoria, the name Queen's ware had not been favoured in court circles, and like other potters, the Wedgwood firm gradually reverted to the term cream-coloured earthenware. At the Great Exhibition they were the only exhibitors of this ceramic. Their catalogue entry reads: "Cream-coloured, or Queen's Ware, with enamelled borders: Etruscan-shaped soup-tureen and stand. Round covered vegetable dish. Dinner plates in various designs.

"Cream-coloured earthenware (Queen's ware): Plates and dishes. High oval soup tureen and stand (by Flaxman). Round and oval soup tureens. Round Etruscan soup tureen and stand. Round covered vegetable dish. Herring dish with embossed fishes. Oval twig pattern fruit basket and stand. Oval quatrefoil-pattern fruit basket and stand. Fruit dishes, various shapes. Quart jugs, Dutch and Roman shapes. Bowls, water-ewers, nursery lamp. Coffee-biggin, with stove and lamp cup. Milk-boiler and cover. Wine funnel with strainer. Egg-beater; blanc-mange moulds; pudding cups. Egg-shaped pudding-boiler. Round and oval milk pans. Pierced milk skimmer."

Josiah Wedgwood's great rival in cream-coloured earthenware was the Leeds Pottery. It is usually assumed that John and Joseph Green in 1760 acquired an already established pottery. But it was ten years later, in 1770, that a *Leeds Mercury* news item referred to "the large Earthenware manufactory now erecting near this town" and another five years before the firm, trading as Humble, Green & Co., was joined by William Hartley.

This was an ideal starting year, earthenware potters being

freed from the effects of Cookworthy's patent monopoly on china clay and Cornish stone, and marked the beginning of Hartley's fantastic success with cream-coloured earthenware. Humble was probably a financing partner, the firm being styled Humble, Hartley, Greens & Co. until 1781, when it became Hartley, Greens & Co. Until his death in 1820 William Hartley was the dominant personality, and thereafter the company's affairs soon became involved and were thrown into Chancery. Production continued until 1825 when the business was bought by Samuel Wainwright and continued under five subsequent proprietorships until 1878.

Hartley organised a highly profitable business in which the sale of cream-coloured earthenware far exceeded the combined output of Egyptian black, pearl ware and tortoiseshell ware. He built up an extensive Continental trade, issuing French and German editions of his pattern books in 1783, forty copperplates illustrating in outline 184 examples of domestic ware. The copy in the Victoria and Albert Museum is titled: "Designs of sundry Articles of Queen's or Cream-coloured Earthen-ware, manufactured by Hartley, Greens & Co., at Leeds-Pottery: with a Great Variety of other Articles. The Same Enamel'd, Printed, or Ornamented with Gold to any Pattern; also with Coats of Arms, Cyphers, Landscapes, &c., &c. Leeds, 1783."

Examples of plain, perforated and woven basket ware were illustrated, covering almost every article of table ware then in fashion for every-day use, including 32 items of tea ware. Reprints were issued in 1785 and 1786 and a second edition dated 1794 included 31 additional plates illustrating 74 new designs. The third and final edition was printed on paper watermarked with the date 1814 and was, no doubt, issued late in 1815 following the reopening of Continental markets after Waterloo. This catalogue reprinted the copper plates used in 1794.

The body of Leeds cream-coloured earthenware was light in weight, thinly potted, with glaze more thickly applied than on similar Staffordshire ware. The glaze has the appearance of having been floated on the surface without bubbling and is seldom crazed. At first the glaze was golden yellow or deep cream in colour, some areas being more deeply hued than others on the same piece. By 1780 the tint was much paler, and by about 1785 had acquired a faintly greenish hue distinctly visible where drops have collected in crevices. This was caused by using Derbyshire lead oxide, a quality exceptionally well suited for ceramic glazes, but marred by an impurity not cleared until after 1810, when a purifying process was evolved by Blair Stephenson, Tipton, Staffordshire. By about 1800 Leeds glaze had become less yellow than formerly, but from about 1810 the tint was greyish green. This was succeeded by a pale bluish tinge, but the examples examined have all been in pearl ware. Some pearl ware has been noted with a yellowish glaze, but this differs in texture and colour from that used on creamware. Searle gives the composition of Leeds glaze as: white lead 60 parts, Cornish stone 20 parts, calcined flint 10 parts.

The glaze-coated biscuit was dried in a heated room, then fired, emerging from the kiln with a clear, brilliant surface. Perfect results depended largely upon securing exact harmony between the compositions of body and glaze (both containing Cornish china stone), and the exact temperatures of firing in biscuit and glost ovens.

Those who have the best claim to know the genuine Leeds are convinced that the glaze supplies the real clue to period, but it is only by long and engrossing study that it is possible to recognise tone gradations and distinguish them from the glazes of other master potters. The tints of glaze on Leeds cream-coloured earthenware have been collated over a period of many years by Mr. Donald Towner.

Lovely and most celebrated was the plain cream-coloured ware depending solely on design for its appeal. Most spectacular were centrepieces, planned to give grandeur to the dessert table. The silversmith set the example with basket-hung epergnes, but he could not offer the warm yellow tone in which elaborate groupings of figures and cornucopias, dolphins and shells, presented sweetmeats and suckets.

Wonderfully light and suggesting fragility were the pieces depending entirely upon pierced openwork for their ornament, their patterns evolved by clever arrangements of a small range of perforations, such as diamonds, hearts, crescents, circles, pales and leaf shapes, cut sharply and clearly. The thickness of the body and the arrangement of the perforations were planned to ensure that the piece was sturdy enough to escape warping during firing. Common ware was quickly pierced with hollow metal punches: more costly pieces were pierced with a sharp, finely pointed knife and perhaps shaped with a fretsaw. Close inspection of the perforations will reveal the method used. Almost invariably they were cut in the clay when it had stiffened somewhat and was known as leather-hard. Occasionally, however, the clay was fired at a very low temperature to produce a light biscuit easily pierced by drill and saw. Perforated ware illustrated in the Leeds catalogue included chestnut baskets and stands, cockle pots, desserts with pierced covers, fish trowels, egg-cups and pierced dishes with openwork rims. There were also "fruit-baskets and stands of elegant basket, twig and open work".

The quality of the enamel decoration carried out in the Leeds factory is obviously by no means equal extending as it did over a period of more than half a century. Without close examination it is often difficult to distinguish enamelling from some underglaze decoration because the enamels in firing sank into the glaze. The colours chiefly used were various tones of yellow, green, red, blue and black, all capable of maturing at a single firing.

Existing examples suggest that much domestic ware was decorated with a bold, round rose, usually in vigorous brush strokes of red and green, the latter having a tendency to flake. This flower is characteristic of the Leeds Pottery. It would be foolish, however, to compare Leeds' somewhat mediocre paintings—Chinese figures, simple landscapes, flowers, insects and so on—with the superb grace of the plain cream-coloured ware with its restrained delight in raised ornament. Some Leeds ware was enamelled by independent decorators. The Leeds potters also introduced some of the coloured glaze decoration known as tortoiseshell ware, and from about 1790 painted under the glaze in high temperature colours.

Transfer pictures printed over the glaze were used throughout the period of Hartley's supervision, from about

1780. L. Jewitt, who inspected the accounts of the Leeds Pottery for the year 1791, has recorded that the stock of copper plates was then valued at £204, a figure suggesting that many transfers yet unrecognised were printed at the Leeds Pottery. Jewitt added that "the yearly balance then [1791] struck was £51,500". Transfers were printed in jet black, purplish black, red and orange red; black outline might be filled with enamel colours. A coffee pot in the Victoria and Albert Museum displays two allegorical scenes in which the name *Leeds Pottery* in script is incorporated in the transfer.

Leeds cream-coloured earthenware was never consistently marked, but throughout the period of manufacture under Hartley, the name Leeds Pottery might be impressed with an asterisk, dot or hyphen between or after the words. In marks dating earlier than about 1790 the letters appear unevenly placed. After about 1800 the name might be impressed twice, forming an X. The name HARTLEY GREEN & Co / LEEDS * POTTERY also dates from about 1800 and might be impressed horizontally, crossed or in the form of an arch. Marks were used more frequently in the nineteenth century than formerly. LEEDS * POTTERY in tall capital letters, sometimes followed by the letter C or G, is found on a coarse, gritty body probably potted by the Leeds Pottery Company, who operated the old factory between 1837 and 1840.

Old Leeds cream-coloured earthenware has been imitated. Even pierced work must be examined judiciously, for highly elaborate work was issued by the potter Slee who worked in Leeds and whose cream-coloured earthenware bears the impressed mark LEEDS · POTTERY. Slee is known to have been operating as late as 1916. Early in the present century reproduction tea ware was imported from Holland.

The number of potters who included cream-coloured earthenware among their productions amounted to hundreds during the century extending from 1775 to 1875. The majority concentrated on plain domestic ware which was not impressed with the maker's name: a few attempted to compete with the moulded and pierced work of Wedgwood

and Leeds. Enamel on cream-coloured earthenware tended
to flake under the onslaught of knives and forks: flat ware,
therefore, was seldom decorated with more than narrow
borders or bands of colour, ornamental or plain, usually in
blue or green or a combination of the two.

Each potter adapted his formula to suit local conditions.
William Evans, in 1846, recorded ten qualities of Staffordshire cream-coloured earthenware in production:

	1	2	3	4	5	6	7	8	9	10
BLUE CLAY	36	30	25	25	28	56	27	25	27	36
BLACK CLAY	18	26	22	23	28	—	33	24	—	24
BROWN CLAY	18	24	18	16	28	—	—	15	27	16
CHINA CLAY	—	—	16	16	--	20	70	15	—	—
FLINT	28	20	16	16	16	20	33	16	44	24
CORNISH STONE	—	—	3	4	—	4	—	5	2	—

A few outstanding potters impressed their name on a proportion of their productions: the majority of earthenware,
however, was issued unmarked. The Schreiber collection in
the Victoria and Albert Museum displays Staffordshire
cream-coloured earthenware impressed with the names of:
Neale & Co., Hanley; Enoch Wood, Burslem; Warburton,
Cobridge; Turner, Lane End; Rogers, Dale Hill, Burslem;
Hackwood, New Hall, Shelton; and Davenport, Longport,
whose ware was of good substantial quality with enamelled
borders.

Elijah and Joseph Mayer, father and son, Hanley, potted
undecorated cream-coloured earthenware described by
Jewitt as of "unusually good style and quality". Production
ceased in 1833, and when Joseph died in 1860 he possessed
a collection of outstanding pieces equal in every way
to Wedgwood's Queen's ware. A teapot recently seen,
impressed MAYER on the tail of the handle, was exceptionally light in weight, and a recent chip displayed a
saffron-coloured body.

Lakin & Poole, Burslem, carried on a large trade in
cream-coloured earthenware during the late eighteenth and
early nineteenth centuries. Invoices in the Jewitt collection
dating between 1792 and 1796 advertise "Table Services

Enamelled with Arms, Crests and Cyphers" such as fashionably decorated porcelain. Among the articles invoiced were "oval concave dishes, flat plates, soups, twifflers, muffins, sauce boats and stands, dessert services, flower horns, candlesticks, baskets and stands". The name impressed was LAKIN & POOLE. The mark observed impressed on a fruit dish with a pierced rim was L & P BURSLEM.

Ephraim Booth & Sons, a large firm of potters operating at Stoke-upon-Trent in the late eighteenth century, are recorded on their billhead as "Potters to His Royal Highness the Duke of Clarence and St. Andrews in the Kingdom of Great Britain, Earl of Munster in the Kingdom of Ireland". Among their productions were "tureens and ladles with green edge and cream-coloured glaze: also other domestic ware such as salad dishes, oyster shells, pickle leaves, sauce tureens with green, blue or green and blue edges." The impressed mark was E B & S .

Lesser Staffordshire potters of the late eighteenth century who impressed their names upon ordinary cream-coloured earthenware included: Shorthose & Co., Tunstall, late eighteenth century to *c.* 1820; Henry Booth, Stoke-upon-Trent; Robert Wilson and his successors, Hanley, but some was enamelled until 1802; Robert Garner, Lane End, examples of whose work are in the Stoke Museum; Thomas Bacchus, Fenton; George Harrison, Fenton, of whom Jewitt possessed an invoice dated 1793 referring to "cream-coloured ewers and blue edged tureen".

Among the cream ware potters of the third quarter of the nineteenth century may be mentioned Powell & Bishop of Hanley, who operated from the late 1860s, and, according to Blacker, "reproduced in all its softness and delicacy of tint and evenness of surface the famous old cream-coloured ware of Josiah Wedgwood, then known as 'Queen's Ware'." Until 1875 this was impressed BEST / P & B and afterwards with a caduceus surmounted by P & B. I. & I. Proctor, Longton, made comparable ware, including pierced hollow-ware vases, from 1855 to the 1880s impressed STAFFORDSHIRE below a crown and the letter P.

Among the Bristol cream ware potters was Joseph Ring, established 1784 and a maker of Queen's ware by 1786, having engaged Anthony Hassells of Shelton as an expert in this ceramic. He bought his plant from Staffordshire. The resulting domestic ware closely resembled finely potted Staffordshire work and is recognised by its stronger yellow colour, due to the use of glaze stained yellow by oxide of iron. Ring was killed in 1788 by the collapse of a kiln: the business was continued by his widow. The Bristol cream ware potters first used transfer printing in 1797: until then the painters experienced in decorating local tin-enamelled earthenware were employed to enamel in colours. In Jewitt's collection was an invoice showing that manufactures included: oval dishes, table plates, soups, suppers, twifflers, tureens, quart jugs, pint jugs, coffee pots, coffee cups and saucers painted, table plates painted, quart mugs variegated. A local song attributed to the year 1786 records:

> "What Labour We had for to Bring it to Bare
> before that wee could make a good cream colour ware."

It is recorded that St. Anthony's Pottery, established 1780 in Sunderland, made common cream-coloured earthenware, and from early in the nineteenth century "two or three kilns per week of Cream Coloured and best Cream Coloured to imitate Wedgwood's Table Ware, was sent to Holland and other Continental Countries." The terms of this letter suggest that the Wedgwood firm still reigned supreme in the manufacture of cream-coloured earthenware. Much transfer printing was done here as well as printing on the glaze direct from wood engravings cut by Thomas Bewick. From early in the nineteenth century the ware was impressed with the name SEWELL in variations, such as SEWELL & DONKIN

William Smith of the Stafford Pottery, Stockton-on-Tees, was a prolific manufacturer of cream-coloured earthenware—he called it Queen's ware, and at a later date for a few years forged the Wedgwood mark—shipping most of the earthenware so marked to the Continent. In 1825 he established a branch pottery at Genappes, near Mons in Belgium, operated by skilled potters sent from Stockton.

Castleford, four miles from Leeds, established in the

mid-1790s, produced cream-coloured earthenware, but coarser and not so highly glazed as old Leeds pottery. Derby made cream-coloured earthenware indistinguishable from Staffordshire common quality. Swansea, under the control of George Haynes from 1786, produced large quantities of tastefully-decorated ware. Several Scottish potteries such as the Clyde Pottery, Glasgow, and the Caledonian Pottery, Rutherglen, made ordinary cream-coloured earthenware.

Chapter Nine

TRANSFER-PRINTED EARTHENWARE

SO great has been the rivalry among collectors of old
Staffordshire blue transfer-printed with views of great
houses and scenery that examples originally costing six-
pence, and more recently selling for a few shillings, may
now command as many pounds. As in postage stamps, it is
the rarity of an item and its condition that determines market value, and only slightly the quality of its printing.

The story behind the achievements of transfer-printing
on pottery is wholly English, originating in the mid-
eighteenth century and applied in this country long before
its technical appreciation abroad. For centuries designs
engraved on copper had been reproduced in quantity on
paper, but the transferring of clear-cut impressions from
copper plates direct to the curved surfaces of ceramics had
been rejected as impracticable. In the early 1750s, however,
a method was developed by which such designs could be
reproduced in quantity on china ware with a similar saving
of time and cost. Consequently there was a vast increase in
the range of decoration which was economically practicable
on wares priced for everyday use.

The men who converted the idea of transfer-printing on
ceramics into a practical proposition were Stephen Theo-
dore Janssen, a leading patron of the arts and a prominent
merchant-stationer in the City of London; John Brooks, a
notable mezzotint engraver with a studio in the Strand;
and Henry Delamain, a Dublin potter and manufacturer of
delftware tiles. Together they solved the various technical
difficulties associated with the transfer paper, the printing,
and the firing, evolving a process by which imprints from

engraved copper could be transferred to an enamelled or glazed ceramic surface. It is unlikely that any of these men fully appreciated the importance of their discovery. At any rate, the immediate result was its application to little enamelled snuff-boxes and similar charming trifles decorated at the celebrated, but short-lived, Battersea Enamel Manufactory founded in 1753, in which they were partners.

Janssen's contact with paper-makers enabled him to gain their interest in devising a paper suitable for transfer work, for none had existed hitherto. This paper, hand-made from white linen rags, needed to be strong, faultlessly hairless, and with a smooth surface free from pinholes. This was made non-absorbent by vigorous calendering, thus ensuring that the oil colour would be completely transferred from the paper to the enamel or ceramic surface.

John Brooks initiated the transfer process, cutting the first copper plates and applying the particular technique required for this specialised work, with deep incisions shaped to hold the enamel-oil ink firmly yet permit it to be printed with clarity on the paper when the copper plate and ink were warmed to an equal temperature.

Henry Delamain was responsible for preparing the finely-ground enamels with printer's ink in such a way that, when transferred to the enamel surface and fired at a temperature of about 550 degrees centigrade, the oil was burned away, leaving the lines of enamel fused to the surface.

Among the elusive figures associated with ceramic transfer printing is Robert Hancock, one of the engravers working for Janssen, then being fresh from his apprenticeship with George Anderton, a minor engraver of Birmingham. The Battersea works operated for less than three years, however, compelling young Hancock to seek work elsewhere. It is considered virtually certain that, to the good fortune of English ceramic manufacturers, he met the situation by introducing the transfer printing process to Bow, then under the management of Thomas Frye, formerly a mezzotint engraver. This association must have begun early in 1756, for the memorandum books of the Bow traveller John Bowcocke show that, on 28th May and 18th June, he received orders for "a sett compleat of the second *printed* teas", "1 pint *printed* mug 5/-", and "1 half pint ditto 3/6." These are the earliest reference in connection with printed ceramics yet noted. Bow porcelain is known to have been printed in four colours: brick red, black, a dull dark purple, and brown. These transferred lines might be used as outlines for transparent washes of coloured enamels.

Later in the same year Hancock introduced transfer-printing to the Worcester Tonquin Manufactory, eventually becoming a director. To ensure sharpness and clarity of line it was essential to apply the transfer over the glaze. An exception was blue, which required a fluxing temperature about 50 per cent higher than the overglaze colours, none of which could survive a kiln temperature exceeding 750 degrees centigrade.

Printing in underglaze blue on porcelain appears to have originated at Worcester under the control of Robert Hancock, whose assistant from March 1772 was Thomas Turner. In October 1774 they both resigned from the firm, Hancock at that time being a director. Turner established the Salopian works at Caughley with the fixed intention of developing blue underglaze transfer printing on table ware.

Cobalt oxide was the source of the blue used in ceramic decoration, smalt producing a rich full blue, zaffre a much coarser colour. Smalt was a carefully prepared vitreous compound—a rich blue glass, in fact, reduced to a fine powder: zaffre was a less purified variety of the same material. The actual colour on the ware depended, however, on the potter's skill.

Turner's first porcelain was made from a formula and by methods similar to those used at Worcester. The underglaze printing, however, was blotchy and coarse. Turner improved both colour and glaze and with Hancock's assistance improved the engraving technique. Lines became vigorous, hard and intensely blue, showing that the costly smalt was used, its colour capable of carrying its brilliance through the film of clear glass glaze. The colour was prepared by Turner personally in a private laboratory: during his frequent absences his sister deputised for him in this work.

So far, earthenware had not proved a suitable base for transfer printing under the glaze. When the efforts of Josiah Wedgwood made purified Cornish stone and china clay available to all earthenware potters, from September 1775, Turner was able to evolve a light, cream-coloured earthenware. This, however, proved unsuitable ground for underglaze printing in blue, although such ware was marketed.

Again Josiah Wedgwood came to the rescue, inventing a much harder and whiter earthenware which he named pearl ware, making the formula available to other master potters. This is described by Josiah Wedgwood & Sons Limited as "a white earthenware body containing a greater percentage of flint and white clay than cream-coloured earthenware. A small amount of cobalt added to the glaze increased the whitening effect."

Pearl ware, at first with a faintly yellow tinge, was found by Turner to be an ideal base for underglaze blue printing, the heavy blue of the pattern being accentuated by the white background and harmonising with the faint blue of the transparent glaze. Underglaze transfer printing in blue, later to become celebrated as Staffordshire blue, was, then, first produced in Shropshire. Compared with nineteenth-century blue printing, Turner's lines were thickly cut, to facilitate removal of the ink by the transfer paper. Characteristic of this early work is the shading in strong parallel lines almost as if drawn with the aid of a ruler. Each transfer included the mark S (Salopian) in various sizes, and the plate number accompanied by the marginal initials T T.

Designs followed the highly fashionable Oriental style painted on porcelain in cobalt blue under the glaze. A collection of original copper plates, some of them worn to paper thinness, is in the British Museum, the gift of Mr. Charles Bruff, a one-time proprietor of the Coalport factory which, in 1799, acquired the Caughley Pottery from Thomas Turner. The earliest is dated 1799.

When Turner marketed his transfer printed ware, Josiah Spode, at Stoke-upon-Trent, immediately realised the immense potentialities of the process of transferring designs in cobalt blue to pearl ware biscuit and covering it with transparent glaze. Spode attracted from Caughley an engraver named Thomas Lucas and a transfer printer, James Richards, and provided them with facilities for developing the transfer-printing technique. He himself improved the pearl ware and evolved a hard, transparent glaze which protected the decoration from the effects of food acids and the wear caused by cutlery.

The glaze gave a rich, soft tone to the blue beneath, which had been partly absorbed by the biscuit. For all but the very well-to-do this ware provided the first opportunity of eating from decorative table ware. Overglaze blue printing soon followed, being introduced to the potteries in the mid-1770s. Credit for this must go to William Adams of Cobridge. The increased wearing qualities of this inexpensive decorated ware brought unprecedented prosperity to the Staffordshire master potters.

Of the eighty Staffordshire potters listed in *Tunnicliffe's Directory*, 1787, no more than three were entered as "blue printers" as opposed to twelve "blue painters". During the following decade at least twenty other potters entered the blue-printing trade.

The process of transfer printing began with the engraving of the design cut very deeply into a flat copper plate in such a way that the lines held enough colour to give a firm, full transfer. Early cross-hatching produced a smudgy effect not overcome until about 1800. Only by about 1810 were fine tone-gradations achieved by combining line and stipple engravings on the one plate. Even then, the decoration was, of course, limited to the single colour which could be printed from a copper plate, and considerable skill was required to make the best use of light and shade effects and achieve a well-balanced picture, clear in detail, yet covering every part of its allotted space. This accounts for the frequent introduction of figures and water in the foreground and massive cloud effects to fill the sky. The complexity of the decoration was designed to conceal minor surface flaws such as might be expected on inexpensive earthenware, and were, indeed, accepted as more or less inevitable on such solid lusty ware intended for everyday use.

The engraved plate was warmed on a stove provided

with an iron plate immediately above a brisk fire. The incised lines on the copper plate were charged with colour mixed with thick boiled oil by means of a flexible steel knife and dabber. The heat kept the colour fluid. Excess colour was scraped off with the knife and further cleaned by wiping with a beaver cushion or "boss", leaving colour only in the incised lines. A sheet of thin, strong paper, known as "pottery tissue", was saturated in a weak solution of soap and water and laid upon the copper plate and subjected to the action of a press. The paper was then carefully drawn off, bringing with it the colour from the lines on the plate.

This impression was handed to the cutter, who removed superfluous paper. The transferer then laid it upon the biscuit ware, rubbing first with a small piece of soaped flannel to fix it, and afterwards forcibly with a rubber formed of rolled flannel. The friction caused the colour to adhere to the biscuit in clear outline. The piece was then immersed in cold water and the paper washed away, the colour, full of oil, being unaffected. This oil was removed, leaving the pure colour, by placing the ware in a low-temperature hardening-on kiln. After cooling the ware was dipped in glaze. As small a portion as possible was held by the dipper who plunged the piece into the liquid glaze. By a dexterous jerk this was made to cover the whole surface with a uniform coating. Being porous, the biscuit earthenware imbibed and retained the glaze which remained opaque until fired in the glost kiln. An experienced workman with two boys to give and take could dip about seven hundred dozen plates in a day.

Although printing in black gave greater clarity of outline the blue obtained from cobalt was the only colour capable of providing numerous gradations of tint. The richest blue came from the purest cobalt, and until the 1790s was known to English potters as Saxon blue or smalt.

This was described by Robert Dossie in his *Handmaid to the Arts*, 1764, as "vitrified oxide of cobalt brought from Saxony and has not long been available in England and is sold at high prices as ultramarine, but more usually under its own name . . . its goodness lies in its being dark, bright and cool although always verging towards purple, but the less so the better." English-made cobalt possessed a violet tinge in varying and unpredictable strength, making standardisation impossible. Manufacture had been discontinued by about 1770, but refiners already established in Bristol, Liverpool and Staffordshire continued operating with imported Saxon cobalt ore. Purifying treatments were progressively evolved, all tending to produce smoother and bluer colour. Early in the nineteenth century all traces of copper, lead, iron, bismuth and nickel were removed. The resulting zaffre, however, gave a less attractive tint than is found on eighteenth-century transfer printing.

Artificial ultramarine, evolved by a French chemist in 1802, resembled the bright blue of genuine ultramarine, which cost £20 an ounce at a time when cobalt was 6s. per pound and artificial ultramarine 1s. 3d. per pound. It was known at first as "bleu de Thenard" for its inventor, and formed the basis of most Staffordshire underglaze transfer printing, being sold under various names such as Canton blue, Broseley blue, bamboo blue and willow blue. Many potters preferred to use cobalt blue and advertised their ware as printed with "genuine zaffre". By 1850 the darkest coloured zaffre printing was known as king's blue.

Flown blue, a method of treating transfer printing to produce a lighter, more delicate appearance, was invented by Josiah Wedgwood II in the 1820s. A mixture of saltpetre, borax and white lead placed in the saggars during glost firing caused the colour to flow slightly, producing a softer texture.

Underglaze transfer printing was carried out in various shades of blue until 1828 when it was discovered that by mixing finely powdered yellow, green, red and black enamels with barbados tar, it was possible to transfer designs in various shades of these colours without distortion or loss of brilliance. Two or more of the colours might be printed on a single piece of ware, a separate firing being necessary for each. There was a vogue for polychrome transfers during the 1830s and, although pictorial examples are now uncommon, they are seldom collected. In 1848 F. W. Collins and A. Reynolds patented a process by which three colours, blue, red and yellow, could be fixed from a single transfer with a single firing. The colours, applied separately to the transfer, were so composed that they would mature at the same temperature. This development was used for the colourful pot-lids made by F. & R. Pratt, Fenton.

Transfer gilding was patented in 1835 by Godwin Embrey and was used mainly to enrich blue printing. The design was transferred to the ware in potter's varnish: this was dusted with gold flux, fired and burnished. Embrey sold prepared transfers to leading potters of the day. Examples are uncommon, but they are as brilliant as when made, having withstood burnishing after firing.

Thomas Minton was probably the first to establish himself as a specialist engraver of copper plates for the Staffordshire trade. In 1802 he was followed by John Aynsley, Lane End, who established himself as a designer, engraver, maker of transfer prints and decorator. His name is to be found on transfers until he retired in 1826. Occasionally the name "Bentley, Ware & Bourne, Engravers and Painters, Shelton, Staffordshire" is found incorporated in a transfer design, frequently a naval scene. That transfers might be bought from specialist printers is shown by plates illustrating a print of Harvard College published by Alvan Fisher in 1823. Identical transfers are found on ware made by Stevenson & Williams, Enoch Wood & Sons, and James and Ralph Clews.

Dinner, dessert and tea sets in Staffordshire blue were made in tens of thousands and exported to the far corners of the world. Yet few today have remained intact: they were never intended for display as "best" like porcelain and enamelled bone china. They were for the most part made by master potters whose names were little known except to the china sellers.

In a typical service each flat piece carried a picture. Hollow-ware might be decorated with three or four scenes on inner and outer surfaces. A cheese dish, for instance, might have a scene on the interior of its flat plate and a different one on each side of the cover. At least twelve different views belonging to a series would decorate a table service.

Transfer pictures were enclosed in borders of geometrical

patterns until 1805 when William Brookes, an engraver of Tunstall, suggested to Stephen Crane, a master potter of the same town, that more satisfactory results would be attained by using reduced versions of the strip borders in the romantic pastoral mood then fashionable with wall-paper hangings. By 1810 these borders had outmoded the geometrical. Typically, repeat patterns of flower and leaf festoons, fruiting vines and floreate scrolls might be used, interspersed with butterflies and bell flowers.

Many views were enhanced with wide borders in more elaborate designs, sometimes incorporating reserves containing miniature views or portraits associated with the central theme. These borders are of particular interest to collectors of Staffordshire blue. The makers of some un-marked specimens have been identified by their border patterns, which were not pirated by competing potters, as were successful designs for the main pictorial ornament until the Registration of Designs Act came into operation early in 1842. The use of identical borders by different potters may perhaps be blamed upon specialist suppliers of transfers to the trade. As further enrichment the borders of flat ware might be moulded with designs copied from late eighteenth-century dinner services.

ADAMS, William, Stoke-upon-Trent, was one of the four leading makers of Staffordshire blue on well-designed pearl ware from the mid-1790s. At first oriental designs were used and from about 1816 a large number of notably fine English views were printed in dark blue. His "London Views" are bordered with foliage designs, including a pine tree on the left side and the name of the scene on the back. Of the fifteen London scenes recorded, nine were of Regent's Park, including Clarence, Cornwall and Hanover Terraces, and York Gate; the Bank of England and the London Institution are also found. The "English Views" —churches, castles and manor houses—number more than one hundred, marked on the back with the title of the scene. The majority are bordered with various flowers, bell-flowers predominating; others have large flowers, leaves and scrolls, or a scroll edge and foliage. The only American design by

William Adams was a picture of Mitchell & Freeman's China Warehouse, Boston, with the handsome foliage border and pine tree found on English views.

The firm became William Adams & Sons in 1829 and large numbers of American scenes were exported, including the Columbus series of nine highly imaginative scenes of Columbus landing in America, such as Columbus with fleet in distance, Columbus with dogs and Indian. The borders are composed of irregular medallions with different animals and in the spaces between are sprays of roses. This series was later printed in red, mulberry and black.

Early examples were impressed W ADAMS and from 1829 W A & S. On ware intended for the American market and on some English views there was, in addition, a blue printed eagle with extended wings, grasping a twig in one claw, four arrows in the other, above a festooned ribbon containing the name of the view.

CLEWS, James & Ralph, Cobridge, were successors of Andrew Stevenson and operated for fifteen years from 1817, potting Staffordshire blue of excellent quality. Examples examined have invariably been in a hard pearl ware, heavier than usual. More than 250 views and pictures were engraved, many of them printed in attractive combinations of dark and light blue. Their "Pictures of Sir David Wilkie" are now diligently collected: the beautifully designed borders contain passion flowers among other flowers and scrolls. These were intended as rack plates in a day when colourful pictures were rare in a working man's home. This series includes "Playing at Draughts", "The Valentine", "Escape of the Mouse", "The Rabbit on the Wall", "Christmas Eve", "Letter of Introduction", and "The Errand Boy".

The Syntax designs, numbering more than eighty subjects, were adapted from Thomas Rowlandson's illustrations to William Combe's *Three Tours of Doctor Syntax*. These were published by Ackermann in three volumes, the first tour in 1815, the second 1820, and the third in 1821. "Dr. Syntax Amused with Pat in the Pond", and "The Harvest Home" are very rare examples that have sold for

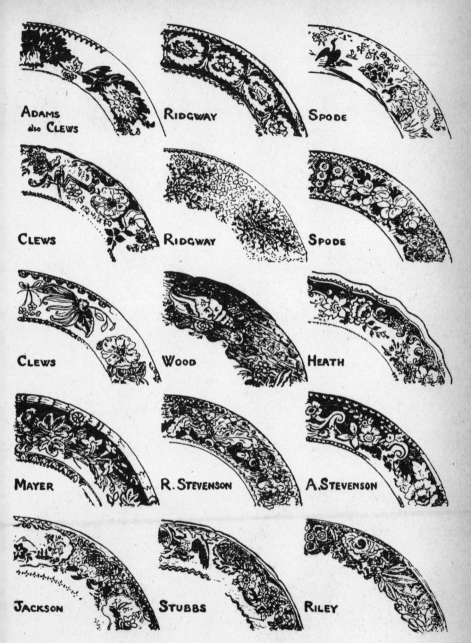

ADAMS also CLEWS

RIDGWAY

SPODE

CLEWS

RIDGWAY

SPODE

CLEWS

WOOD

HEATH

MAYER

R. STEVENSON

A. STEVENSON

JACKSON

STUBBS

RILEY

Fig. 1. Transfer-printed blue and white plate borders.

133

a

b

c

d

e

f

Fig. 2.

a. Design from Spode's famous Oriental Field Sports series: "Groom leading out a horse."

b. Design for a Spode plate decorated with Chinese emblems known as "trophies" enclosed by a willow type border.

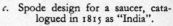

c. Spode design for a saucer, catalogued in 1815 as "India".

d. A transfer from Spode's "Grasshopper" pattern.

e. A transfer from Spode's "Man Riding on a Buffalo".

f. A transfer from Spode's "Net" pattern for a ten-inch plate.

g. A transfer from Spode's "Severn" pattern printed in Rhine blue.

h. A transfer for Spode's "Camilla" pattern in Rhine blue.

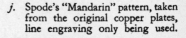

j. Spode's "Mandarin" pattern, taken from the original copper plates, line engraving only being used.

Fig. 3. Transfers from old copper plates at the Spode Copeland factory, showing the earliest type of engraving employed.

136

Fig. 4 (*Above*) Spode's blue "Italian" pattern, a brilliant example of transfer printing in which line and stipple engraving are combined. Produced extensively in the earlier period and reproduced from about 1900. (*Below*) Spode's "Tower" pattern taken from the original copper plate. The design was adapted from an aquatint "The Bridge of Salaco", published 1798.

about £50. The Syntax series is bordered with large flowers and small scrolls and back-stamped in blue with the title of the picture in script in an ornamental rectangle. Scenes from the *Life of Don Quixote* followed, consisting of twenty-four different pictures enclosed in borders of flowers alternating with irregular points, and with beading to edge the scalloped rim. The pictures were pirated from the books: there was no adequate protection against this until the Registration Act of 1842.

The Clews brothers carried on a considerable trade with the United States of America, and at least sixty American views have been catalogued.

One series of twelve American views, including three aspects of the White House, has a scalloped border bearing the names of fifteen states with stars between. A set back-stamped "Picturesque Views" bordered with birds, flowers and scrolls includes twelve scenes on the Hudson River. These were taken from water colours painted on the spot by W. G. Wall, and published as engravings in 1823. Also included were designs drawn and engraved by Samuel Maverdick, New York, illustrating the "Landing of Lafayette", made to celebrate his visit to America in 1824. A dinner service of 112 pieces made to commemorate this visit was sold for £1,050 in 1947.

English scenes were grouped into three main series, back-stamped "English Views", "Select Views", and "Picturesque Views". More than fifty cathedrals, abbeys and castles have been catalogued in "English Views", including Windsor Castle, Fonthill Abbey, Rochester Castle, and Rothesay Castle. These are bordered with a design composed of bluebells and other flowers, or with foliage and intricate scrollwork. The name of each view is back-stamped in a ribbon scroll within a wreath of flowers. "Select Views" such as Cheddar, Fountains Abbey and St. Catherine's Hill near Guildford were encircled with borders composed of large asters and bell flowers. The "Picturesque Views" have a border containing four other views in medallions, and are back-stamped with a scene consisting of trees and a lake with a small boat through which runs a bar inscribed with the title. The "Zoological Garden Views" such as

"Bear Cages" and "Bird Cages" are bordered with twisted scrollwork.

The firm's name was impressed on every piece, either CLEWS or a crown above CLEWS WARRANTED / STAFFORDSHIRE.

The Clews had ceased production by 1834 when James emigrated to America and joined Jabez Voudry and Jacob Lewis in establishing a pottery at Troy, Indiana, to specialise in the manufacture of Staffordshire blue. Lack of suitable materials made impossible the production of white pearl ware and within two years the project was abandoned and Clews returned home. Later, large deposits of fine quality kaolin were discovered in Troy.

DAVENPORT, John, Longport, was established in 1793 as a maker of earthenware, painted and blue printed, achieving outstanding success with plates rimmed in openwork. He does not appear to have made scenic views, but numerous chintz-like designs, the willow-pattern and Anglo-Chinese scenes have been noted. Davenport was celebrated for *dejeuner* services in willow pattern of a beautiful blue, with massive gilded handles, gilded borders, rims and feet, and raised ornament. His earliest work was unmarked, but by about 1800 he began to print DAVENPORT in red with three small irregular circles beneath. Early in the nineteenth century his name was lettered in an arc shape above an anchor. From 1806 he used the mark DAVENPORT / LONGPORT / STAFFORDSHIRE printed in red and surmounted by an anchor. After 1830 the anchor was superseded by a royal crown.

EDWARDS, James and Thomas, Burslem, occupied Kiln Croft Works from 1825 until the late 1840s, potting blue printed wares for the United States and Canada. They were well known for nautical pictures such as the "Boston Mail" series dating from 1841, in which scenes aboard sailing ships were depicted. Their borders were composed of bunches of roses and festoons of roses. They issued about fifty American views. The impressed mark was J T & E.

GODWIN, Thomas, Navigation Road, Burslem Wharf, potted in transfer-printed stone china with handsome effect from the early 1830s. Godwin is named in Ward's list of Staffordshire potters, 1843, and is entered in White's *Staffordshire Directory*, 1851. His work was of consistent excellence, and the transfer-printing reproduced with notable clarity in a combination of line engraving and stipple. He printed in all the colours available, sometimes in a brilliant dark shade of green or in lilac. He never used dark blue. Godwin's borders were usually a composition of morning glory and nasturtium flowers: from about 1835 he also used, less frequently, intricate geometric designs carried well into the bouge as on some of Herbert Minton's bone china.

Pictorial decoration was confined to city views and pictures of American scenes such as Boston and Bunker Hill; Brooklyn Ferry; City of Baltimore; The Capitol, Washington; The Narrows from Fort Hamilton; Utica, New York; Columbia Bridge, Pennsylvania; Schuylkill Water Works; William Penn's Treaty and many others. Godwin issued a series of pedestal-footed toddy bowls with three scenes around the body and another within. His plates and dishes might be eight-sided or scallop-edged. The fine quality of his stone china and the beauty of his transfer printing made his ware more costly than most of his competitors on earthenware.

Godwin's usual mark was impressed THOMAS GODWIN WHARF. The omission of the name Burslem with no appropriate space between "GODWIN" and "WHARF" has given many collectors the mistaken impression that the potter's name was Wharf. Later a transferred mark was used THO' GODWIN BURSLEM / STONE CHINA, and this might be accompanied by a charming little engraving in line and stipple of a house and tower surrounded by trees, with a scroll beneath containing the title of the picture displayed on the front. This was signed T.G., the initials of Godwin himself, this proving him an engraver of more than average ability. Because of their rarity Godwin's transfer printed wares make high prices in America.

HALL, Ralph, Swan Bank Works, Tunstall, who potted from the late 1790s to 1832, appears to have made all his blue transfer-printed ware for the home market. His potting was of poor workmanship and his printing in dark blue shows signs of haste in application, probably with the intention of underselling his competitors. Hall's twenty-five "Select Views", including Pain's Hill, Surrey, and Knole and Wildernesse in Kent, are framed in lace-edged borders of fruit and flowers. "English Views", enclosed in lace-edged borders of large flowers, are views of celebrated residences. Hall's name is found on earthenware decorated with all-over designs adapted from fashionable chintz. The mark impressed is R HALL and a blue printed scroll titling the picture and its series.

JACKSON, J. & J., Churchyard Works, Burslem, issued English and American pictures in light blue from 1831 to 1843. Their productions are rare and command high prices.

MAYER, Thomas, Cliff Bank, Stoke-upon-Trent, acquired Joseph Stubbs's pottery as a going concern in the early 1820s. He continued blue underglaze transfer-printing in a more attractive shade of blue. Trumpet-shaped flowers and vine leaves compose his typical border pattern, and a fine lace edge encircles many of his central pictures. Rims are edged with overlapping scale motifs broken at regular intervals by spoked wheels.

Mayer's views appear to have been issued haphazardly, not in the series that were usual with his competitors. About forty of his English views have been catalogued and thirty American views. He was responsible for a very elaborate—and today extremely valuable—series of twelve dishes displaying in dark blue the arms of various American states. Nearly £500 has been paid for a 21-inch plate bearing the arms of Pennsylvania. A 19-inch dish with the arms of New Jersey sold at the same sale for about £250. The remaining ten bear the arms of Rhode Island, Connecticut, Maryland, New York, Georgia, Virginia, Massachusetts, North Carolina, South Carolina and Delaware, which is perhaps the most handsome of the series: all command high prices. When discovered, these armorial dishes are usually in mint condition, without scratches or greasemarks: apparently they were intended as wall plaques.

The impressed mark is T. MAYER STOKE STAF-FORDSHIRE WARRANTED, in a circle surrounding an eagle. Most of his blue-printed ware, however, is unmarked.

MINTON, Thomas, Stoke-upon-Trent, after leaving Thomas Turner of Caughley in 1786, was employed by Josiah Spode at his London warehouse, Fore Street, Cripplegate, where he engraved copper plates with designs adapted from oriental originals. Among the patterns he cut for Spode at this time were versions of the "Broseley dragon" and willow pattern. On New Year's Day 1789, Minton married Sarah Webb of Bruton Street, and shortly afterwards moved to Stoke-upon-Trent where he established himself as a master engraver to the trade.

By 1793 Minton began making earthenware on a small scale with the assistance of Joseph and Samuel Poulson. Joseph, formerly manager to Josiah Spode, was a highly skilled potter, and Samuel a mould maker and modeller. The order book became so full that he sought and received financial assistance from William Pownall, a merchant in Liverpool. Joseph Poulson was also taken into partnership and the firm traded as Minton, Poulson & Pownall. They issued a great amount of transfer blue, imitating the designs of Nankin. By 1803 the pay-roll numbered fifty. Although Minton made Staffordshire blue throughout the period of great demand, no pictorial or scenic examples impressed with his name are known.

PHILLIPS, E. J., & Co., Longport, operated during the 1820s and are known for their Eton College series of pictures in ornate flower and scroll borders in dark blue. Many of these views have been found on wash-stand jugs and basins, suggesting that the original order was for the College. American views were also issued and a long series of carefully printed "British Flowers", with the names of the series and the flower printed on the back in a floral wreath, together with the impressed mark E & G P.

RIDGWAY, Job, Cauldon Place, Hanley, founded his pottery, with his brother George, in 1792 at the Bell Works,

Shelton, They parted in 1802 and Job built the celebrated Cauldon Place pottery, eventually becoming one of the most prolific potters of blue-printed earthenware. After Job's death in 1813, his two sons, John and William, continued the business, trading as J. & W. Ridgway. Their copper plates were so cut that the transfers were clearer of line and contained more differentiation of tone than those of most other potters. The colour was paler than usual.

They appear to have concentrated on the American trade from 1816, their chief contribution being the "Beauties of America", a series of twenty-four views transfer-printed to table services. The "beauties" include churches, but are chiefly alms and court houses, lunatic asylums and the like, enclosed in borders of medallions each containing a conventional rose and a few leaves: a three-figured sum has been paid for a plate bearing one of the rarer views. Another valuable series consists of the colleges of Oxford and Cambridge, numbering eighteen in all, the views set in eight-sided panels with borders composed of flowers and rectangular medallions containing children and goats. There is no record that the series was continued after 1830 when the brothers separated; John to continue at Cauldon Place, whilst William acquired the Bell Works and established six other potteries, eventually becoming the most important potter in the district and employing more than 1,200.

William Ridgway concentrated on the profitable American market. So great was the demand for his wares that he visited America with the intention of establishing a pottery there. Although he selected a suitable site in Kentucky, the project was abandoned. For ten years he successfully printed a series of fifteen American views in light blue and black, bordered with small sprays of moss or seaweed, sometimes with a scale pattern or crackle ground. A series of eight views marked "Catskill Moss" and "C C" have been attributed to William Ridgway. The most interesting of these is the Albany and Schenectady Railroad, sixteen miles long and opened in 1830: this shows a locomotive of English make known as the "Stourbridge Lion". For the first two years after opening the carriages were horse-drawn.

John Ridgway continued the manufacture of Staffordshire blue at Cauldon Place, the borders of his American views being composed of five-pointed stars in various sizes.

The Ridgways impressed their names in full and printed the name of the scene in blue.

ROGERS, John and George, Dale Hall, Burslem, potted from 1802 until 1815, when George died and John took his son into partnership. The firm traded as J. Rogers & Son until 1842 when the business was sold to James Edwards. The Rogers firm was specially celebrated for versions of the willow and Broseley dragon patterns in a particularly radiant dark blue. Many of their pictures are enclosed in a border of roses and forget-me-nots, including such titles as "The Adopted Child", "The Maypole", "Love in a Village" and so on. The mark was ROGERS impressed or printed, sometimes with the addition of the sign of Mars.

SPODE, Josiah, Stoke-upon-Trent, printed in blue on pearl ware from about 1785. This earthenware he progressively made whiter, and he used a rich luminous blue for printing, not available to other potters. Evidence has been found on the works site that the Spodes refined their own cobalt: excavations have produced large samples of cobalt ore. In my small book *The Story of Spode*, 1950, it is pointed out that Spode's blue and white ware, painted and printed, "made from about 1800, has a white body of exceptional purity, greatly enhancing the beauty of the prints. This is particularly noticeable in a long series of blue and white designs cleverly adapted from contemporary engravings of English and Continental scenery.

"The printing of the pictures on the central panels has always been clear and unsmudged; the borders never overrun the rims, and transfer joints are almost imperceptible. One-colour printing necessitated the skilful interplay of contrasting colour and background. Spode found that discriminating use of water and figures supplied the need. The edges of the plates and dishes were moulded in a style influenced by contemporary silver ware: some of them were suggested by the scalloped outline found on large silver meat dishes."

Llewellyn Jewitt in *The Ceramic Art of Great Britain* (1883), listed Spode's blue and white designs with their dates of first production, many originating between 1820 and 1826. These have been edited and divided into groups by Sydney B. Williams in his book *Antique Blue and White Spode* (1943).

These groups may be summarised as

(*a*) A fine series displaying Indian scenes and dating from about 1820. The designs were adapted from illustrations in Thomas Williams' *Oriental Field Sports*, first published in 1805. Engraving, colour and glaze are all of outstanding excellence.

(*b*) More typical of the period, reflecting the romantic Italian mood. This series includes the Tiber, Castle, Tower, Lucano, and Blue Italian patterns.

(*c*) Blue and white showing oriental influence, including Willow, India, Marble, Two Birds, Hundred Antiques, Net, Nankin, Gothic Castle (in a Chinese setting), and Old Peacock patterns.

(*d*) Caramanian pattern in which views of Asia Minor are depicted, mainly in Caramania. The Spode version consists of composite pictures taken from a book published in 1803.

(*e*) General designs including the Milkmaid introduced in 1814; the Woodman, a composite design from sections of various contemporary engravings, 1816; Waterloo, 1818; Warwick Vase, 1821; Blue Rose, 1824; Persian, 1824; Greek Pattern, 1825; and numerous others.

(*f*) Outline designs in which blue-printed patterns were coloured by hand. The Peacock pattern in this medium was copied in 1814 from a contemporary Chinese porcelain plate. Comparison has shown that Spode's version was far superior for table use to the Chinese original, with its rough, sharp edges and somewhat rough surface. Spode used stone china and a softer glaze. The Spode records show that the design was highly successful on the Continent. Other outline patterns include the Ship, 1819; and the Oriental, 1820, in which lotus, prunus, chrysanthemum, and peony motifs predominate.

STEVENSON, Andrew, Cobridge, made Staffordshire blue from about 1810 until the mid-1820s. The pottery was established in 1808 by Bucknall & Stevenson, but by 1812 Bucknall had resigned his partnership. Their productions displayed a high degree of technical ability and they printed in a rich dark blue which many collectors consider to excel that of Spode, or in a combination of dark and light blue.

When Andrew Stevenson became sole proprietor he entered the American market, with great success so far as orders were concerned. Unfortunately his costs proved higher than those of his competitors, and by 1818 the pottery had been acquired by J. and R. Clews.

In addition to copying published American views he commissioned W. G. Wall, a young Irish artist, to sketch American views on the spot. Twelve of these were taken into production and are back-stamped in blue with the artist's name. A border was specially designed for each American view, consisting of varying arrangements of large flowers, small wreaths and scrolls. Stevenson's American views, numbering about twenty-four subjects, include six of New York City by W. G. Wall. The "Battle of Bunker Hill", in dark blue with a wide fruiting vine border, is rare: a 12-inch meat dish has sold for as much as one hundred guineas. "The Temple of Fame" illustrating the memorial to Commodore Perry with a willow tree to the left in a combination of dark and light blue has sold for £30, and "New York from Brooklyn Heights" in medium blue for £25.

Stevenson issued more than thirty English views such as Tonbridge Castle, Mereworth House, Summer Hall, all in Kent; Walsingham Priory, Haughton Hall and Culford Hall. At first these were bordered with roses and other flowers, later with vine leaves. In some instances, such as "Writtle Lodge", the border incorporated two or four medallion portraits.

Andrew Stevenson impressed his name on all his earthenware, either A STEVENSON or a crown-encircled A STEVENSON WARRANTED STAFFORDSHIRE. Some American views are imprinted in blue with the name of the picture accompanied by an eagle or a draped urn.

STEVENSON, Ralph, Cobridge, a brother of Andrew, potted blue-printed earthenware of outstanding quality from 1816 to 1840. About three dozen designs have been identified, including three groups of English back-stamped "Panoramic Scenery", "British Lakes", and "English Views". Examples of the rare "Panoramic Scenery" are in dark blue with a foliage border. "English Views" with the attractive oak leaf and acorn border are: Harewood House, Endsleigh Cottage, Kenmount House, Oxburgh Hall, Windsor Castle with portraits of Washington, Lafayette, Jefferson and Clinton, and a view of Rochester Aqueduct Bridge at the base. "British Lakes" is also a short series, with flower and scroll borders.

"American Views" number eighteen subjects including eight of New York and six of Boston, all with the oak leaf and acorn border. These command high prices. A small plate printed with The Battery, New York, in dark blue has been sold for thirty guineas, and another small plate of Fort Gansevoort, New York, in dark and medium blue, twenty guineas. The Battle of Bunker Hill, from a print engraved by Annin, Smith & Co. after a drawing by J. R. Penniman, always fetches high prices.

Ralph Stevenson was joined in partnership during the late 1820s by a potter named Williams. They traded as Stevenson & Williams, but apart from additions to the repertoire of engravings there was little change in technique. Oak leaf and acorn borders are separated from the central design by small beading. An additional eighteen American scenes were issued including five of Harvard College, three of Columbia College as it was after 1820 when two wings and a belfry were added, and the Capitol at Washington. The Capitol is sometimes to be found with the border broken by four medallions containing portraits of Washington, Lafayette, Jefferson and Clinton.

Until joined by Williams, Ralph Stevenson impressed his name STEVENSON: during the partnership the mark was R S W or R STEVENSON & WILLIAMS.

STUBBS, Joseph, Longport, made Staffordshire blue in which colour, design and finish are of high standard.

English scenes are bordered in a design of foliage and pointed scrolls and American scenes in borders composed of eagles, flowers and scrolls generally arranged on plates with three equidistant eagles: on dishes there are four eagles. The American views, numbering twenty-four prints, include "View at Hurlgate, East River" showing a steam ferry in the foreground and a sailing boat in the distance. A small plate showing this view in dark and light blue has sold for £50, and the rare "View of New York Bay" and "Boston State House and Common", also in dark and light blue, have sold for near £100 each. For long the attractive milkmaid scenes have been attributed to Stubbs, but marked examples bear the impress SPODE.

Much of Joseph Stubbs' work was issued unmarked, but border patterns were not used by any other potter. A few pre-1816 pieces have been noted with the name STUBBS impressed. The mark thereafter was JOSEPH STUBBS LONGPORT, in a circle enclosing a star; perhaps to distinguish his work from that of William Stubbs, Hanley. The impress STUBBS & KENT LONGPORT is evidence that a partnership existed at some time before he retired in 1829.

TAMS, S. & Co., Crown Works, Longton, from about 1830 to 1850 issued a series of six "London Buildings" including Drury Lane Theatre, Covent Garden Opera House, Somerset House, and the Royal Exchange in foliage borders. Many American views and portrait pieces were made, all in foliage borders. They may be impressed S TAMS & Co; TAMS; TAMS & ANDERSON; TAMS ANDERSON & TAMS, indicating changes of proprietorship from time to time. Blue-printed ware was also marked with a large, heavy back-stamp bearing the title of the picture and, in the 1840s, the name SEMI-CHINA.

WOOD, Enoch, Burslem, established his pottery in 1783 with Ralph Wood as partner as a maker of "all kinds of useful and ornamental earthenware, Egyptian black, cane and various other colours, also black figures, seals and cyphers." The partnership ended in 1790, and Enoch Wood, financed by James Caldwell of Lindley Wood, began manufacturing domestic earthenware at Fountain Place, Burslem, trading as Wood & Caldwell. By 1793 they had entered the blue-printing trade, and eventually became prolific and prosperous in this medium. Wood and his sons were responsible for more than five hundred English, American and French views, and a further three hundred of a miscellaneous character. The majority of these date from 1819 when Enoch Wood bought out Caldwell and was joined in partnership by his sons.

The hundred or more English views consist of cathedrals, castles and country seats, such as York and Durham cathedrals, Fonthill Abbey, Belvoir, Rochester, Warwick and Windsor Castles, Dorney Court, Buckinghamshire and Harewood House, Yorkshire. These views entirely fill the centres of dishes and plates and are encircled with borders of flowers and fruiting vine edged with a narrow twisted motif. The title of each picture is imprinted in a foliate ribbon scroll. The series known as "English Cities" contains adaptations from contemporary engravings including Chichester, Coventry, Ely, Leeds, Liverpool, Norwich and Rochester. The flower and scroll border contains six medallions and is separated from the picture by a narrow ornamental ribbon. These are impressed E W & S and imprinted in blue with the title of the view in two scrolls accompanied by a bishop's mitre and staff.

The "London Views" number twenty-five pictures, each within a rectangle enclosed in a fruiting vine border, with exceptionally large bunches of grapes. Most of the scenes are of the newly built Regent's Park area and include Doric Villa, Coliseum and Cumberland Terrace. Imprinted in blue on the back of each is a scroll with leaves and the inscription ENOCH WOOD & SONS BURSLEM, with a separate imprint containing LONDON VIEWS and the name of the view.

"American Views" are found with various borders, but early examples are composed of sea shells. These are in two arrangements: first, the central view displayed in a circle with the border containing a conspicuous cockle shell, and the title back-stamped; later there is an irregular opening for the picture view which is named on the front, and the

Index to the letters for each year and month from 1842 to 1883

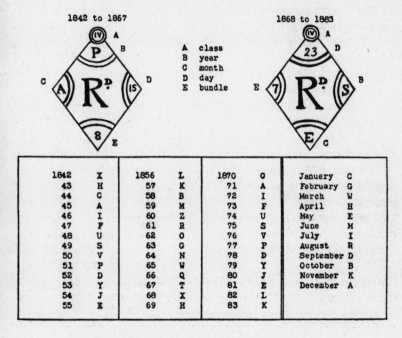

1842 to 1867   1868 to 1883

A   class
B   year
C   month
D   day
E   bundle

1842	X	1856	L	1870	O	January	C
43	H	57	K	71	A	February	G
44	C	58	B	72	I	March	W
45	A	59	M	73	F	April	H
46	I	60	Z	74	U	May	E
47	F	61	R	75	S	June	M
48	U	62	O	76	V	July	I
49	S	63	G	77	P	August	R
50	V	64	N	78	D	September	D
51	P	65	W	79	Y	October	B
52	D	66	Q	80	J	November	K
53	Y	67	T	81	E	December	A
54	J	68	X	82	L		
55	E	69	H	83	K		

For September 1857 ?R used from September 1st to September 19th.

For December 1860 ?K used.

For March 1st to March 6th 1878 the following mark was issued:

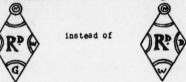

instead of

Fig. 5. Much ware between 1842 and 1883 bore a registration mark to prevent design piracy and the corner letters and figures are here explained. Class IV covered all ceramic wares. The "bundle" contained the original design filed at the Patent Office, and the date was that of the design's introduction, not necessarily that of the ceramic so marked.

shell border contains no cockles. These were adapted from prints sent from America such as "Niagara Falls" engraved by J. Milbert in 1818, and "Lafayette at Washington's Tomb" after a drawing by D. W. Jackson for Harris & Channcey, a well-known firm of china importers. "American Views" include the series "Landing of the Pilgrims" dating from 1820, when Wood was commissioned to make a dinner service for a commemorative banquet to be held at Boston in connection with the founding of New England. The border is handsome, with scrolls and four medallions, two of them containing ships and two inscriptions. The pattern was also placed on the market, and plates now sell at £20 each.

"Scenes from the New Testament" are enclosed in a border of scriptural motifs, flowers and scrolls. Wood also issued innumerable scenic views of India, Africa, and Italy, and twelve French views in a border of fleurs-de-lys, hollyhocks and bunches of grapes. Four of these are of La Grange, the home of Lafayette.

The early mark was WOOD impressed, together with a blue-printed trade mark. After about 1830 the impressed mark was circular: in the centre an eagle with a shield, and below SEMI CHINA, and encircling the whole, E WOOD & SONS BURSLEM WARRANTED. In addition to this there is often a blue back-stamp consisting of the title of the picture, an eagle with a branch in its claws, and a scroll flowing from its mouth with the words E PLURIBUS UNUM.

A full list of the master potters whose impressed name is to be found on blue transfer-printed earthenware would number at least two hundred. In addition to the foregoing, the following potters issued some excellent work: Josiah Wedgwood & Sons, Etruria; Joseph Heath & Co., Tunstall; Charles Meigh, Hanley; Heathcote & Co., Fenton; Belle Vue Pottery, Hull; Dillwyn & Co., Swansea; Brameld & Co., Rockingham.

The willow-pattern has claimed an unshakable, but remarkable, position in the collector's affection. This pseudo-Chinese design in blue underglaze transfer-printing has never been out of production since it was evolved in about 1780 by Thomas Turner of Caughley. The original copper plates as used on earthenware engraved by Thomas Turner, with his signature in the margins, are now in the British Museum.

Turner adapted the design from a blue and white Chinese plate decorated with a celebrated tea-house in Shanghai, with its inverted umbrella-shape roof turned up in pagoda-like points. No Chinese design closely resembles this: in any attempt to compare details the likeness vanishes. The London china sellers at once appreciated Turner's willow pattern, first hand-painted in blue on soft porcelain and almost immediately adapted to engraving and transfer-printing under the glaze.

In the original printed design, used exclusively on earthenware, the pagoda is on the right of the picture, surrounded by conventional willow, peach, fir and plum trees, the mysterious tree with dark circles, and the tallest tree of all, bearing three tiers of apples, thirty-two in all. This arrangement applies to flat-ware only, the design being adapted to suit the space available on hollow-ware. In the original Caughley plates no figures appear on the little bridge spanning the river, but later one, two or three figures are to be seen hurrying across the rounded-arch bridge. The wooden zig-zag fence, familiar in fashionable English gardens of the period, extends across the foreground, each section in different geometric pattern. The design slightly differs on Caughley porcelain: the pagoda appears on the left of the picture, the bridge arches are pointed, and the sky and water are slightly shaded.

Caughley willow pattern dates from c. 1780 and is printed in a deep, sparkling blue. The mark on earthenware is a roughly drawn C or S to which may be added a small cross. SALOPIAN in outlined capitals was also used. The mark on porcelain is a filled-in crescent in blue underglaze. John Rose of Coalport acquired the Caughley factory in 1799, continuing the production of willow pattern earthenware printed from the original plates. In 1812 Rose incorporated the Caughley plant with that of Coalport on the opposite bank of the Severn.

Thomas Minton when he established himself as a copper plate engraver to the pottery trade at Stoke-upon-Trent in 1790 designed versions of the willow pattern for other potters. In these little more was changed than the fence patterns and the number of fruit on the tree. John Turner, Lane End, one of the earliest potters to decorate with the willow pattern, omitted the bridge from his design. Plates and dishes have rims perforated with narrow pales and are impressed TURNER.

Josiah Spode I printed willow pattern on pearl ware from 1785 to 1797, but this bore little resemblance to the Caughley version. The pagoda is on the left of the picture, and the bridge, with only two men crossing, is on the right beside a peach tree and an apple tree. The fence, shorter than in other designs, contains the swastika in its design. Borders are of the honeycomb variety copied from the Chinese. The mark is impressed SPODE in roughly formed capitals.

Josiah Spode II used a willow pattern more closely resembling that of Caughley, with an apple tree bearing thirty-two fruit—reduced to thirty on flat ware with perforated borders. After about 1805 dragon and butterfly borders were fashionable: separating the butterflies and dragons are sceptres filled in with trellis work. Elsewhere the trellis work resembles basketry. The engraving is clear and soft. The impressed mark is a scroll containing the name SPODE, or SPODE 10, but examples have been noted with SPODE hand-painted in blue. Later the name was printed in blue. Job Ridgway's willow pattern is almost identical with Spode's and is marked with an R contained in a square resembling a Chinese seal.

Josiah Wedgwood appears to have produced little willow pattern. This, on pearl ware, reproduces the Caughley version with the fret on the fence slightly different: the apples number thirty-four on plates and more on dishes. The blue is not very intense and after the mid-1820s flown blue was preferred. The mark is WEDGWOOD impressed. From the early 1830s the Wedgwood firm produced willow pattern earthenware printed in black and often enriched with gilding. This sombre-looking ware is rare.

John Davenport, Longport, potted willow pattern services

by the ton. The apple tree on the flat ware bears only twenty-five apples, but considerably more on hollow-ware. Only good quality ware is impressed DAVENPORT or DAVENPORT LONGPORT with or without an anchor, or with an anchor alone.

Benjamin Adams, Greengates, potted a large quantity of conventional willow pattern in stone china with fifty-two apples in the tree. The design on the bouge of flat ware is squarer than Caughley's. Until about 1805 Adams printed on pearl ware and the apples numbered thirty-two. The mark is TURNER impressed. The willow pattern of James and Ralph Clews shows thirty-four apples. The Rockingham version differs from all others in showing the boat in the foreground, no fruit on the tree, no fence, and only two men upon the bridge.

W. T. Copeland who succeeded Spode in 1828 was a prolific maker of fine willow pattern on pearl ware, following the Spode tradition. From 1832 to 1846 it was impressed COPELAND & GARRETT; from 1847 to 1869 COPELAND LATE SPODE.

Chapter Ten

THE STONE CHINAS

***

ENGLISH ceramics of the early nineteenth century tend to be decried by those who fail to appreciate their technical excellence. Improved methods of potting produced stronger, more colourful ware capable of giving enduring service, yet within purse reach of a wider public than ever before. Outstanding among these was stone china, brilliantly decorated and immensely strong, an entirely English development perfectly attuned to its period. Refinements during the first half of the century included ironstone china, semi-porcelain, opaque porcelain, opaque china and the inexpensive granite ware. Staffordshire potters began experiments towards stone china in the late 1790s, a few years after a high tariff had been levied upon imported porcelains in 1794. This protective measure had long been urged by English porcelain potters competing with the State-subsidised porcelains of Europe and oriental importations by the East India Company. The sale of luxurious porcelain services had been the mainstay of the London china-sellers whose stocks were quickly depleted with no prospect of comparable replacements from English sources.

One of the principal porcelain importers had been Miles Mason, 131 Fenchurch Street, London, whose sales were now reduced to unremunerative proportions. He realised, however, that finer wares would be possible after the lapsing of the Champion patent in 1796 (see p. 110) which had monopolised the use of Cornish china clay and china stone as regards porcelain. With this in view he financed and rebuilt the Islington China Manufactory, Liverpool, with two practical potters, Thomas Wolfe and John Lucock, as partners. The work produced here was of little consequence in itself. They turned out a poor quality bone china in no way comparable with that already being made by Josiah Spode. An existing plan of the Islington China Manufactory shows transfer-printing and gilding rooms. Miles Mason simultaneously established an earthenware pottery at Lane Delf, Staffordshire, with George Wolfe as the practical partner.

By 1800, therefore, Mason had familiarised himself with the recipes and processes of both branches of potting. He then withdrew from the Liverpool venture and became sole proprietor of the Lane Delf pottery, apparently abandoning the manufacture of coarse earthenware in favour of bone china and hard porcelain. His entry in *Holden's Triennial Directory*, 1805, reads: "Miles Mason, china mfr, Lane Delf."

He now conducted experiments in an endeavour to evolve a ceramic comparable with the hard porcelains of Europe. Although not successful in this, two years later he was making stone china, a fine opaque earthenware closely allied to fine stoneware, but containing considerably less flint than ordinary English earthenware of the period and more Cornish stone. Stone china, tough and with a glaze impervious even to the cutting edge of dinner knives, was first of the semi-porcelains which were to bring great wealth to master potters of Staffordshire. This hard earthenware, possessing porcelain characteristics, was a fused body, the temperature of the kiln causing the alkalis in the clays to combine with the silica and alumina. The time of firing was six to seven hours according to the size of the kiln and the type of ware. When unusually large objects were to be fired, the heat was raised very gradually. The opacity of stone china was due to a deficiency of flux and the temperature of the firing, which was too low to produce translucency. A standard formula, evolved later, consisted of Cornish stone 40 parts, china clay 35, ball clay 18, calcined flint 7, but each potter varied this to suit his own preferences. Poor qualities of stone china are distinguished by their greater opacity and slightly yellowish tinge.

Mason's success was such that he closed his London

warehouse and concentrated entirely on production. One of his tea services, fully marked on each of the forty pieces, is in the Symes collection. In the *Morning Herald*, 15th October 1804, he advertised:

"It has hitherto been the opinion, not only of the Public, but also of the Manufacturers of this Country, that the earths of these Kingdoms are unequal to those of Foreign Nations for the fabrication of China.

"Miles Mason, late of Fenchurch Street, London, having been a principal purchaser of Indian Porcelain till the prohibition of this article by heavy duties, has established a Manufactory at Lane Delph, near Newcastle-under-Line, upon the principle of the Indian and Seve China. The former is now sold at the principal Shops only, in the City of London, and in the Country, as British Nankin. This article is warranted from the Manufactory to possess superior qualities to Indian Nankin China, being more beautiful as well as more durable, and not so liable to snip at the edges, more difficult to break, and refusable or unitable by heat if broken.

"Being aware that to combat strong prejudices with success something superior must be produced: he therefore, through the medium of his Wholesale Friends, proposes to renew or match the impaired or broken services of the Nobility and Gentry, when by a fair trial in conjunction with Foreign china, he doubts not that these fears will be removed, and, in a short period, the Manufactories of Porcelain, by the patronage of the Nobility of this country, will rival, if not excel, those of Foreign Nations.

"N.B. The articles are stamped on the bottom of the larger pieces to prevent imposition."

Josiah Spode II, meanwhile, was working on similar lines and in 1805 was able to market a much finer stone china, with a dense body closely approximating porcelain. It was, indeed, the missing link between ordinary earthenware and porcelain. The delicate blue-grey tint of its body formed an ideal ground for the old Chinese designs in brilliant enamels with which it was decorated. Effects were produced impossible with earthenware. These colours consisted of metallic oxides combined with an alkaline flux, which, when exposed to a high temperature, formed a smooth glaze.

By 1810 Spode had discovered that potash felspar vitrified more slowly than soda felspar, thus reducing the warping risk and lessening the tendency of the biscuit to absorb smoke: the bluish grey tint was lightened. Pores were filled more regularly and completely than formerly, producing an unflawed surface, smooth and without undulations. This was marketed for a few years as "New Stone China" and later as "Stone China".

Stone china was particularly in demand for table services, as one of its practical advantages was that it retained heat longer than other ceramics.

Some exceptionally fine decoration was obtained by painting under the glaze. Its fusibility permitted a larger palette to be used, and resulted in brighter colours than were possible with underglaze decorations on porcelain and bone china. The slightly absorptive quality of the biscuit necessitated the employment of skilled artists with a sure touch: once the colour was applied it was impossible to remove it. After painting, the stone china was fired to a red heat to drive off the oils used in the colours so that glazing would not be clouded. The colours that matured at the same temperature were purple, violet, brown, grey, black, red, orange, yellow, green, blue and a bluish green. These were all dull until glazed. Overglaze decoration was also used. The enamels were made by mixing stoneware glaze and adding colour and a little plastic clay made to the same formula as the basic body to ensure adhesion. Should glaze and flux fail to correspond the colours would virtually vanish under firing, or scale off or craze.

The reddish-brown edges of oriental hard porcelain were rough and sharp and, according to Miles Mason, were inclined to snip. Spode rounded the edges of his stone china. The oriental hard paste covered with glaze did not permit the enamels to sink and thus gave a raised, slightly rough surface to decoration. In stone china the colours sank into the surface and did not flake in use.

Because Spode's stone china was without specks and pitting there was no need for him to use crowded design, as did competing potters. Characteristic decorations included copies of *famille rose* patterns, chiefly in pink, blue and red, applied in flat washes over printed outlines, simple and heavy, but inexpensive. Patterns adapted from the Imari style and known to china-sellers as "Japans" were used by every potter of note. Many services were fashionably painted with family coats of arms in full colours. Others displayed fantastic birds with long tails and crested top knots, among flowers of impossible colour and form, fierce dragons with knobbly claws and rolling eyes, and rivers thickly sprinkled with tiny fairy boats.

Among Spode's outstanding successes was the peacock and peony pattern, in which a pair of colourful peacocks confront a huge, pink peony flower and a spray of prunus blossom, believed to have been introduced in 1814. The parrot design was equally popular set against a mountain and lake background. The mosaic pattern, with grounds of various colours such as blue and deep yellow overprinted with a network design to suggest cracking ice, continued until the end of the period when W. T. Copeland controlled the firm. After glazing the mosaic was enamelled with a single large spray of prunus blossom and a bird. The Chinese version signified the death of winter and the coming of spring. Marbling might be substituted for the cracked ice in early examples. In some of Spode's dinner ware the plate centres were coloured, their borders ornamented with a design in transfer-printed blue and their rims coloured Indian red imposed with gold diaper work.

Extensive table services in stone china were greatly in demand. Families were large and entertainment lavish. Dinner services were standardized to twelve covers, but frequently extended to thirty-six, with thirty serving dishes for game and meat. Plates for the three main courses were of the same size and the services now included soup plates. Dinner and dessert services combined became fashionable, the pieces matching. These ranged from soup and vegetable tureens to shell-shaped dessert dishes and dessert plates. The old practice of serving dessert on ware of a different type and design continued, however. A typical family dessert service contained a pair of tazze, four dishes and twelve plates.

Special services were evolved for supper, and from about 1815 were made up of about 130 separate pieces: four fan-shaped dishes and covers, four square dishes and covers, one octagonal dish, liner and cover, two sauce tureens and stands, with ladles, two oval egg stands, each with twelve egg cups, six octagonal meat dishes, four oval dishes, a salad bowl, twenty-four each of soup, dinner and dessert plates. Combined tea and coffee services with but a single set of saucers now gave way to sets with their full complement of saucers.

For drawing rooms, entrance halls, passages and the like in middle-class homes there were massive vestibule vases, sometimes exceeding a yard in height, supported on separate pedestals rimmed with pierced galleries of ormolu, a feature of the 1820s. Oval jardinieres and fish cisterns might have dark blue grounds with reserves containing appropriate designs and rims encircled with non-repeating flower patterns and mounted with elaborate ormolu work.

Spode's huge warehouse in Portugal Street, London, became the fashionable centre of the trade in stone china. In response to requests from noblemen and wealthy citizens already possessing Chinese dinner services, he extended these to fashionable proportions by copying them in stone china. In 1945 a most interesting record[1] of this was given to a member of the Copeland family, by a lady whose grandfather had been a solicitor in Bideford, on the coast of Devonshire. Her father (1831–1920) had bequeathed a large dinner service for division among his ten children. The service contained a number of Chinese plates acquired in the way of barter by their grandfather from a sea captain who, like most sea-faring men of the eighteenth century visiting Bideford and Appledore Quay, paid his personal bills with merchandise brought from the East. These Chinese plates were later sent to Spode, who incorporated them in a gigantic dinner service. A number of these Chinese plates with their Spode counterparts are now in the possession of a member of the Copeland family.

Spode quickly perceived that Chinese models were admirably suited to his stone china, as is shown by his use of a square pseudo-Chinese seal mark to distinguish this ware. His early efforts before 1805 were marked SPODE STONE CHINA in a cartouche, printed in blue under the glaze. From 1805 he used a Chinese square seal containing bogus characters and the name SPODE across the middle, with STONE CHINA below: this was also in blue. This usually

[1] *The Story of Spode*, G. Bernard Hughes, 1950.

appears on the underside of rims and is found in two sizes, the larger being the older. During the period 1810–15 the mark SPODES/ NEW STONE was impressed. The seal mark was then brought into use again but was printed near the centre of the base. During the Copeland-Garrett period (1833–46) the mark was NEW STONE JAPAN. When W. T. Copeland became sole-proprietor stone china continued in all the fashionable Victorian styles marked COPELAND STONE CHINA.

Other potters made varying qualities of stone china. Honey noted heavy dishes roughly glazed over a brownish body, "which are at times difficult to distinguish from the Chinese, which themselves had been copied from English models, perhaps even from the productions of Josiah Spode himself, who in his turn had adapted many of his patterns from earlier Chinese and the designs found on tea papers." It is interesting to note that Spode's stone china has been collected for more than fifty years.

John Davenport, Longport, possibly was first to equal Spode's new stone china, production extending from about 1815 until 1882. He, too, adapted oriental patterns to the English taste, also painting purely English landscapes, flowers, fruits and birds, with lavish gilding. He made octagonal jugs in the style usually associated with the Masons. Blue-printed outlines to painted decoration were used during the 1820s. Jewitt described Davenport's stone china as remarkably good and effective. "Dinner and dessert services as well as jugs and other articles are of faultless quality, and many decorations are adaptations of old Indian patterns. In some of these the spirit of the oriental artist has been so thoroughly caught that, to the casual observer, they might well pass for genuine foreign pieces."

Two marks were used by the Davenport firm on stone china: DAVENPORT in a ribbon supported by a pair of pillows with an anchor between and STONE CHINA beneath, all impressed; a red printed mark consisting of a circular garter bearing DAVENPORT LONGPORT STAFFORDSHIRE encircling STONE CHINA in script, with an impressed anchor. The presence of 82 FLEET ST., the address of Davenport's London warehouse, shows manufacture between 1824 and 1842.

Josiah Wedgwood made stone china for a short period, possibly ten years, ending in about 1825. Examples are rare and are impressed WEDGWOOD or Wedgwood. These should not be confused with the stone china made nearly half a century later by Enoch Wedgwood & Co., Unicorn Pottery, Tunstall. This firm operated in the third quarter of the nineteenth century, employing nearly seven hundred workers. It introduced the "Asiatic Pheasant" which became a standard pattern on inexpensive ware throughout the Potteries. This backward-glancing bird was depicted in black outlines with a plumed tail and usually perched on a branch. The bird might be in yellow, red or green. The impressed mark was STONE CHINA / WEDGWOOD & Co.

.Herbert Minton, Stoke-upon-Trent, was potting unflawed stone china by about 1820. Early designs included the well-known "Amherst Japan", named for Lord Amherst, Governor-General of India, 1823–1828. This ware is found impressed NEW STONE and when accompanied by the name MINTON dates later than 1861.

John and William Ridgway, Bell Bank, Hanley, potted stone china from the 1820s. Their printed mark was a lopsided shield surrounded by scrollwork and containing the name of the pattern such as "Indian Temple" and the name STONE CHINA / JWR. The brothers parted in 1830, William remaining at Bell Bank and impressing his stone china W RIDGWAY / STONE CHINA. Ridgway, who owned several other potteries, including the Charles Street Pottery, Hanley, failed in 1854. The Charles Street branch was acquired by J. W. Pankhurst & Co., who continued making fine quality table services in stone china, mainly for the American market. Their mark, printed in black, was an adaptation of the royal arms above STONE CHINA / J.W. PANKHURST & Co.

Pountney & Allies, general potters of Bristol, from 1816 made stone china and by 1825 more than two hundred persons were employed. In 1835 Allies withdrew from the partnership. The mark was impressed: POUNTNEY &

ALLIES in arch shape with a cross in the centre, and STONE CHINA.

J. & M. P. Bell & Co., Glasgow, made stone china dinner services from the time of their establishment in 1842. Many of these were decorated in blue transfer-printing: there was a particular vogue for views of the Italian Lakes and the Warwick vase pattern of the 1850s. The several marks included the impressed bell which might incorporate the initials J.B. Early printed marks included an eagle with outspread wings, grasping a roll inscribed with the name of the pattern and the initials J. & M.P.B. & Co.

Among the many Staffordshire firms whose marks included the term STONE CHINA were John Ridgway, Cauldon Place, 1834–40; Cork & Edge, Burslem, 1831–64; Hicks, Meigh & Johnson, Hanley, 1822–30; Thomas Carey & Sons, Fenton, 1826–41, whose magnificent printed mark includes a bishop's mitre, a coat of arms and the name SAXON STONE.

Stone china was the precursor of the immensely strong ironstone china from which, in its turn, was evolved granite ware. By 1804, as described on page 156, Miles Mason closed his London china and glass retail shop, then termed a magazine, and was devoting his entire energies to potting at Lane Delph. In 1807 he built up-to-date and more extensive Minerva Pottery, Lane Delph, and took his eldest son William (1785–1855) into partnership. In 1811 William broke away to operate his own pottery nearby, specialising in blue transfer-printed earthenware until 1824 when he closed down and became a china seller in Manchester. His productions are marked W MASON impressed or printed in blue.

Miles Mason in June 1813 retired a rich man, transferring his business to his sons George Miles Mason (1789–1859) and Charles James Mason (1791–1856). Within six weeks Charles James had been granted a fourteen-year patent to manufacture the now celebrated and collected Mason's ironstone china. This, described in the patent as "English Porcelain" was, in fact a hard earthenware, slightly transparent, but of great strength, compactness, and density of texture and durability, and possessed some porcelain characteristics. The name ironstone was given on account of its ironstone slag content, its hardness and its clear ringing tone when struck. Ironstone china was, however, clumsy in appearance at first, thick of section, but brilliantly and lavishly decorated. In 1815 the brothers, trading as G. M. & C. J. Mason, built more extensive premises, which were eventually finished as a long row of four-storied warehouses and workshops with kilns and mills at the rear.

George Mason retired in 1829 to devote himself to politics, and Charles James operated the business as Charles J. Mason & Co., with Samuel Bayliss Fereday as partner. After Fereday's death in 1844 he traded alone. At this time he introduced a machine for making plates and saucers, but mechanical defects and opposition from employees caused him to lose money and by 1848 he had become bankrupt. Three years later he established another pottery at Daisy Bank, Longton, but four years later he was compelled to close. The moulds, plant and goodwill were then acquired by Francis Morley.

Ceramic authorities have long discussed the composition of Mason's ironstone china as detailed in his patent specification, and have concluded, wrongly, that his formula was bogus. In forming this conclusion they have overlooked the important fact that Mason's specification was signed "under my hand and seal" on 31st July 1813, eight days after the granting of this patent and two weeks before it was enrolled. It was illegal then, as now, to enter a false specification, even if it were possible to deceive the officials concerned. Such a specification when unmasked was immediately pronounced void and such instances are recorded.

The patent specification, headed with George III's coat of arms (see page 163) with a bearded unicorn, begins:

"Charles James Mason of Lane Delph,
    "near Newcastle-under-Line, in the County of
Stafford. Potter.
    "1813, No 3724, 31st July.
    "A process for the Improvement of the Manufacture
of English Porcelain.
    "NOW KNOW YE, that in compliance with the said
proviso, I the said Charles James Mason, by this
present instrument in writing under my hand and
seal, do describe, declare, ascertain, and

specify the nature of my said Invention, and the
methods in which the same is to be performed,
in the manner following, that is to say:
"The iron stone which contains a proportion of
argil [a trade term for clay] and silex is
first roasted in a common biscuit kiln to
facilitate its trituration, and to expel sulphur
and other volatile ingredients which it may
contain. A large earthen crucible is constructed
after the exact model of an iron forge [furnace],
a part of the bottom of which is filled with charcoal
or coaks; these having been previously strewed with
ore and about one-third part of lime, are raised to
an intense heat by a strong blast of air introduced
under the coaks at the bottom. By this heat the ore
is fused, and the fluid iron drops through the fuel
to the bottom, then follows the scoria, which floats
upon the top of the fluid iron. This latter scoria,
or as the workmen call it, slag, is the material
used in the manufacture of the china and is much
impregnated with iron, and of a compact and dense
structure. The slag is next let off by a hole through
the forge into a clean earthen vessel, where it cools.
This last vessel is then broken, in order to detach
the slag from it with hammers. The above part of the
process we do not consider essential as it is merely
conduces to the cleanliness of the ware.
"The scoria is next pounded into small pieces
and ground in water to the consistence of a fine
paste at the slip mills. This paste is next
evaporated to dryness on a slip kiln well known
amongst potters. Thus evaporated to dryness it is
used with the other ingredients in the following
proportions: Prepared iron stone 3 cwt; Ground
flint 4 cwt; Ground Cornwall Stone 4 cwt; Cornwall
clay 4 cwt; Blue oxide of cobalt 1 lb. These having
been mixed together with water by the slip maker,
are again evaporated on the slip kiln to the proper
consistency for use. The clay thus prepared is, of
course, used in the usual way in the fabrication of
several kinds of vessels."

The glassy frit prepared as in the first part of the specification is equivalent to top slag tapped from commercial blast
furnaces of the period. Mason was well aware that iron blast
furnaces were producing such a frit and he fairly described
the process. Until 1813 it had been considered a useless dross

and thrown upon the slag heap. I discuss this subject fully in my book *Victorian Pottery and Porcelain* (Country Life). "Patent iron stones" were marketed by Aaron Manby, an iron-master of Wolverhampton in the same county. These were made under a patent granted in May 1813, to John Manders, chemist; Aaron Manby, and Joseph Vernon, furnace men. These patent ironstones were composed of molten slag that flowed from iron furnaces. This was drawn off into moulds shortly before the puddlers tapped the iron and was gradually cooled in annealing flues.

"The top layer of this slag was a glassy material, pale green in colour, closely resembling frit, and about as transparent. No doubt its resemblance to frit prompted Charles Mason to incorporate it in his patent as 'Prepared Iron Stone'. This is not to be confused with the lava-coloured blast-furnace clinker or slag referred to in the Mander-Manby-Vernon patent as converted into 'Forms that may be used for any Purpose to which Brick, Quarry, Tile, Slate or Stone are now applied'.

"Some at least of the transparent slag was obtained at a later date from the blast furnaces of Edward Giles, Wednesfield Heath, near Wolverhampton, who despatched it to the Potteries by the canal that bordered his premises. Giles built an extensive rockery in his garden from large irregular blocks of this glassy slag, and when this was examined a few years ago it was possible to discern objects through a block nine inches thick despite a 120-year film of smoke. Thin slivers were virtually transparent."

Improvements in puddling processes by the early 1840s caused the glassy slag floating on the molten iron below the dross to display a deep purple tinge, thus making it useless for ceramic purposes, but desirable to the glassmakers of Stourbridge and elsewhere for pressing into now collected ornamental ware. As these processes became more widely used in the blast furnaces, the supply of transparent slag lessened. Mason then changed his formula, replacing it with flint-glass cullet. Ure's *Dictionary of Arts*, 1875, states that the improved ironstone china was composed of 42 parts each of felspar and china clay, 10 parts pulverised flint, and 8 parts flint-glass and the writer adds that "slag from iron smelting is sometimes introduced".

The Masons potted immense quantities of their patent ironstone china. There was little difference in its original cost and that of most other stone chinas, but a service made

by the Mason firm would outlast several of the more fragile
ones in daily use. Like the porcelain potters before them,
George and Charles Mason held periodic auction sales in
London. *The Times*, early in May 1828 reported the sale of
1,004 lots of Mason's ironstone china at prices ranging
between £20 and £30 a service, the sale totalling approxi-
mately £30,000. Their prior advertisement in the *London
Morning Herald*, 21st April, 1828, announced the sale of:

"Many hundred table services of modern earthenware, breakfast
and tea ware, toilet and chamber sets, many hundred dozen of baking
dishes, flat dishes, broth basins, soup tureens, sets of jugs, and
numerous other aticles.

"The China is of the most elegant description, and embraces a
great variety of splendid dinner services, numerous dessert services,
tea, coffee, and breakfast sets, of neat and elegant patterns, ornaments
of every description that can be manufactured in china from the
minutest article calculated to adorn pier table and cabinet, to the
most noble, splendid and magnificent jars some of which are nearly
five feet high."

A further advertisement in *The Times*, 24th May, announced a sale of "patent ironstoneware for coffee houses,
tavern keepers and hotels." It will be noted that the patent
had expired in July 1827 and the Masons were now facing
competition from other Staffordshire potters.

Mason's ironstone china jugs, now assiduously collected,
were at first given a heavy, faintly blue glaze and the base
usually had a "wiped" appearance. The well-known octagonal jugs with the reptilian handle touched with scarlet and
the head turned to the right became immensely popular and
were made in sizes ranging from 2½ inches to more than 10
inches in height. The most frequent colours were red, pink
and blue, but examples in rich blue with gilding are not uncommon. Complete sets, decorated to match, are difficult to
collect for many patterns were used, superficially alike. The
demand for these was such that stone china potters made
close copies. The quality of the potting of those made by
Davenport usually surpassed that of the Masons, and he was
equally successful in colourful decorative schemes appealing
to a wide public. Jugs modelled in relief with scenes from
Shakespeare's plays were also made by the Masons: a set of
three sizes with different scenes has been recorded. Mugs of

all shapes were made too, some fluted, some plain, some with a toad inside to shock the unwary drinker. Octagonal mugs might have outspreading bases and width might exceed depth.

The colours on ironstone china were hand applied in flat washes over printed outlines and consisted at first of pink, blue and red. After 1818 the colours consisted chiefly of vermillion reds, brilliant deep blues and apple greens. Pink, puce and pale green sometimes appeared and occasionally patches of black and brown. All of these colours matured at a single firing. Many types of quaint, jumbled designs were used, particularly in quickly copied Imari patterns in the style of the costly enamelled bone china of Spode, Bloor of Derby, Brameld of Rockingham, and Rose of Coalport. The motifs to be expected include the following, either singly or more generally in a combination of several: large flowers resembling peonies, a full blown rose, sprigs of hawthorn, daisies, all with appropriate foliage; exotic birds, and waterfowl on the wing; with butterflies, dragon-flies, gnats or other insects on the reverse.

Domestic table ware was virtually covered with brilliant colours and gilding to disguise black specks that tended to disfigure the surface. These will be noted on unpainted surfaces of ironstone china actually made by the Mason brothers. Patterns adapted from the Chinese included anglicised versions of *famille verte* in which clear green predominated and the *famille rose* dominated by opaque shades from delicate pink to deep crimson. Flowers and foliage included "Flowers of the Four Seasons": peony of spring, lotus of summer, chrysanthemum of autumn, prunus of winter. The peach, double cherry, magnolia and gardenia were among other flowers used. Other designs showed vivid scenes from Chinese domestic life with landscapes and gardens.

From about 1825 the Masons used a blue ground in which white reserves were painted with landscapes, flowers, birds and other motifs. The blue ground was either left plain, enriched with gilding, or decorated in colours with thickly applied enamels. From about the same time plates and dishes with blue scenes and views surrounded by gilt borders were made for the American market. The "Bandana"

4. Teapot, basin and coffee cup and saucer from a combined service in felspar porcelain by Chamberlains of Worcester. The set includes twelve teacups, twelve coffee cups and twelve saucers. Marked *Chamberlains, Worcester*, in red script.

4a. Part of a combined tea and coffee service in felspar porcelain, made by Josiah Spode II in the early 1820s. This fine earthenware, invented by Spode in about 1805 and in production until the early 1830s, is as translucent as porcelain.

pattern dates from about 1840. This pattern was composed of Indian foliage and grotesque animals printed in red and black on a buff or other light ground. Gilding, when used lavishly, might be signed by the gilder such as Lawton or Sellers.

In addition to dinner and dessert services, tea ware and jugs the Mason brothers made large pieces such as toddy bowls and pitchers of gallon capacity. In the 1820s some huge pieces of ironstone china were in production, such as so-called fish tanks—really wine coolers—and vases three to five feet tall, lavishly painted and gilded in pseudo-Chinese style.

Fireplaces were also made in ironstone china, showily enamelled and gilded. Six different models have been noted, each in two sizes with 42-inch and 22-inch openings and each requiring a separate set of moulds. They were cast in eight sections: a pair of supporting pillars resting on plinth bases curved to bear the weight of the upper portion; a cross-piece in three segments, the central one acting as a keystone; and the mantelshelf resting upon these and projecting over the front.

The drawing and dining rooms of Charles James Mason's home, Heron Cottage, Fenton, were fitted with fireplaces of ironstone china. One of these is now in Hanley Museum, showing signs of damage caused by Chartists who raided the cottage in 1842. Each pillar is a half-hexagon with flat sides decorated with birds and foliage in moulded relief, painted in colours against a yellow or patterned ground. The 22-inch opening of this fireplace is fitted with a cast-iron grate in late Georgian style.

Some were patterned in a Chinese style. Others were moulded in high relief with large trailing acanthus leaf patterns and masks thickly gilded and burnished, and so designed as to provide smooth panels painted with flower and foliage sprays in pink, puce, pale green, apple green, vermilion and blue. Decoration of these panels differed in each fireplace. Flowers and insects included those found on table ware. The ground colours of dark blue, apple green and yellow were applied by a process introduced by Henry Daniel of Shelton in 1826. These grounds were less fusible than those used by the enamellers and were unaffected by the firings required for subsequent decoration. A small example in blue is in Sir Arthur Conan Doyle's writing room at Windlesham. Several miniature models of ironstone china fireplaces are known, distributed by Mason for display in the windows of builders' merchants.

Each fireplace was marked on one of its sections with what is surely the largest transfer-printed trade marks to have been used on English ceramics. On those examined the mark has been printed in brown and measured about 6 inches across and about 4 inches deep. Its main feature was the coat of arms as used by the Prince of Wales during his regency of 1810 to 1820. This coat of arms, that of George III with the label of the Prince of Wales, headed C. J. Mason's patent specification. Above was the printed inscription CHINA CHIMNEY PIECES MASON & Co., PATENTEES STAFFORDSHIRE POTTERIES and below PATENT IRONSTONE CHINA.

The style of the firm on these marks shows that the fireplaces were made after the withdrawal of George Miles in 1829 and before 1838 when the use of the royal arms by potters, other than holders of the royal warrant, was forbidden by Queen Victoria. Many bogus versions of the royal arms were designed for potters and continued in use until the 1880s.

C. J. Mason eventually made garden seats in ironstone china: an example displayed at the Great Exhibition, 1851, was catalogued as "decorated in a mixture of Anglo-Indian and Japanese patterns, representing an old dragon, in raised enamel on a gold ground". Gravestones and monumental tablets were also made, lettered under the glaze.

The Masons are believed to have marked all their ironstone china. First, impressed in capitals, was MASON'S PATENT IRONSTONE CHINA, in a line when convenient, but on small ware in a circle without the name Mason's. From 1815 the impressed mark was accompanied by a transfer-printed mark in jet black, puce or blue. This consisted of a crown below the name MASON'S. In a few years the impressed mark was abandoned and PATENT IRONSTONE CHINA inscribed on the printed mark in a wide cartouche

beneath the crown. Some early marks in black were stencilled: a tea set inspected recently was so marked beneath
the large pieces. The crown appears to have been taken from
the crest of the Prince Regent's coat of arms heading C. J.
Mason's letters patent. Mason's crowns are found in several
variations, but the reason remains obscure. This mark continued until the formula was changed when the word
PATENT was substituted by IMPROVED.

A printed mark used during the period that the firm
traded as C. J. Mason & Co. illustrates the front elevation of
a substantial block of four-storied workshops with kilns and
chimney stacks behind, above an escutcheon inscribed
FENTON STONE WORKS CJM & Co with STAF-
FORDSHIRE POTTERIES below. To this was added
IMPROVED CHINA and later GRANITE CHINA.

When in 1854 Francis Morley & Co. acquired Mason's
goodwill, the manufacture of ironstone china was continued, impressed REAL IRONSTONE CHINA with the
printed mark adapted from the royal arms and IRON-
STONE CHINA below.

In *Ceramic Art in Great Britain*, 1878, L. Jewitt recorded
that Francis Morley in his turn sold during 1859:

"The entire business, moulds, copper-plates to ms. Geo. L. Ashworth
& Taylor Ashworth who continued to the fullest extent the manufacture of the 'Patent Ironstone China', which they and their prede-
cessor had named REAL IRONSTONE CHINA on their marks.
They produced all Mason's best patterns in services, vases, etc., made
from his original models. They also manufacture Meigh's ironstone
from his old moulds. . . . The ironstone china from its extreme hardness (for it is not easy to break even a plate) is specially adapted, in its
simpler styles of decoration, for services used by large steamship
companies, hotels, clubs, colleges, and other places where hard usage
has to be undergone; while in its more elaborate and rich styles it is
eminently fitted for families of the higher ranks. No climate affects
this ware. The usual style of decoration for dinner services in imitation of Oriental patterns—Japanese and Indian flowers etc.—and
the colours and gilding are rich in the extreme. In vases and jugs the
handles are usually dragons and other grotesque animals. The Indian
vases are of perfect form, of exquisite design, rich in their colours,
and massive in gilding. They are priceless Art-treasures."

Mason's Fenton Pottery was acquired in the late 1850s by
E. and E. C. Challinor who made ironstone china and white

granite decorated with transfer-printing and sponging. The marks were: IRONSTONE CHINA E & C CHALLINOR impressed or printed with a version of the royal coat of arms above a ribbon inscribed IRONSTONE CHINA E & C CHALLINOR FENTON.

Cookson and Chetwynd, Cobridge, in 1866 abandoned the manufacture of bone china and concentrated upon their more profitable ironstone china for the American trade. Their mark, a printed adaptation of the royal arms with the name IMPERIAL IRONSTONE CHINA COCKSON & CHETWYND, is seldom seen in England.

T. Furnival & Sons, Cobridge, potted improved ironstone china from the late 1840s. Jewitt in 1878 referred to their ironstone china as

> "beautiful, and among their most recent productions are table services of rich Italian design, plain white with a china-like surface and glaze; the ornamentation, which is indented, is produced from an embossed mould, the lines being as fine and delicate as if cut by the graver, so as to have the appearance of chasing; and the lines being filled with glaze the surface is still even. Some of their ironstone china is attractively painted with grasses and insects."

This clearly demonstrated the extent of the improvements in ironstone china since the original Mason patent. The mark was FURNIVAL impressed.

Ironstone china bearing the mark of Holland & Green is always of a clean, white quality. A marked dinner service examined showed the ware could be classified as transparent. This firm was particularly celebrated for the clarity and brilliance of its brunswick green and *rose du Barry* ground colours. The printed mark was an adaptation of the royal arms above IRONSTONE HOLLAND & GREEN.

Ironstone china enriched with coats of arms and crests in full colours is collected. Some of these appear to have been bogus and produced to satisfy a fashionable whim on the part of some mid-Victorians, including the railway companies. Among the makers of such ironstone were the firms of Holland & Green, Thomas Hughes, Brownhills, and Wedgwood & Co., Tunstall (not to be confused with Josiah Wedgwood & Sons, Etruria). Wedgwood & Co. potted an enormous amount of ironstone china transfer-printed in various colours and often partly hand-painted. Their Asiatic pheasant patterns were exceptionally well painted. The printed mark was WEDGWOOD & Co., encircled by IMPERIAL IRONSTONE CHINA.

During the late Georgian years several improved stone chinas were evolved, all having a marked translucency. They were fine felspathic earthenwares of varying qualities and sold under such names as opaque china, opaque porcelain, semi-china, semi-porcelain and demi-porcelain. All were of outstanding strength, moderately hard, uniform in texture, pure white at their best, and rather less transparent than bone china. Evenly and durably glazed by the same methods then current for bone china, these wares became successful competitors of French hard porcelain and were largely demanded in America, the entire output of several potters being exported to that country.

The glaze was composed mainly of Cornish stone, powdered calcined flint, white lead, flint-glass cullet, whiting and other fusible materials ground together in suitable proportions with water until of a fine creamy consistency. The glaze was opaque until fired so that underglaze decoration became clearly visible beneath a film of hard gloss.

The earliest use of the term opaque china for this felspathic stone china is believed to have been by the Swansea firm of Baker, Bevan & Irwin, who potted between 1814 and 1839. The mark BB & I OPAQUE CHINA has been found impressed on many skilfully decorated table services. Others bear a transfer-printed mark composed of a scrolled escutcheon containing "Opaque China   B B & I" in script.

Among the many Staffordshire potters who used the term opaque porcelain was Job Meigh & Son, Old Hall Works, Hanley. The pottery was established in 1790 by Job Meigh whose successors, son and grandson, were named Charles. Their business has been described by J. F. Blacker as one of the largest in the Potteries in the years around 1850. "Upwards of 700 hands were employed in manufacturing 80 tons of clay into various articles by the use of 250 tons of coal every week." Their output was enormous. Meigh's opaque porcelain was hard and white with a clear, unflawed glaze. The firm's reputation for unusual decoration and excellence of artistic design on this ware was unrivalled. One pattern in which they excelled was the naturalistically coloured convolvulus. This was registered at the Patent Office in the early 1840s, but later was copied by other potters, two of whom displayed it at the Great Exhibition. It was also copied by the japanners of South Staffordshire. Meigh's dessert services in opaque porcelain were elaborate and costly, but cheaper than those in bone china. Transfer-printing was clear and brilliant, and, following the vogue of the period, might be associated with painting. Collectors look for the Koh-i-noor shape in dinner ware. The catalogue of the Great Exhibition describes the covered dishes as "standing upon well-modelled feet, and the handles formed by folds of ribbon held together by rings."

An early mark was a pseudo-Chinese seal, used on stone china from 1835 to 1847. This was contemporaneous with a printed escutcheon containing the pattern name and CM / IMPROVED STONE CHINA. Other marks included OPAQUE PORCELAIN impressed; INDIAN STONE CHINA impressed; ENAMEL PORCELAIN within a rectangle.

In 1861 the Meigh business was converted into a company, the Old Hall Earthenware Company, the initials OHEC being added to the former mark in 1870. The name was changed to Old Hall Porcelain Works in 1887 and until production ceased in 1902 its opaque porcelain was marked with a red transfer-printed three-turreted castle above OLD HALL and the date 1790 in a Staffordshire knot.

Sampson Bridgwood & Son, Fenton, called their version porcelaine opaque. Table ware shaped and decorated in the style of French hard porcelain was made in immense quantities. This was impressed LIMOGES in an oval garter enclosing the initials PG (Parisian granite). In addition it bore the printed mark of a shield of arms and PORCELAINE OPAQUE BRIDGWOOD & SON. In about 1858 Sampson Bridgwood acquired an additional pottery in Burslem and took Edward Clarke into partnership: they traded as Bridgwood & Clarke. The mark impressed was BRIDGWOOD & CLARKE with a printed mark inscribed PORCELAINE OPAQUE B & C BURSLEM. Clarke became sole proprietor after Bridgwood's death in 1864, using the impressed mark EDWARD CLARK with a transfer-printed mark containing an adaptation of the royal arms above a flowing ribbon inscribed EDWARD CLARKE PORCELAIN OPAQUE TUNSTALL. In 1877 Clarke transferred his pottery to Longport.

The term "opaque china" is said to have been used at Swansea late in the 18th century. It was, however, and Honey has confirmed this, the production of Baker, Bevan & Irwin, Glamorgan Pottery, Swansea, from the early 1820s to 1839. The mark, printed in red, consisted of OPAQUE CHINA enclosed in scrollwork with B B & I beneath.

The term semi-china appears to have been the invention of John and Richard Riley, Hill Street Works, Hanley, early makers of stone china from about 1814 until 1828 when the partners died. Their ware was marked with an oval garter labelled RILEY'S, enclosing the name SEMI CHINA.

Several potters used the term semi-china during the next half century, including Harvey Adams & Co., Longton, established 1862. They introduced several registered designs in semi-china such as "shamrock" tea ware; embossed foliage dessert services; fern and foliage dessert and tea services, in which the designs were composed of about fifty arranged groups of trees, leaves and ferns in relief, modelled from specimens supplied by the Duke of Sutherland and painted in tints of spring, summer and autumn. There were also primrose flowers and leaves in relief, naturalistically coloured.

G. Grainger & Co., Worcester, introduced semi-porcelain in 1850, and at the Great Exhibition in the following year displayed a selection of dinner and dessert plates, soup tureens, vegetable dishes, ewers and basins. Attractive appearance and low cost brought substantial orders from the china-sellers. Grainger's semi-porcelain was completely vitrified and superficially resembled bone china, so that in the event of chipping, white was displayed instead of a disfiguring cream or brown flaw. Production continued until 1889 when the firm amalgamated with the Worcester Royal Porcelain Company. The mark was GRAINGER & CO SEMI-PORCELAIN.

Samuel Alcock & Co., Hill-Top Pottery, Burslem, who in

1839 had rebuilt Ralph Wood's old pottery and made popular types of earthenware and china, produced semi-porcelain table ware, including teapots, during the late 1850s. This was impressed SEMI PORCELAIN and printed S ALCOCK & Co.

Granite ware was a cheap, white, stone china. Its name, suggesting great strength, was given by the American china-sellers who admired its hardness, even surface, durable glaze and capacity for withstanding the rigour of transport. The name granite china appears to date from its use by Ridgway & Morley, stone china potters, 1842 to 1844. This bears no resemblance to the earlier granite ware made by Josiah Wedgwood, an earthenware with a greyish or bluish mottled glaze made in imitation of granite. Two types of granite ware, each in several qualities, were potted in thousands of tons during the third quarter of the nineteenth century: pure white and light weight for the city trade; faintly bluish in tinge and heavy for the country trade. It was the first ware strong enough and cheap enough to replace pewter on ships. Immense quantities were despatched in the white: some was dipped, sponged or painted. Little of it was marked.

Jewitt described the granite ware made by E. & C. Challinor, Fenton Pottery, as "of good, hard, sound and durable quality: some of their most successful embossed patterns being Ceres or Wheat, the Garland, and the Vine-leaf patterns. A large variety of jugs were made embossed with Wheat, Garland, Barbary, Lily, Lotus". Challinors impressed their granite ware with a Staffordshire knot enclosing the name GRANITE, also with E & C CHALLINOR within a border and surmounted by a version of the royal arms. Other marks were transfer-printed, GRANITE E & C C being incorporated in each. W. Davenport & Co., Longport, advertised in 1860 that they made "the hardest and most durable earthenware in white granite." This was impressed DAVENPORT.

Several potters marketed their best granite as "Parisian Granite", such as Sampson Bridgwood & Son, Fenton.

The entire output of stone china and its associated ceramics made by a few of the Staffordshire potters was exported. Examples decorated in relief, with transfer-printing and sponging, have been found in America impressed with the name of William and Thomas Adams, Tunstall, and Moore & Co., Old Foley Pottery.

Even stronger than granite ware was the mid-Victorian lava ware, coloured with oxides of iron, manganese, and cobalt. Its hard, indestructible glaze, consisting chiefly of flint and felspar, required intense heat to fuse it. Lava ware was used chiefly for cottage ware, spittoons and the like.

A superfine stone china evolved in 1805 by Josiah Spode II was named felspar porcelain. This body incorporated a considerable amount of felspar, enabling it to be fired at a higher temperature than other English ceramics. This increased hardness, making it less brittle and not so liable to fracture. By 1818 virtually pure felspar was used from newly-discovered deposits in the Bredon Hill, Montgomeryshire. This resulted in one of the most technically perfect ceramics made in England, free from surface flaws and as translucent as anything that came out of China.

Felspar porcelain was used mainly for costly table services, its remarkable translucency and whiteness greatly enhancing the radiant colours of the unflakable enamels and eminently suitable for lavishly gilded ground colours. Old gold colour might be substituted for gilding which was purposely omitted to create a more harmonious effect. So closely did this fine earthenware approximate to oriental export porcelain that owners of small services could have them enlarged or replacements supplied in felspar porcelain. Much was marked SPODE / Felspar Porcelain printed in blue and after the early 1820s Spode in Gothic letters above a wreath of rose, thistle and shamrock containing "Felspar Porcelain" in script printed in puce. Production ceased in 1833.

John Rose of Coalport potted felspar porcelain from about 1815 until the 1840s. He was first to utilise the newly-discovered felspar deposits thus producing his "improved felspar porcelain". Decoration included every subject associated with early Sèvres porcelain, displayed against beautiful ground colours of dark blue, light blue, turquoise, apple green and soft pink. Chamberlain of Worcester and Bloor of Derby made felspar porcelain table services as well as a number of small firms in Staffordshire.

Chapter Eleven

CHIMNEY ORNAMENTS

WHEN Queen Mary II set the seal of her royal approval on contemporary taste in the early 1690s, London became as much of an Eastern bazaar as Amsterdam, the aristocracy flocking to meet incoming ships carrying lacquer, porcelain and other oriental wares. Porcelain appeared in every well-to-do home: "Scaramouches, Lions, Monkies, Mandarines, Trees, Shells and a thousand odd Figures in Chinaware" were noted by Addison in 1711, long before the days of Meissen's Italian Comedy figures.

These costly trifles were essentially for the opulent: tastes of the less wealthy gentry and middle classes were met by English potters possessing a rich store of native craftsmanship and working local clays into earthenware image toys and chimney ornaments. It is one of the fascinations, but also one of the problems, of English earthenware ornaments that innumerable unknown potters made small but significant contributions to this basic art-form. Today's collector has to be content with knowing the names and styles of comparatively few of these men, but concentration on important potters such as the Astburys, Thomas Whieldon and the Wood family should not cloud the fact that each had numerous rival contemporaries. Nevertheless, knowledge of the advances in techniques and materials, of modelling, moulding casting, pressing, of colours and glazes, greatly assists the collector in classifying and authenticating his specimens, not only to reject the spurious, but also to derive renewed pleasure from comprehending the way these potters combined old skills with new inventions to meet the ever-increasing demands upon their craft.

Earthenware figure ornaments were long known to potters and china-sellers as image toys, a term used by Josiah Wedgwood when recording experimental work in 1753 and in his "book of trials" ten years later. By the end of the century they were known merely as toys. From the 1820s the larger figures were known as chimney ornaments and small examples as toys.

Early image toys were hand-modelled from clays which, fired at moderate temperatures, produced close-grained earthenwares either beige or a rich warm red in colour (see Chapter 8). One firing only was required to bake the clay and fuse the finely sifted smithum or lead ore into a rich, yellowish-tinted glaze. These early figures, fragile and now extremely rare, should not be confused with later issues dating from the 1750s, dipped in liquid glaze and twice fired.

Figures in white salt-glazed stoneware came from Staffordshire (see Chapter 3). Contemporary advertisements refer to this as flintware to distinguish it from other types of salt-glazed stoneware. White salt-glazed stoneware figures were shaped by pressing into two-piece moulds or by hand-modelling. By the mid-1750s, however, the earthenware potters of Staffordshire were using the porcelain potter's technique of figure-making. Parts of figures were shaped in separate moulds and assembled, being joined together with liquid slip prepared from the same ingredients as the earthenware itself.

It is probable that the earliest figures in white salt-glazed stoneware came from the pottery of Robert Astbury (see Chapter 3). By 1730 he was making small figures in forms moulded from Chinese originals. Traces of japan gilding are visible on some examples. Gold leaf was applied to the stoneware over a film of smooth red slip that enhanced the brilliance of the gilding.

Collectors may expect to find in white salt-glazed stoneware the dog of Foo, hawks, and manikins copied from Chinese soapstone models, and a variety of birds purely English in design such as peacocks and barnyard fowl. Other figures included such domestic animals as dogs, horses, cows and sheep with eyes and other details in brown or blue slip. Small arbour groups were made and figures depicting various craftsmen, huntsmen, musicians and the equestrian pieces known to collectors as mounted hussars. These were hand-modelled throughout, the various anatomical units being shaped by rolling, cutting and pinching. Clothing was fitted over the skeleton core modelled from an almost plain cylinder formed by rolling clay between the palms of the hands. The upper end of such a cylinder was shaped into a neck and a spherical ball of clay was modelled into a head. Arms of rolled clay were then attached to the body, their flattened ends tooled to represent hands and fingers.

When Thomas Whieldon established himself as a master potter in 1740 he quickly achieved a reputation for small figures such as cats, dogs and hens in an improved agate ware that closely resembled the genuine stone (see Chapter 4). He also made image toys in dark cream-coloured earthenware decorated with coloured glazes that were the lineal descendants of the earlier slip-decorated figures and those combining different kinds of clay to produce varying colours in a single figure, thus accentuating details of costume or character. The simple modelling methods of the day permitted the fused smithum glaze to move freely and smoothly over the surface of the earthenware. By adding to this glaze a small range of metallic oxides he produced the effect known as tortoiseshell glazing (see Chapter 4). In liquid glaze this met with enormous popularity and was copied by many Staffordshire competitors. This was Whieldon's first important contribution to the Staffordshire trade in image toys.

Most of the figures that may be attributed to the Whieldon pottery have all the quality of sketches by a master potter. It is probable that Whieldon himself was responsible for many of the original models, but improbable that any of his productions sold after the early 1750s were from his own hand, as is so often stated: his time as an executive was so valuable that he took Josiah Wedgwood into a managing partnership in 1754 (see Chapter 8).

Whieldon was the first earthenware potter to manufacture cow milk jugs, following the pattern introduced in about 1755 by the London silversmith John Schüppe. They continued in popular favour until the 1850s, when the question of their cleanliness was discussed adversely during the great cholera epidemic. A chronological collection of such cows illustrated a century of progressive changes and improvements in English pottery technique and ornament. There has been a revival of early styles in the present century.

Some outstanding figures were produced by Ralph Wood (1715–72) of Burslem. In 1750 he established himself as a potter of salt-glazed white stoneware and before the end of the decade was producing earthenware figures in styles evolved by Whieldon. He often applied a deep brown slip to the biscuit before coating it with transparent glaze. Ralph Wood soon began mixing powdered metallic oxides, such as were used by the enamellers, with the liquid glaze and laying on separate washes of colour with a brush. This development is described in Chapter 4. The early colours were soft-toned greens, blues, manganese purples and greyish olive: by 1775 brown, orange and chrome green had been added to the palette. These could be applied either to the unfired ware, or to the biscuit, or as an overglaze. The colours, ground to flour fineness, were added before fritting, so that transparency was not appreciably reduced. Form and glaze so completely harmonised that such figures represent the purest pottery technique, encroaching in no way upon fashionable porcelain styles.

Ralph Wood's figures decorated with a few soft underglaze colours became increasingly ambitious, eventually covering a wide range of subjects from men, women and equestrian groups to animals such as deer and foxes. In the mid-1760s Wood was caught in the tide of the new evangelism then sweeping the kingdom: this prompted him to abandon rustic figures and to issue vigorously sculptured figures illustrating Old Testament characters.

Wood's elaborate groups were intended for the gentry who preferred chimney ornaments more elegant than quickly moulded single figures. The equestrian figure of *Hudibras*, adapted from an engraving by Hogarth, and *St. George Slaying the Dragon* were among the largest, the latter measuring about 12 inches in height.

Ralph Wood was succeeded by his sons Ralph (1748–95) and John (1746–97) at a time when the demand for white salt-glazed domestic ware was declining in favour of cream-coloured earthenware. This department came under the control of John, who in about 1780 parted from his brother and established an independent pottery at Brownhills. Ralph remained at Burslem as a specialist figure-maker, producing a great deal of new work, but retaining in use many of his father's moulds. Mr. Bernard Rackham points out that Ralph Wood junior introduced two new decorating techniques to the Staffordshire figure-makers. The first of these was to increase the range of the high-temperature underglaze colours—mainly blue—already in use. This colour technique was quickly seized upon by Felix Pratt III, who operated a family pottery at Fenton from about 1802 until 1828. So successfully did he manipulate these colours that earthenware decorated in this way is now known to collectors under the generic term of Pratt ware, although dating from about 1790. The colours include blue, drab green, yellow, orange, dull brown and purple brown, often applied in spots or mottled with a sponge, or dabbed on with a stippling brush. Figures so decorated were made by Ralph Wood junior, Pratt, and other Staffordshire potters as well as by the Herculaneum Pottery, Liverpool, and in Sunderland.

Ralph Wood's further innovation was to decorate figures with bright overglaze enamels in styles following those of the porcelain potters. This method was more expensive than underglaze painting, requiring a third firing, that necessitated additional plant, fuel and labour. In addition, the colours themselves were more costly, so that they were used sparingly except on occasional elaborate, highly worked groups. This type of decoration brought Wood vastly increased orders, and many other potters followed his lead.

Figures and animals in unglazed biscuit porcelain were at that time fashionable and expensive, intended to rival white marble statuary, then considered the ultimate in interior decoration. The finest came from Sèvres: they were made less exquisitely at Derby. Ralph Wood competed by issuing figures in white glazed earthenwares: porcelain delicacy was of course impossible, but their comparatively low price influenced demand from the gentry and middle classes.

Aaron Wood (1717–85), younger brother of the older

Ralph, and father of Enoch Wood, influenced the trend of Staffordshire figures more than any other potter. He was apprenticed to Dr. Thomas Wedgwood in 1731 at about the time that the process of casting earthenware came into use (see Chapter 3) and became an outstanding block-cutter in alabaster. When he left Wedgwood he found employment with Thomas Mitchell of Burslem, but in 1746 he joined Whieldon.

At about this time Ralph Daniel, Cobridge, introduced plaster-of-paris moulds for figure casting. These were made from models carved in hard wax, measuring about one-tenth larger than the finished figures to allow for shrinkage during drying and firing. In casting figures liquid clay was run into the porous moulds and allowed to stand for a few minutes. Remaining slip was then poured out, leaving a clay shell which was removed when dried to leather-hardness. Unlike moulded figures, cast figures showed only slight individual deviations from the basic design. Casting was brought into use only when a long run of simple figures was proposed.

Aaron Wood quickly saw the commercial advantages of using the new method of casting, and by 1750 was established in a pottery of his own at Burslem as a maker of white salt-glazed stoneware. Ten years later he was making outstanding figure work, at first in the Whieldon style, then decorated with underglaze colours in the style of Ralph Wood junior. He was responsible for the original full-length figure of Benjamin Franklin, copied by other potters, some of whom in the nineteenth century inscribed the plinths with the name of Washington or Wellington in gold. On the evidence of marked pieces that remarkable figure group "The Vicar and Moses" has been attributed to Aaron Wood. It was often copied during the nineteenth century by less gifted potters and is reproduced today.

James Neale (1740–1814), who had been a potter's agent, first at the Mug Warehouse, Liverpool, and later in London, acquired Humphrey Palmer's pottery at Hanley in 1776. He then issued many very effective small figures during the last quarter of the eighteenth century. These were shaped by pressing in two-piece moulds, carefully finished by hand, and sparsely coloured in a restrained way with good quality un-flawed enamels. In 1786 Neale took into partnership David Wilson, and two years later they began to make figures in pearl ware, a ceramic evolved by Josiah Wedgwood in 1779 and defined as "a white earthenware body containing a greater percentage of flint and white clay than cream-coloured earthenware with a small amount of cobalt added to the glaze to give a still further whitening effect." Small figures were in production by 1790, displaying a high standard of modelling, closely resembling that of porcelain and always carefully enamelled with fine quality pigment. They stand upon square, shallow plinths with smooth surfaces, sometimes lined with gilding. Large figures in pearl ware were being made by 1800. When in 1801 the firm came under the control of David Wilson, the glaze was so deeply tinted that the body appeared bluish in hue. It is usually stated, incorrectly, that chalk was incorporated into the body used for these figures. Lustred figures were also made. Marked examples incorporating the name of NEALE or NEALE & WILSON are known. Those impressed NEALE & Co. were sold by Neale's London warehouse.

Lakin and Poole, Burslem, who made many excellent figures and groups from the time of their establishment in 1791 until their bankruptcy six years later, specialised in pieces reflecting contemporary social life. One of their most spectacular groups represents the gruesome scene of the "Assassination of Marat by Charlotte Cordé of Caen, in Normandy, 1793". They were among the several potters who issued in earthenware the ever-popular "Tithe Pig" group, in 1765. The "Tithe Pig", made in several sizes, represents a peasant wife offering her baby in payment of tithe, instead of the pig held by her husband. Lakin & Poole's figures were usually on high square plinths with colours discreetly applied without garishness. The mark was the name impressed.

Salt-glazed figures usually stood directly upon thin, flat-surfaced solid plinths. Under the Whieldon influence plinths became taller and hollow with inward sloping outer faces which might be ornamented with simple motifs such as flowers and leaves in slight relief, often coloured green.

Interiors of bases were unglazed until the introduction of dipping into liquid glaze. From then until the 1770s figures followed the lead of the porcelain potters, standing upon rusticated or rocky mounds, which themselves were superimposed upon shallow square or rectangular plinths. An elaborate figure might be supported upon a cube-shaped plinth with relief decoration in the neo-classic style upon the four vertical faces.

The industrial potters preferred quickly made square plinths, shallow and smooth on all surfaces, encircled by a line of colour or gold. The title of the subject might be painted upon the front. In finer work the plinth was deeper with in-sloping faces decorated in relief. Groups continued upon rocky bases supported by plinths.

Earthenware figures became less pretentious from about 1800, the majority being unmarked and the product of unrecorded potters working in a small way. The high speed of production and low rates of pay associated with the figure-making branch of the pottery trade were recorded in *The Report on the Employment of Children in Factories*, 1842. Here nine-year-old William Cotton, employed by Deakin & Sons, Longton, is shown to have been paid two shillings a week, producing forty-two figures an hour through a week of seventy hours, nearly 3,000 figures in all. Another nine-year-old, Richard Morton, employed by Hilditch & Hopwood, Longton, stated in evidence: "I work by the piece and can make 40 dozen small figures in a day: I get one penny for ten dozen, that is, about two shillings a week." This child in a year of fifty-two weeks—holidays were rare—might produce about 145,000 figures, for which he was paid about five guineas. The annual production of figures must indeed have been vast.

A prolific maker of portrait busts and inexpensive figures was John Walton who potted at Hadderage, Burslem, from the early 1800s to 1835 when he was succeeded by his widow Eliza. Walton used a cheap, brittle earthenware capable of being fabricated at high speed. Although as a rule these figures were crudely made they have an enduring charm that endears them to many collectors.

Walton was among the earliest Staffordshire potters to

adapt earthenware to the manufacture of the *bocages* made by the porcelain potters. This he accomplished effectively, introducing a vogue that spread to other potters and continued until the end of the Georgian era. A tree, rising behind the figure or group, consisted of a short trunk supporting a few branches thickly covered with conventional leaves, carefully arranged by hand and decorated with bright green enamel, each bunch having in its centre a coloured flower. Walton's *bocage* containing a sheep with a lamb in the rocky recess of the base must have been made in tens of thousands. This is always vigorously modelled and the animals coated with clay chippings from a pottery turner's lathe to represent wool. This figure was made by other potters, but the "wool" was produced by mechanically tooling the surface of the animals whilst they were in the leather-hard grey state. The name of the subject might be inscribed on the front of the plinth of a Walton figure, no matter how obvious the legend, such as "Lion" or "Lovers". A scrolling motif painted towards the lower edge of the base is a distinguishing feature of many Walton figures: many, too, bear the impressed name WALTON in a large blue scroll on the back of the plinth. In some instances the mark is beneath. During the early 1830s Joshua Walton, Hanley, made inexpensive figures, some of which were impressed WALTON beneath.

Walton's technique was followed by other potters, notably Ralph Salt (1782–1846). He started business at Miles Bank, Hanley, as a decorator in about 1812 and by 1828 was established as a potter of figures, particularly *bocage* pieces, sheep with hand-raised wool, and sporting dogs. He enamelled in bright colours and also lustred. By 1834 he built a larger pottery in Marsh Street. Salt marked some of his finer figures with the name SALT impressed in large letters on a raised scroll at the back of the plinth. His son continued the business but his figures were less well finished, even when made from his father's moulds.

Obadiah Sherratt, Hot Lane, Burslem, was another prolific figure maker, but no marked example has been recorded. He was operating as a potter by 1815 and is thought to have been responsible for large figure groups usually raised on square or rectangular plinths with a bracket foot at each corner, such as appeared on chests of drawers of the period. The expansive entrance to "Polito's Menagerie" was considered a triumph of firing in the flat. It is painted with an inscription reading "The Menagerie of the Wonderfull Burds and Beasts from Most Parts of the World, Lion and Giraffe". The giraffe was introduced into England during the 1820s. This is sometimes found bearing the name "Wombwell". Small details often enable a figure to be dated closely, such as Sherratt's figure of Paul Pry carrying a hat box. The play in which Paul Pry was a character was originally produced in 1826. Among other figures and groups attributed to Obadiah Sherratt are "The Sacrifice of Isaac", "Ale Bench", "Teetotal Bench", "The Death of Monrow" depicting Lt. Munroe being carried off by a tiger, and "W. Corder and M. Martin", the murderer and his victim of the celebrated Red Barn. In 1828 Sherratt built larger premises in Waterloo Road. After his death in about 1846 the pottery was operated by his son Hamlet, and from about 1850 by Obadiah's widow, Martha. Production ceased in the late 1850s.

Among other potters whose names have been noted impressed on early nineteenth-century Staffordshire figures are John and Ralph Hall, Swan Bank, Tunstall, and the Sytch Pottery, Burslem, who made small figures and blue-printed earthenware. The partnership, dating from about 1800, was dissolved on New Year's Day, 1822, Ralph then operating the Tunstall factory while John continued with his sons until 1832 when they became bankrupt. Figures from all these sources appear to have been impressed HALL in large capitals.

Edge & Grocott, Burslem, made *bocage* groups in the Walton style during the early nineteenth century. Examples are recorded impressed with their name on a raised tablet at the back of the plinth. William Walker, Shelton, specialised in sporting dogs during the nineteenth century. Robert Garner, Lane End (1786–1800), according to Jewitt—who possessed some of his accounts for 1797—operated a large business and made sets of figures inscribed with titles on their plinths. Joseph Dale, Burslem, of whom little is known apart from his marriage in 1825, made Walton type figures.

These might be impressed J. DALE BURSLEM. A set of "Four Elements" and a bust of John Wesley are in the British Museum. Turner & Abbott, Lane End, potters to the Prince of Wales in the late eighteenth century, impressed their name on some very small figures.

From the early 1820s an excellent series of figures was made from an improved "pearl pottery". The *Operating Mechanic*, 1825, described this as "a superb kind of elegant and tasteful ornaments and is so much valued that the workmen are usually locked up and employed only on choice articles." The ingredients were stated to be "blue, and porcelain clay, Cornish stone, a little flint-glass and red lead." The result was a dry earthenware body with a finely textured unglazed surface, and it was used only for figures and busts.

The fine, hard pearl ware was discovered to be an excellent base for decoration with gold, silver and purplish pink lustre. The finest quality, burned until almost pure white, gave a unique brilliance to the metallic coating.

Sunderland figures in a rather coarse earthenware have a decorative merit entirely their own. At their most ambitious they might be in pearl ware, figures being adapted from those of eighteenth century Meissen and enamelled. More frequently, however, they were quickly produced. The Sunderland potters—there were about fifteen different firms —made competitive use of lustre. As early as 1818 a set of the "Four Seasons" was sold at Christies for fourteen guineas. The majority, however, were made for the cheap market. The Sunderland or Garrison Pottery marked many of its figures. Established early in the nineteenth century, it operated under various proprietorships until 1865.

Animal figures were made in huge numbers, usually in matching pairs. These included the well-known Sunderland lions, also made successfully by John Walton, Burslem, and at Portobello, Scotland. The Sunderland Pottery also made some magnificent bulls in dark-hued copper lustre, remarkable examples of industrial earthenware statuary.

A familiar chimney ornament is the dog somewhat suggestive of a spaniel, but known to the nineteenth century as a comforter or spaniel's gentle, a cross between the

Maltese dog and a King Charles' spaniel. It was painted with a collar around its neck from which hung a small gold padlock and a slender gold chain falling across its neck and disappearing over the back. It was almost invariably white with long ears and scattered spots in copper or pink lustre. In Sunderland these popular chimney ornaments were made in five sizes ranging from about six to eighteen inches in height. Greyhounds in a variety of positions, pug dogs and French poodles are also to be found. Sunderland cats sitting upright on square cushions were made and copied by several small potters in Staffordshire.

Bocages in the Staffordshire manner were less meticulously finished than those of Staffordshire. Vases filled with similar leaves and flowers rising to the height of about a foot were popular. In early *bocages* the figure of a soldier or sailor might stand among the leaves encircled with a wreath. The watch stand in the form of a grandfather clock or a church tower was given stability by the addition of a couple of moulded figures standing on the plinth: these date from about 1820.

Among the earthenware portrait figures that have been discovered impressed with Sunderland marks are Queen Victoria, Wellington, Nelson, Napoleon, Wesley, Joan of Arc. There were also pairs of shepherds and shepherdesses, fishwives, sailors and soldiers, crudely cheap to ensure a ready market.

In the late 1830s began a long vogue for flat-back figures, the base generally consisting of a smooth flattened oval. The earliest to which a definite date may be attributed appears to be the seated Queen Victoria with Prince Albert, issued on the occasion of their marriage in February 1840. These Victorian figures were for the most part shaped by means of two-part or three-part press-moulds invented in about 1830 by an American. Press-moulds speeded up modelling and reduced the quantity of materials required. The combination of a whiter body, more brilliant glaze, and the sparkling underglaze oven-blue—now known to most collectors as Staffordshire blue—quickly superseded earlier methods of potting chimney ornaments.

In addition to the dominant oven-blue, the overglaze enamels used were chiefly red, green, yellow and black, all of which when applied thickly have a tendency to flake off the glaze. The Staffordshire potters were well aware of this defect, and when William Cornelius in 1853 invented a liquid gold, much less costly in its application than mercury gilding, figures began to be sparsely ornamented in black and gold, large areas remaining white. Press-mould figures were also made in other pottery centres such as Sunderland, Newcastle, Bristol and in Scotland.

Mould-pressing was found to be ideal for the quick production of full-length figures of celebrities, although twenty different processes went into the production of each. Portrait figures have been grouped into nine classes by Mr. Thomas Balston whose *Staffordshire Portrait Figures of the Victorian Age* (1958) lists and annotates more than 170 persons in nearly five hundred variations: royal family, statesmen, naval and military, religious, authors, stage, sport, crime, miscellaneous. Enormous numbers were sold during the third quarter of the nineteenth century, the demand continuing in a lesser degree until the end of the century. Seldom do the portraits bear much resemblance to their originals.

The only potter so far identified as a specialist in these figures is Sampson Smith, Sutherland Works, Longton, a number of whose press-moulds have been discovered and taken into use. Other figures are obviously from a small group of potters whose names have not been identified: although various original moulds are still in use their source remains a mystery. Marked examples are very rare indeed.

Chapter Twelve

LUSTRE AND ENGLISH MAJOLICA

OLD English lustre is a joy to handle. Its colours and sheen are an undemanding delight to the least observant eye, even while to many the special charm in collecting this ware lies in the range of decorative detail to which the lustre serves merely as an additional garnish. Its semblance to metal shot with all the colours of the rainbow makes one wonder how it came to be discovered. Many collectors imagine lustred earthenware to have been a purely English invention: it was, however, an early nineteenth-century revival of an art once practised in Egypt by Saracen potters. In about the eleventh century lustring was carried out in Persia, where patterns in the metallic film were displayed against a richly coloured glazed surface. Ceramic lustres were soon developed in Spain, and by the fifteenth century patterns had become highly complex, colours richer and more varied, shading into violet and opalescent tones. At this time Italy was making lustred earthenware, shell-like in tone and showing exquisite reflections. So far the lustring of earthenware had been a highly individual craft. In the early years of the nineteenth century the Staffordshire potters adapted the process to their industrialised methods, the result being in effect metallised earthenware, although known by the old name of lustre.

Any survey of lustre ware must cover an immensely wide range of lustre effects and decorative techniques. In order to clear up frequent misunderstanding, however, it must be stated at once that the basic principle consisted in covering the smooth, opaque-glazed surface of the earthenware with a film of prepared metallic oxide, so thin as to be more or less translucent. It must be appreciated that to display iridescence the lustre had to be applied thinly: if thick it became merely the colour of the metal used. "Copper" and "silver" are no more than convenient names for lustres: practically all the familiar tones appear to have been derived from the metals gold and platinum, applied over various colours and qualities of glazed earthenware to achieve lustrous effects in gold, silver, copper, pink and purple or plum and the rare yellow. Gold and platinum were used because they are virtually non-oxidising under atmospheric influence: silver was never used as it quickly became oxidised. William Evans in 1846 recorded the basic formulae:

"The components for the lustres are thus combined.

"Gold—in nitro-muriatic [acid], sufficient, dissolve gold, 120 and grain tin, 5; mix with, by heat, balsam of sulphur, 60 and spirits of turpentine, 40. Drop the acid solution in whilst stirring the medium; and when well mixed, add the best turpentine. One ounce of gold makes 32 of lustre.

"Persian gold lustre—in fat oil on a tile placed on a hot stove, mix dry oxide of gold, and when eliquidation commences, stir with a palette knife, and add more oil till 25 be used, and the colour resemble that of balsam of sulphur; then diminish the temperature and gradually add turpentine 75.

"Silver or steel lustre—in muriatic acid, concentrated, dissolve platinum till the acid be saturated. Then at 112 degrees Fah., to 25 of solution, add very carefully and in small doses, 75 spirits of tar. Chlorine will be evolved by the heat, and the chloride of platinum will remain in the tar. The metallic solution is applied to the ware by broad hair pencils; and this last, baked in a muffle at enamelling heat is *steel* lustre.

"Then in water mix the oxide of platinum (obtained by sal-ammoniac precipitating it from the acid solution) and cover the steel lustre; again bake and it will be silver lustre. If the glaze be opaque white, not brown, the latter will at once give *silver* lustre."

It will be observed that two coatings and firings were essential to produce a burnished silver effect, cost being proportionately increased.

Evans states that William Stennys, Burslem, had improved gold lustre, and John Gardner, Stoke-upon-Trent, had improved silver lustre: unfortunately he gives no facts or dates. The identity of the potter responsible for introducing lustring to Staffordshire is disputed. John Hancock, in a letter to *The Staffordshire Mercury*, 1846, claimed to have "discovered and first put into practice the making of gold, silver, and steel lustre at Josiah Spode's pottery at Stoke during 1789." If any was produced its brilliance was probably quickly discovered to be impermanent because of atmospheric action upon some impurity spread throughout the lustre. There is no evidence that Josiah Spode I marketed such wares.

It is probable that the earliest lustre to be marketed was produced by a potter of white salt glazed stoneware. Examples exist with the typical orange peel pitted surface covered with lustre resembling polished steel. The potter was probably Enoch Wood, a maker of white salt glaze in the late eighteenth century and, in the nineteenth, of solid silver lustre. The process was probably perfected by the Wedgwood firm on pearl ware. Josiah Wedgwood and Sons Ltd. possess records proving the use of silver lustre on a commercial scale in 1805 in the form of encircling bandings and usually in association with coloured enamels.

Collectors divide lustre earthenware into eight main groups, most of which are self explanatory: ware wholly covered with plain metallic lustre to give the piece every appearance of gold or silver plate or beaten copper: similar lustre sprigged with ornament in relief; the lustre in all its different colours applied in bands to enrich pottery decorated with scenes and other ornamental motives handpainted in enamels or transfer-printed, usually in blue; designs painted or stencilled in lustre on white grounds; the reverse of this, known as resist lustre, in which the lustre appears as the background to white or coloured patterns; mottled lustre; lustre figures; reproductions.

It will be readily understood that a film of metal thin enough to be applied easily and economically will vary in colour and appearance according to the body it is fired upon, the metal used, and the conditions under which the final firing is made. Many of these effects in English lustre were the result of tedious technical experiment: others were involuntary and could not be foreseen by the potter. Whilst certain colour distinctions and classifications may be listed, many of these merge so imperceptibly into others that it is neither practical nor possible to differentiate entirely, particularly among the gold oxide lustres ranging from dull brown and deep bronze through the coppery hues to glittering gold. Silver is usually brilliant as the pure burnished metal, but examples dating between the late 1840s and the 1860s may now have become a dull leaden colour.

Silver lustre derived from platinum could not possibly date earlier than the late 1780s, for the first crucible capable of accepting the great heat required to make platinum oxide was not invented by Achard until 1784. A comprehensive technical work on platinum published in 1800 contains no reference to the potter's use of it; neither does a paper on the subject read to the Society of Arts in 1803. It seems, then, that its use in this connection was not known outside the Potteries.

One purpose of silver lustre was to imitate solid objects of silver or Sheffield plate, such as tea and coffee services and other ware including salt cellars, pepper pots and mustard pots. Most of the early all-over silver lustre was excellently lustred, but displayed no ornament other than beading and fluting in the Georgian style, producing brilliant high lights on the curves. This solid silver hollow ware was at first lustred within and without in an endeavour to complete the illusion at least to a casual glance. This was immediately dispelled, however, by weight and thickness. This all-over silver lustre ware obviously followed the shapes of contemporaneous silver, some being duplicates. Among the ware the collector may expect to find may be mentioned chamber candlesticks with extinguishers, loving cups, combined toast racks and egg-frames with eggcups, goblets, chalices with covers and stands, and all kinds of dinner and tea ware.

By the early 1840s all-over silver lustre was lined with white glaze and might be over-painted with banding or simple flower motifs. John Ridgway, Cauldon Place, Hanley, patented in 1852 an electro-chemical method of lustring. This was described in the specification as the application of "the art of electrotype or electro-metallurgy . . . provided that the surface of the non-conducting body [the ceramic] is so prepared that the metal deposited thereon shall become combined therewith." This patent was basically dependent upon Elkington's newly-lapsed patent covering the process of electro-plating. The film of electrically deposited lustre was not, however, strong enough to withstand continual washing. Production was considerable for about a quarter of a century.

Resist lustre which swept the market during the period 1810 to the 1840s derived from the earlier stencilled work in which delicate patterns in silver lustre were stencilled to the surface of glazed pearl ware. In these the design tends to be ragged at the edges. Designs might also, of course, be painted in a thin film of lustre on white grounds. John Davenport evolved and patented the technique of what collectors term resist lustre. Cut-out paper or parchment patterns were pasted upon the white glaze and the entire surface waxed. The designs were so skilfully cut with scissors and penknives that details might be of pen-and-ink fineness. When the patterns were removed the design was exposed in white glaze against the wax. The surface was brushed with lustre and when this was dry the wax was removed with benzine and the ware fired. This type of silver resist lustre—a silver pattern against a white ground—is uncommon and does not appear to have been reproduced.

The standard method of producing white patterns against silver grounds was evolved a few years later. The design was painted on the white glaze, not in lustre but in a resist material such as finely pulverised china mixed with glycerine or honey, or brown shellac in spirits of wine. This withstood the metallic solution in which the entire surface of the ware was then covered and when dry could be washed off, before the ware was fired, to reveal the pattern in white against the lustre background.

Gold lustre dates from early in the nineteenth century. In 1807 the Cambrian Pottery Warehouse, 62 Fleet Street, London, advertised "Ware ornamented with an entirely new Golden Lustre." This was the London warehouse of the Swansea Pottery, indication that Wales was ahead of Staffordshire in the manufacture of fine quality gold lustre. This was applied to a white body and displayed a beautiful golden glister The glaze might be stained with purple of cassius which made the lustre sparkle like shot silk and gave a purple or plum-coloured hue. The tints of gold lustre, ranging from deep bronze through ruddy coppers and purples to the palest lilac and pink, are so gradual that no two people would agree as to where one begins and another ends. Later gold lustre was applied to a red body that caused the metal to shine warmly while beneath there was an intensity of colour. It is thought that this change was the result of joint efforts by William Henning and John Gardner.

According to Evans the Staffordshire potters used a body consisting of Bradwell Wood clay, 25; yellow brick clay, 10; blue or black clay, 40; flint, 25. This was well blunged and filtered through lawn, then fired to a reddish brown biscuit and glazed to a smooth, mirror-like surface.

The ground colour upon which these lustres were fixed was normally white or cream, exceptions until the late 1820s being hand-painted grounds distinguishable by their slightly uneven finish. Coloured grounds in pink, apricot, blue, canary yellow and buff date later than 1826 when Henry Daniel of Shelton patented a process of ground laying that produced a level, glossy surface.

An attractive reddish-brown lustre with a greenish hue was made from the mid-1820s until about 1840. This lustre was obtained by mixing oxides of gold, iron and ochre with lavender oil and painting this to the ware with a hair pencil brush. This was gently fired in a reducing atmosphere. The effect was obtained by rubbing the lustre, before it became cold, with a piece of beaver to remove an obscuring film. This lustre has not been reproduced.

Designs in resist lustre, both silver and gold, include the fruiting vine in many arrangements; geometrical and scroll patterns in wide encircling designs and in narrow bands; patterns with birds predominating, either naturalistic or exotic; roses, thistles, strawberries, ivy, unidentifiable flowers and foliage and so on, in a wide range of combinations.

This generation of late Georgians delighted in possessing serving jugs painted or transfer-printed with sporting scenes enclosed in designs of resist lustre. These, often monogrammed and sometimes dated, were principally intended as gifts for garnishing the chimney piece and for use only on special occasions. Resist lustre jugs differed little in form. The fashionable limits set on shape of body, spout and handle virtually precluded originality. Since shape was restricted these jugs demanded and received elaborate decoration in which the colour and intensity of the metallic film played a major part.

Fox hunting jugs encircled with huntsmen and hounds against landscape backgrounds were issued by several lusterers. Most common were those with huntsmen standing in nonchalant attitudes accompanied by three or four bored-looking hounds. Such jugs are to be found inscribed with the name of the hunt. It was sometimes a pleasant gesture of the master of the hunt to present the brush in a lustred hunting jug. Hand-coloured printed fox hunting scenes were often adapted from Henry Alken's engravings and several have been recorded from *Hunting Recollections*, 1829. Stag hunting, horse racing, hare coursing, bull baiting, cock fighting, fishing, archery and prize fighting jugs are also found. This series includes too the magnificent coaching jug transferred and/or hand painted, with a resist lustre neck and a silver band encircling the base. Sporting jugs with pictures printed in blue and surrounded by solid silver lustre were made during the 1820s. The quality of sporting jugs deteriorated from about 1830.

Copper lustre, contrary to much expert opinion, dates from about 1840 and no earlier, despite the existence of dated pieces. This lacked the brilliance of gold lustre and was, obviously, much less costly, much being disfigured with flaws such as specks, pinholes, pimples and bubbles. The basic pottery, red in colour, was notably strong and heavy. Hollow-ware was usually lustred inside and the exterior decorated with simple flower and foliage devices in gaudy colours, such as blue, green, yellow and red. Relief moulding was used and this might be accentuated with enamels. Serving jugs and mugs might be decorated with quickly enamelled scenes between horizontal rings.

The mottled pink or purple lustre effects were introduced by the Wedgwood firm. Although this is usually known as

Sunderland ware, the potters of Newcastle, Staffordshire, Bristol, Swansea and Liverpool produced precisely the same effects. This distinctive lustre, found on dull cream or dead white earthenware, is recognisable by its untidy splashes, waves and marblings. These inexpensive effects were the result of using the old Chinese method of spraying. The metallic solution was applied to the glaze and sprayed with thin oil blown down a tube and through a filter of fine muslin. The muffle heat caused the oil to expand and form tiny bubbles which burst upon the surface of the ware. In some instances there might be additional decorations in reserves, including transfer figure subjects and inscriptions.

Perhaps the greatest range of quality in lustre, however, is found among the purely decorative figures which have an appeal all their own. At their most ambitious these consisted of beautifully modelled classical figures adapted from eighteenth century models. Their most eminent makers included David Wilson, Hanley, Enoch Wood and Ralph Salt. The celebrated figure of a mounted Hussar in the British Museum, attributed to Wilson, is the most ambitious piece of lustre statuary in existence. Salt's delicately modelled figures are very different from those made by his contemporaries in Staffordshire, whose figures were irregular in form and carelessly lustred.

Although English lustre is especially associated with Staffordshire, much splendid ware came from Swansea. The body is harder than that of any other pottery and a much warmer brown in tone which gives it an individual brilliancy. Some authorities believe that Swansea made the first successful use of decorative bands encircling the necks of jugs, red and green designs being applied to a pale blue ground incised with lustrous lines. Among the best known of the Swansea ornament was the strawberry design, with berries in red, green hulls and leaves, and pink stems and runners. This factory also made what was known as "Cottage Swansea" with vertical or horizontal ribbing designs, often in association with a pair of black transfer panels sometimes hand tinted.

Some lustre is found with a small ring impressed beneath. It has been assumed that such examples were made at Leeds, as were many of the beautifully designed goblets in silver resist. A series of large jugs was decorated with farm and hunting scenes in high relief. Other early lustre pottery from Leeds was gaily oriental, and when this phase passed panels of transfer-printed views came into favour.

Lustre ware for the most part was marketed anonymously, both high quality productions and the heavier, cheaper wares. Even the beautiful lustre in the Munster Collection at the Hanley Museum is entirely unmarked. The list of lustre potters is extensive but fewer than twenty marks have been reliably recorded.

The Wedgwood firm was one of the few potters to impress their name upon lustre, and then merely WEDGWOOD. The majority of marked lustre appears to have been made at Longton between about 1830 and the 1870s. The demand for this ware appears to have increased so greatly during the late 1820s that in 1831 at least two specialists in gold, silver and resist lustre established themselves in Longton. The longer lived of these was Charles Allerton and Sons, Park Works, many of the old shapes and methods continuing uninterruptedly for at least a century. The impressed mark ALLERTON is found on some early productions. Robert Gallimore began simultaneously at St. James's Place, but abandoned manufacture during 1844 in favour of bone china. The impressed mark R G has been noted.

HARVEY impressed indicates manufacture by G. and W. K. Harvey, Longton, between 1841 and 1853. Thomas Cooper also began the manufacture of lustre at the High Street Pottery, production continuing for more than thirty years under various proprietors. Some exceptionally fine gold lustre may be found impressed with a large B. This was the mark used by Thomas Barlow during the third quarter of the nineteenth century. P & U within a diamond was the mark of Poole and Unwin during the early 1870s. All-over silver and copper lustre impressed M P & Co or LONDON above a foul anchor was made by the Middlesbrough Pottery Company between 1834 and 1852.

Signs of use are invariably to be detected on early lustre, even if it has merely been dusted for a century or more.

During this period atmospheric action has slightly dulled its original brilliance, no matter what its colour. Later lustre, with few exceptions, is less smooth to the touch. Modern reproductions in gold and silver display an impossible brilliance: even if the surface of modern gold lustre is good its coppery-gold effect is too brown. Reproduction copper lustre is apt to be coated too thickly and when decorated the enamelled sprays and flowers are stiff and disproportionate, while the blue, green, yellow and rose have unreal hues as though a dark tinge has been added to antique them. Where deliberate faking of marks is suspected an investigation should be made into the period during which the potter in question operated.

The lustre techniques used so successfully on majolica wares in Italy and elsewhere differ materially, but in no species of ceramics is the metallic gleam more beautiful. In some lights this early majolica is fiery red, in others golden, in others copper, purple, blue, pink, colours that play as the rays of light strike the dish, bowl or jar.

When Herbert Minton, the celebrated Victorian potter of Stoke-upon-Trent, showed at the Great Exhibition, 1851, he introduced imitation majolica ware, a colour-glazed earthenware devised by his art director, M. Leon Arnoux (1816-1902). In appropriate moulded patterns and seen under gaslight this could well be mistaken for some Italian lustred majolica. Its foundation was a cane-coloured calcareous earthenware capable of being shaped and pressed with high relief ornament in clear, sharp detail. This was dried and baked to a biscuit in the usual way, and then dipped into a bath of white opaque enamel glaze composed of pure silica, oxide of lead, oxide of tin and water. The cane colour of the unglazed biscuit so affected the hue of the white covering glaze that it reflected into the colour glazes which decorated it.

These glazes were derived from the type evolved by Ralph Wood (see Chapter 4). Technical advances had by now made possible greater brilliancy and purity of colours in a wider range of hues including various tints of red, pink, blue, green, purple, mauve, orange, yellow and brown. These colours were obtained by adding colouring oxides to clear glaze which had a thermal expansion similar to that of the earthenware. If these were unequal the glaze eventually became covered with numerous fine fissures known as crazing.

English imitation majolica remained fashionable for more than thirty years and continued in production until Edwardian days. The Minton firm, for instance, advertised their majolica as late as 1902. Architectural ornament included tiles, façades, fireplaces, wall panels, string courses, garden seats; domestic majolica included umbrella stands, wall plaques, flower vases, jardinieres, hot water bottles, wall brackets for trailing ivy, ladies' work baskets; table majolica appeared in wine coolers, dessert services, cheese stands, bread trays, jugs, egg-holders, teapots, candlesticks and so on.

Herbert Minton's entry in the catalogue of the Great Exhibition reads: "Vases etc., in imitation of Majolica ware . . . Wine Coolers of porous ware ornamented with festoons of vine leaves and grapes and coloured in the majolica style . . . a variety of flower pots and stands and garden pots coloured in the old majolica style." At the American Exhibition, 1853, Herbert Minton displayed in "Majolica style, a large flower pot in bright colours with lilies of the valley and fern design in relief, in a deep, wide-brimmed saucer to match." The firm continued the terms "imitation majolica ware" and "majolica style" until in about 1860 competitors entered this profitable branch of the industry and the name "majolica" became general.

Herbert Minton at this time commissioned statuary models from the finest sculptors of the day for reproduction in parian ware. Among these was Baron Marochetti who also undertook the modelling of several large pieces of imitation majolica. For the Great Exhibition he designed a large circular flower vase of which many examples were sold. This was mounted with a pair of goats' heads, large and modelled in meticulous detail with long curving horns. Between these hung elaborate swags of fruit, flowers and foliage in high relief against a spirally gadrooned body.

This stood upon a circular dish, its rim moulding matching that of the vase. The Jury of the Great Exhibition commended this piece of majolica "because of its design and colours and great size".

Majolica tiles for facing the ever-popular scented mignonette boxes for indoor and outdoor use were made in many effective designs, in particular various painted tulips in bold relief and other flowers in their natural colours.

By 1860 the Minton firm had introduced small figures in non-porous cane-coloured stoneware decorated with majolica glazes in delicate tints. These were copied or adapted from porcelain moulds and are sometimes mistaken for eighteenth-century figures. These, like all other Minton majolica, are impressed with date symbols.

An early follower of Minton in the imitation majolica trade was James Woodward, Swadlincote Pottery, Derbyshire, who, from 1860, began potting every conceivable article appropriate to this earthenware. This was marked with a foul anchor, the cable twisted around the stem forming the monogram J W. The Wedgwood firm in the same year introduced imitation majolica on a white earthenware body: a broken dish shows that close-grained pearl ware was used. Dessert services were made with relief ornament in brilliant colour effects. Green glazed dessert ware was made extensively.

Among the majolica potters who marked their ware was John Adams and Co., Victoria Works, Hanley. From about 1860 until 1873 they made majolica in a quality much above the average, impressed ADAMS & Co. Flower vases measuring about four feet in height and supported by well-modelled cupids; vases with cupid handles; and others on mask feet were a feature of this firm.

Banks and Thorley, Hanley, established 1873, made a great variety of unmarked majolica. Associated with this firm are the notable dessert services glazed with a chocolate ground against which are arranged, with striking effect, groups of ivy, ferns, and anemones, slightly embossed and glazed in naturalistic colours. Another pattern utilising the chocolate ground has rope-bordered panels in buff enclosing thistle leaves in green with a twisted rope handle. Other hollow-ware with chocolate-coloured grounds was decorated with flowers and foliage in relief, extending from base to rim, such as sprays of corn, ferns and bulrushes naturalistically coloured.

Parian statuary ware might also be used as the basic ceramic for majolica glazes. Large pieces were not profitable in parian biscuit, but the creamy richness of this porcelain increased the brilliance and clarity of the glaze and gave a delightful softness to flesh tints. Typical of the centrepieces that immediately became fashionable was a design with a delicate openwork dish supported by graceful nude figures mounted on a pedestal. It is believed that this was introduced in the early 1860s by George Jones, Trent Pottery, Stoke-upon-Trent, established as makers of parian ware in 1861. Within a few years Jones was making majolica centrepieces for the table, with parian statuary supports. His range of productions was strikingly varied and included candelabra and two-lidded vases. Bee skips for the service of honey were made in several designs, and plaques measuring up to 30 inches have been noted. Jones was awarded gold medals for his majolica at the exhibitions of Paris, 1867, London, 1871, and Vienna, 1873. His impressed mark was the monogram GJ. Another majolica-parian specialist was Edward Steele, Hanley, whose body and colours were of unusual excellence. His work included elaborate figure centrepieces but none was marked.

Chapter Thirteen

SCOTTISH POTTERY

THE craft of earthenware potting in Scotland, as in England, was a peasant industry until the mid-eighteenth century. The trade then followed the English pattern, and during the nineteenth century at least eighty sizeable potteries were operating, in addition to numerous family works. Earthenware manufacture on a large scale was introduced to the country in 1748 by Dinwoodie & Company, Delftfield Pottery, Glasgow. The firm was established to manufacture delft ware of a quality equalling that of Bristol and Liverpool. The essential calcareous clay was obtained from Kirk & Cobham, Carrickfergus, Ireland, at 5s. 6d. per ton in hundred-ton lots. This was the firm supplying the Liverpool potters. Production continued until the 1790s. White stoneware was made from 1766; cream-coloured earthenware from 1770; black basaltes in the Wedgwood manner from the mid-1780s. In the 1770s the firm was advertising dinner services painted with coats of arms and crests at prices reaching £30.

Following the lead of Spode in England, the Dinwoodie firm was producing bone china by 1800. Collectors search for the rare tea ware coated with a soft velvety umber-brown glaze, declared by cynics to have been intended to make the infused liquor appear stronger than it really was. Another Delftfield innovation in bone china was table ware enamelled in matt black and painted with brilliant flowers and foliage. In flat ware the face only was enamelled. This decoration was then fashionable in France, but does not appear to have been copied by English potters. In 1805 the firm was honoured by being granted the royal appointment of "Potters to H.R.H. the Prince of Wales". Delftfield failed to compete successfully with Staffordshire, however, and closed in 1810. None of its ware was marked. It is interesting to note that in 1791 pottery exports from Port Glasgow included: queensware, 45,330 lb.; delftware, 14,900 lb.; earthenware, 6,400 lb.

Among the better known of the Scottish potteries founded in the late eighteenth century is the Portobello Pottery, Midlothian. Admiral Vernon's victory over the Spanish at Puerto Bello, Panama, on 23rd November, 1739, made "Portobello" a household word and was commemorated by salt-glazed white stoneware appropriately decorated in relief. To many, this small range of stoneware, briefly fashionable, constituted Portobello ware. The considerable potteries at Portobello, covering more than a century of manifold activities, suggest possibilities to today's collector that are considerably more rewarding.

In 1750 Portobello was merely a thatched cottage on the Firth of Forth, newly built and named, presumably, after the still-famous victory. But William Jameson, an architect-builder from Edinburgh, two miles away, took over in 1763, building a brick kiln and later various factories and dwelling houses so that by 1799 *Scotland Delineated* could describe it as "a rising village of about 300 inhabitants employed in the manufacture of bricks, tiles, brown pottery and white stoneware." Most important of all, the manufactures included cream-coloured earthenware, as has been proved by authenticated specimens.

This is noteworthy because pottery manufacture in Scotland only attained significant proportions after 1775 when Josiah Wedgwood successfully contested the validity of the monopoly in Cornish china clay and china stone enjoyed by Richard Champion of Bristol. Wedgwood made his pearl ware formula available to all potters interested and this was directly responsible for the establishment of many new potteries in Scotland. Three of these were at Portobello. The clay was found suitable for the manufacture of pottery; there was coal at near-by Niddrie; and shipping to import china clay and china stone from Cornwall. Jameson, in 1786, built an extensive pottery, no doubt to plans provided by the brothers Scott who leased the premises. In the following year Jameson built a harbour to facilitate the loading of goods to the property he was developing and directly accessible to Scott's Pottery. Formerly all shipping had been beached.

The Scott brothers manufactured dark red earthenware covered with a film of white engobe; white pearl ware; and cream-coloured earthenware of varying qualities. Dinner and dessert services in earthenware were then in great demand, replacing heterogeneous collections of earthenware, metal and wood. Red earthenware might be dipped in chocolate coloured engobe, decorated with designs in yellow and finished with a brilliant lead glaze. Formal designs of fern and foliage have been noted, and there are records, too, of grotesque figures. In the British Museum is a bowl of dark red earthenware covered with white engobe, transfer-printed in blue under the glaze. Portobello pearl ware of this period in the British Museum includes a marked flower pot decorated with acanthus leaves in low relief and a plate with classical patterns transfer-printed in blue.

Chimney ornaments, known in Scotland as dabbities, were made in a style closely allied to Staffordshire Pratt ware, decoration being carried out with underglaze high temperature colours in a palette limited to blue, green, yellow and dull or purplish brown, all maturing together with one firing in the kiln. These are sometimes painted in spots or dabbed on irregularly with a stippling brush. Soldiers, fishermen and fishwives, and also classical figures, were made, as well as candlesticks and watch stands.

The mark impressed was the name SCOTT with the conjoined letters PB immediately below. A dish of the dark red earthenware characteristic of Portobello, decorated with a floral pattern in white slip with a honey-tinted glaze, is marked SCOTT BROTHERS: this is in the Royal Scottish Museum. Portobello's first venture into the manufacture of pottery was unsuccessful, however, and production ceased in about 1793. This earthenware should not be confused with similar ware made by Scott & Company, Sunderland, from 1789. This might be impressed SCOTT.

The Portobello Pottery was reopened in 1795 by Cockson & Jardine of Edinburgh. Their skilled potters and decorators were attracted from nearby potteries at Prestonpans and Newbigging. Pearl ware and reddish brown pottery were the chief productions. Existing examples attributed to this period include plain white domestic ware and hollow-ware with figures and foliage in low relief, often with underglaze decoration in four colours. One recorded teapot in the contemporaneous silver shape resembles the Castleford style and its lid is surmounted with a well-modelled swan finial.

The Portobello Pottery in 1808 passed into the possession of Thomas Yoole, whose son-in-law Thomas Rathbone had been a managing potter in Glasgow. He became a partner almost at once for when a new lease was granted in 1810 it was to "Thomas Yoole and partners under the name of Thomas Rathbone and Coy; stoneware manufacturers."

William Baird in *Annals of Portobello*, 1898, has recorded that Rathbone's "principal output was plain ware, such as bowls, jugs, basins, jars, filters, etc. But besides these articles they did an extensive business in ornaments of a florid kind, their vases, yellow with brown spots, being richly embellished with leaves, and occasionally figures. Ornamental jugs, cream pots, classic and rustic figures, male and female, as fishwives, soldiers, sailors and shepherds for mantelpiece ornaments, found a ready market, being sent in carts and retailed in all parts among the country people."

Carpet bowls was a favourite indoor winter game during the second half of the nineteenth century, particularly in the Border counties where carpet bowling clubs were formed. Lord Henry Bentinck has recorded that the game was played in the galleries of great country houses. A handsome set is preserved at Holker Hall, Lancashire.

The game was played with six pairs of balls in granite ware, a tough, heavy stone china, capable of withstanding the hazards of hitting each other and the furniture without breaking. Examples are found decorated with bands and lines of brown, pink, blue and green in designs resembling tartans and various mottled underglaze colours. Others were painted with conventional designs of foliage or starry patterns in green, red and black. The jack remained white. Sets were made at Portobello and also at Sunderland and various Glasgow potteries.[1]

Retailers of Portobello pottery discovered that inexpensive models of cows, horses and lions were favourite figure subjects with Scottish folk. Rathbone's Florentine lions, modelled from the celebrated lions carved in marble at the entrance to the Loggia dei Lanzi, Florence, were made in large numbers. They were copied successfully by John Walton of Burslem. Baird illustrates an example coloured greyish blue under a glaze of unusual brilliance. The lion, head turned to the right, with right paw upon a large ball, stands squarely upon a flat, oblong plinth, the edge encircled with olive leaves in relief. This example measures $10\frac{1}{2}$ inch long by $7\frac{1}{2}$ inch high.

The small figures made by Rathbone have an enduring charm although usually crudely made to keep prices within reach of low income families. There was a Scottish demand for earthenware *bocages* in the Staffordshire manner. A tree rising behind a figure consisted of a short trunk supporting a few branches thickly covered with conventional leaves and flowers, carefully arranged by hand. Vases might be filled with similar leaves and flowers to the height of about a foot: in early examples the figure of a soldier might stand in the bocage. Watch stands incorporating several figures in the design were made from about 1820.

Until the mid-nineteenth century there were few ornaments except ceramic plaques for ordinary folk to hang on their walls. Rathbone's wall plaques included pictorial subjects in relief, sometimes coloured and glazed: others were in hard terra-cotta painted after firing. The frame and picture were in a single piece. A framed plaque measuring 5 inches by $3\frac{1}{2}$ inches was issued to commemorate George IV's military review on Portobello sands, 23rd August 1822. This displayed a relief portrait of the king painted in colours and inscribed "Welcome George IV". A circular plaque, 1 foot in diameter, was made to commemorate Queen

[1] Bibliography: *Scottish Pottery*, Arnold Fleming, 1923; *Cassels Book of Games*, 1872; Country Life, correspondence, June 12, July 3 and 31, 1956.

Victoria's first visit to Scotland in 1842. This displayed an equestrian portrait of the queen with a page in attendance. Other Rathbone wall plaques with decorations in relief included the royal coat of arms; "Bacchus and Venus"; "Flora"; a winged lion; and an equestrian figure in armour.

Thomas Rathbone was succeeded by his son Samuel who employed nearly one hundred workers until the late 1830s. A trade depression in 1837–8 brought about temporary closure. The firm's former prosperity was never recovered and production ceased in 1850.

After seven years the Portobello Pottery was reopened by Dr. W. A. Gray, who operated it under the name of the Midlothian Stoneware Potteries. The chief production was an improved white stoneware known in Staffordshire as granite ware, and notable for its cheapness, even surface, gaudy colouring, and long wearing glaze. Dr. Gray was joined by his son Alexander in the 1860s and under his management the factory's former prosperity was revived, about eighty operatives being employed. The Grays also made general stoneware such as spirit bottles, spirit barrels, jugs, water filters, foot and carriage warmers. The mark impressed was W. A. GRAY & SONS.

A second pottery was established at Portobello in 1830, manufacturing salt-glazed stoneware to the exclusion of white goods. Productions included hunting pots, goblets, tumblers and bucket-shaped water filters. Many of the latter were ornamented in high relief with figures of men and women often grouped in drinking scenes, as well as animals, hunting scenes with horses and hounds in full cry, flowers and numerous other motifs. In the same ware the firm made well-modelled figures, horses and cows. The mark was impressed MILNE CORNWALL & Co.

Ten years later the business was sold to John Tough, proprietor of the Newbigging Pottery, who continued the manufacture of salt-glazed stoneware until 1867. By then the Portobello clays had been worked out. Plant and premises were acquired by G. W. Buchan who developed a flourishing industry in granite ware. For a short period an art ware known as Portobello faïence was made, cleverly designed and enriched with brilliant colour glazes. This was soon discontinued owing to formidable competition from Staffordshire and Lambeth. Buchan's mark was an impressed star.

A third pottery was established at Portobello in 1830 by John Hay who acquired a brick and tile works that had been operating from 1781. Inexpensive earthenware was made including vases and simple chimney ornaments. Clay from the brickfield was used as well as from Cornwall. Upon Hay's death in 1885 the pottery was continued by his sons, employing about forty men and women.

ALLOA POTTERY (Fife) was established in 1790 and continued under various managements potting coarse earthenware until about 1860. Then Peter Gardiner, finding the density and colour of the Alloa clay ideal for majolica, pioneered this decoration in Scotland. Rockingham teapots were also made in attractive designs with matching jugs. Although at one period, 26,000 teapots were made and glazed weekly, examples are difficult to acquire. Jet ware was also manufactured, a feature peculiar to Alloa being the decoration of hollow-ware with colour transfer prints of ferns. A gold medal was awarded to Gardiner for this ware at the Philadelphia Exhibitions, 1876. The pottery closed in 1908. No mark has been recorded.

ALLANDER POTTERY (Milngavie, Glasgow) was established in 1904 as an art pottery by Hugh Allan. Vases were decorated with glazes coloured and curdled by the addition of raw metallic oxides. Some were also decorated with crystalline enamels. This pottery closed in 1908.

ANNFIELD POTTERY (Glasgow) was established in 1812 by John Thomson employing potters and decorators from Staffordshire and specialising in pearl ware of good quality, particularly tea services clearly printed with Eastern scenes in a mulberry tint. Most of the output was exported to Australia. The factory was closed in 1884. The marks, printed, were JT & S, JT / ANNFIELD, JT & SONS GLASGOW with the name of the pattern which might appear in a garter above the initials.

BO'NESS POTTERIES (Linlithgow) were established in 1766 as "The South Pottery", manufacturing coarse brown-ware from local clay. The factory was acquired in 1784 by Dr. John Roebuck who adapted the plant to make excellent cream-coloured earthenware and white stoneware, importing materials from Cornwall and flints from Gravesend. Bo'ness, a contraction of Borrowstounness, operated under a succession of managements during the nineteenth century until closed in 1889. In 1836 Jameson & Co. introduced potters, painters and printers from Staffordshire, skilled in the newest processes. Their blue-printed pattern "Bosphorus" became a best-seller.

Bo'ness specialised in cottage chimney ornaments, vigorously modelled and notable for their individuality. Bright colours were painted under the glaze, thus facilitating washing. Among their better-known pairs of animals and birds were alert fox terriers, comforters, and other dogs standing on four feet without pedestals; self-satisfied cats, lions and rabbits; cocks, hens, ducks, cockatoos and other birds.

BRITANNIA POTTERY (Glasgow) was established in 1857 by Robert Cochran, who installed modern plant and mass-produced thick, hard-fired ironstone china and white granite in forms and decorations resembling those of the heavy, white hard porcelains which had for long predominated in the American market. Cochran's ware, heavy, tinged with cobalt blue to match the French porcelain, with a thick, stiff glaze replacing the former thin cobalt-blue stained glass, scooped the American market, where it was found eminently suitable for travelling unscathed over rough tracks.

Cochran's best-selling pattern was Ceres, modelled by David Chetwynd, Hanley, in about 1865. This consisted of wheat and barley sheaves in relief encircling the ware and coloured under the glaze. The Britannia Pottery, with six hundred operatives, virtually subsisted on the Ceres design for fifteen years. Blue-printed pearl ware was also made, three best-selling patterns being Syria, Damascus and Oriental in clear pale blue lines. A set of copper plates for printing a dinner service was costly: the bill for the original Syria plates was £687.

White stoneware jugs were decorated in relief, the ornament enriched with a brilliant underglaze matt blue. These jugs were smear glazed on the exterior, the interior being lead glazed. Simple cylindrical three-spouted puzzle jugs (see page 40) were issued over a long period, the Robin pattern being particularly popular. The pattern in relief was brightly coloured, the lower part of the body being painted to resemble a wall, with a leafy spray rising from behind it to serve as a perch for the robin. Ivory ware largely replaced the cold blue tint of ironstone china and its associated earthenwares from about 1890, square shapes then being fashionable.

The firm became Cochran & Fleming in 1896 and continued under this management until 1920, when it was acquired by the Britannia Pottery Co. Ltd., for the manufacture of semi-porcelains.

Printed marks included the figure of Britannia with the pattern title above and the name Cochran below—C & F after 1896; COCHRAN crown SEMI PORCELAIN; ROYAL IRONSTONE CHINA. Impressed might be COCHRAN, after 1896 C & F G.

CALEDONIAN POTTERY (Glasgow) was established in about 1790 by Reed, Paterson & Co., and then known as The Glasgow Pottery. It is believed that soft porcelain decorated in the Worcester style was made until 1807 when the factory was acquired by Aitchison & Co. who renamed it Caledonian Pottery, manufacturing table ware in bone china and earthenware. Shortly afterwards they bought the moulds, patterns, plant and goodwill of Delftfield (see page 204). From about 1810 the firm specialised in bone china table ware with grounds of egg-yellow enamel, white reserves containing colourful posies, and elaborate gildings. Earthenware was decorated in underglaze colours.

Murray & Couper bought the pottery in 1840, James Couper being Glasgow's leading china-seller. Fine bone china was made, various semi-chinas, and earthenware. Unfortunately sooty specks emitted from the furnace of a near-by ironworks made yellow stains in the white ware, causing a large proportion of wasters. These productions ceased in 1857 and stoneware was produced including vigorously modelled statuettes, cane handles, flasks and jugs encircled with hunting scenes in relief, or with such figures as Tam o' Shanter and Souter Johnny. From 1891 excellently modelled Egyptian black was made in an attempt to restore to favour what had formerly been a very popular body. This was impressed with a Scottish lion rampant.

CLYDE POTTERY (Greenock) was established in 1816 by Andrew Muir & Co., who advertised in the *Glasgow Courier* of that year; "The Clyde Pottery Company . . . are manufacturing Cream-coloured, Fancy-coloured Edge, and printed Earthenware of a quality which they can with confidence recommend." The pottery at this period specialised in punch and toddy bowls, their lily of the valley pattern, painted and enamelled in bright colours with a yellow lustre border, being a best-seller for many years. In the early 1840s the factory was acquired by Thomas Shirley whose earthenware was impressed TS & Coy. Shirley sold to a group of merchants in 1857, the pottery operating until 1903 under a succession of proprietors using the trade mark C P C° G impressed or printed in a garter.

DUNMORE POTTERY (Airth, Stirlingshire) was established early in the nineteenth century to manufacture coarse domestic crockery and tiles from red clay. Peter Gardiner (see Alloa Pottery) acquired the factory in 1860 and quickly converted a sluggish business into a prosperous concern, utilising his expert knowledge of glazes. Much admired by collectors are Dunmore teapots in deep mazarine blue, cobalt blue, copper green, and crimson glazes. Dunmore's pure copper green glaze on terra-cotta successfully rivalled a similar glaze by the Minton firm. These coloured glazes required skilful manipulation in the kiln as one colour was liable to "strike" and discolour another, even if in different saggers. Blues were particularly liable to stain other ware. In addition, blues and greens tended to strike the interior walls of saggers and cause stains on future contents. The rare early examples and terra-cotta were made from Dunmore clay: later Cornish materials were used.

The Earl and Countess of Dunmore recommended Gardiner's productions to the china-sellers of London, the countess herself designing rustic vases and ornaments which had a considerable vogue. When the Prince of Wales stayed with the Dunmores in 1871 he visited the pottery, with the result that, for a time, the possession of Dunmore pottery was highly fashionable, particularly dessert services, leaves, fruit and animals surface-splashed with glazes in rich tints of brown, yellow and green. "Wicker" baskets were woven from slender strands of clay and glazed in the majolica style. Teapots in the form of a tortoise with its head forming the spout were made during the fourth quarter of the nineteenth century. It is claimed by Scotsmen that Dunmore introduced the celebrated golliwog as a chimney ornament. The factory closed early in the twentieth century. The impressed mark DUNMORE has been noted.

FIFE POTTERY (Sinclairtown, Scotland), known also as Gallatown Pottery, was established in about 1820 and manufactured a variety of common earthenware and yellow caneware. In the mid-nineteenth century the factory came under the control of Robery Heron, who introduced the well-known Wemyss ware. This was well designed and skilfully potted white earthenware, boldly painted with large flowers and foliage, fruits, and cocks and hens. The decoration does not appear to have been duplicated elsewhere with any success. Only rarely does an example bear the mark WEMYSS WARE.

GLASGOW POTTERY was established early in the nineteenth century by John and Matthew Perston Bell to make fireclay ware. In 1842 they entered the bone china and semichina trade and soon were making parian ware and terracotta too. No other Scottish pottery issued such a wide variety of wares. Collectors of Victorian ceramics will be interested in a list of these Scottish productions on view at the Great Exhibition, 1851, at which the firm of Bell & Co. was the only Scottish exhibitor.

"Dinner services in stoneware: Blue printed, landscape pattern, Italian lakes. Flowered ware, mulberry coloured centre with azure border. 'Warwick vase' registered pattern.

"Tea services and jugs in stoneware and porcelain [bone china]. Common stoneware, in dipt, sponged and painted. Scent jar in stoneware, antique shape, with Turkish centre, printed in five colours. Wine coolers, antique shape, with stands.

"Articles in Parian: Small vases with figures in bas-relief, the body and handle modelled after a vase found in Pompeii. Antique vase with upright handles. Jugs modelled after the antique, with bas-reliefs from the Elgin marbles, representing the Battle of the Amazons. (Registered shape). Jugs, same shape but plain, with same subject enamelled. Bas-reliefs from the Elgin marbles.

"Specimens in terra cotta: Large vase (Piranesi) with flowers and scrolls in bas-relief. Large vase, similar, but plain. Large fluted columns, serving as pedestals for these, with capitals and bases complete. Shorter columns without capitals."

Bone china was decorated by Scottish artists, landscapes of Scottish scenery, flowers and fruits being the principal ornaments. The glaze is soft to the touch and entirely free from iron specks. Vases might be painted all over in black enamel as a background to painted pictures of Roman soldiers with accoutrements in highly raised white enamel: this style of decoration is not known to have been produced by any other potter. The majority of blue and white printed ware was based on oriental designs made fashionable by Spode half a century earlier. A leading copper plate engraver was David Roberts, later knighted and a Royal Academician (see page 217). The pottery closed early in the twentieth century.

The trade mark was a bell impressed or printed. After 1869 B or J B was placed inside the bell.

GORDON'S POTTERY (Prestonpans) was established early in the eighteenth century and from about 1770 operated two kilns manufacturing common earthenware until the nineteenth century. Then blue and white printed pearl ware was made, the "Bird and Fly" pattern being a best-seller for many years. Two types of Gordon ware jugs are now collector's prizes. These are circular and oval with figure and other designs in high relief painted underglaze in light orange, brown and grass green with black or blue lines on brims and handles. The narrow-mouthed oval jug displayed Jacobite emblems and mottoes in side panels. Jacobites placed such a jug, filled with water, on their dining tables so that they might inconspicuously toast "The King over the Water". The war-like scenes encircling the round jugs are supposed to represent scenes from the Battle of Prestonpans. Teapots were made of an earthenware that vitrified in the biscuit kiln, the interior only being glazed. Basaltes were made with a fine smear glaze distinguishing them from their English counterpart. The pottery closed in 1832. The impressed mark GORDON has been noted.

NORTH-BRITISH POTTERY (Glasgow) was established 1810 as the Osley Pottery to manufacture bone china. The paste was flawed and production had ceased within ten years. The premises were then occupied by a series of stoneware potters until 1874, when they were acquired by Alexander Balfour. He concentrated upon strong granite ware, gaudily coloured for the African market and often inscribed in a native language. Balfour issued a highly successful series of cow cream jugs, the animal lying on an oval plinth coloured in underglaze green. White stoneware jugs were made with encircling designs in relief and superficially resembling the more expensive parian ware. These were heavily lead-glazed inside and smear-glazed outside. Production quickly ceased, however, for the smear glaze on stoneware held dirt and was difficult to clean. Thistle-shaped egg cups with transfer-printed Scottish scenes were made here as well as egg-hoops such as were formerly turned in woods and horn.

OLD CUMNOCK POTTERY (Ayrshire) was established in 1786 by James Taylor, inventor of steam navigation, to make coarse earthenware. Upon Taylor's death in 1825, the pottery was acquired by the Nicol family, by whom it was operated until closed in 1919. Under the Nicol management the pottery became celebrated for motto ware made from local red clays covered with yellow engobe. This was decorated with line sketches and inscriptions scratched into the engobe by means of a sharp pointed tool, revealing the design in red. This ornament was displayed with considerable effect when suitably glazed. Fleming lists the following typical mottoes: "a cream jug would have 'Straught frae the coo'; a butter dish, 'Help yersel, dinna be blate'; a bowl, 'I'm no greedy but I like a lot'; plates, 'Hane yer breath to cool your parritch', 'The proof o' the puddin is i' the preein' o't."

PRESTONPANS POTTERY: records show that more than seventy earthenware potters were employed in two potteries operating on this site during the third quarter of the nineteenth century. Forty years later two large and two small potteries employed 252 potters. It is believed that porcelain was made here for a short period from the 1750s. The *London Chronicle*, 1755, reported: "Four potters well-skilled in the working of English china were engaged to go up to Scotland where a new porcelain factory is going to be established in the manner and process of that carried on at Chelsea [and] Stratford-by-Bow. But we know nothing definite of the locality of this pottery." The Royal Scottish Museum exhibits two pint mugs attributed to Prestonpans, about 1760. These are of porcelain, closely resembling the soft paste and glaze of Chelsea, painted with the Dalrymple arms, flowers and foliage in colour.

ROBERTS, Sir David, R.A.: began his career as a potter's copper plate engraver, employed by Bell & Co., Glasgow Pottery. His best-selling transfer was "Triumphal Car", an oriental scene depicting a chariot drawn by two leopards against a background of temples, palaces and palm trees. The border was panelled with chariots drawn by other wild beasts, the whole design being full of vigorous movement.

ROSSLYN POTTERY (Fifeshire) was already established in the third quarter of the nineteenth century. It was known to Victorians and Edwardians for its "penny banks" or "Pirley pigs" in the form of farmyard animals such as pigs, horses, sheep, sitting hens, rabbits' and dogs' heads, and also furniture, such as chests of drawers and chests. These have a rich dark brown Rockingham glaze, displaying the embossed ornament to the full. Hand-power was used until 1883, when the pottery was enlarged and Victorian majolica made and also yellow caneware.

SARACEN POTTERY (Glasgow) was established in 1875 by Bailey, Murray & Bremner to manufacture cane, Rockingham and jet ware, as well as majolica jugs sold by grocers containing one or two pounds of jam. These were impressed BM & Co SARACEN POTTERY. Late in the century ornamental and useful china was produced in the style of Belleek and marked NAUTILUS PORCELAIN.

SPRINGBURN POTTERY (Glasgow) operated from about 1860 to 1880, potting white earthenware marked SPRINGBURN below a thistle flower with two leaves.

VERREVILLE POTTERY (Glasgow) was established in 1777 as a flint-glass house and by the late 1780s manufactured cream-coloured earthenware. The business came into the possession of John Geddes in 1806 who introduced steam power and modernised the plant. Lack of skilled labour prompted Geddes to establish in about 1810 Scotland's first Academy for Potters, introducing highly skilled Continental potters and decorators to teach Scotsmen. Bone china was made from 1817, and by the early 1820s exceptionally fine biscuit and enamelled figures were modelled. Flower encrustations, exquisitely painted in enamel colours with grounds enriched with butterflies and insects, were equal to anything that came from Rockingham and Coalport. Twig baskets in the later Belleek style were also made. China, earthenware and glass were in simultaneous production.

Geddes' son was taken into partnership during 1824, and three years later they were joined by Alexander Kidston and traded as Geddes, Kidston & Co., a style continued until 1834, when Geddes and his son retired, selling their shares to Kidston and Hugh Price for £9,000. Kidston considered the plant outmoded and, in addition to new machinery and kilns, he introduced potters, gilders and flower and landscape painters from the leading English bone china works. Verreville became celebrated for its fine table services and ornamental ware, the majority of it exported.

In 1847 the factory came under the control of Robert Cochran, who abandoned the manufacture of unprofitable ornamental ware in favour of domestic productions. Cochran was primarily a technician: in 1852 he patented the down-draught kiln; a "batting" machine in 1864; and his money-spinning two-pound necked jam jar in 1865. Previous to this, jam jars or jelly cans were pure cylinders. When factory jam, packed in boxes for transport, became accidentally inverted, the jam slid down to the paper cover and spoiled the contents. The neck of Cochran's jar prevented this.

In 1856 Cochran ceased the manufacture of bone china, utilising the plant for the manufacture of heavy semi-porcelains, and, in the following year, established the Britannia Pottery (page 211). He operated both factories until his death in 1869 and was succeeded by his son Robert. The pottery was sold in 1918 and demolished. When a mark was used the name Cochran was incorporated in the design.

VICTORIA POTTERY, POLLOKSHAWS (Glasgow), was established as an earthenware pottery in 1855 by David Lockhart and Charles Arthur. In addition to table ware, many models of chimney ornaments in the Staffordshire manner were issued, mainly white and touched with gilding and black and red enamels. Productions were rarely marked but L & A impressed and LOCKHART & ARTHUR printed have been noted. Arthur resigned in 1865, the firm then trading as David Lockhart & Co., and from 1898 as David Lockhart & Sons. The impressed marks were DL & Co and DL & SONS.

WATSON'S POTTERY (Prestonpans) was established in about 1750 to make coarse earthenware. The production of cream-coloured earthenwares dates from the 1780s and excellently modelled chimney piece figures were also made, birds and beasts being popular. Steady employment was given to about eighty operatives, many introduced from Staffordshire. The bulk of the eighteenth-century Scottish figures were potted at Watson's with underglaze colours less profuse than elsewhere in Scotland. Punch and toddy bowls were a feature, painted with flowers and foliage in the Staffordshire style, but with floral or Greek fret borders printed in underglaze blue. Stoneware was also made and late in the eighteenth century the firm advertised "plates, bowls, bottles and greybeards, the latter being Bellarmines such as has been made in England for more than two hundred years." In about 1800 the pottery was acquired by John Fowler & Co., whose family managed the business until 1840 when it was closed.

Little of the eighteenth-century ware was marked, but examples are known impressed WATSON. Under the Fowlers' printed marks included WATSON & Co in a rectangle; the name of the pattern in a double-lined diamond; and SEMI CHINA in a diamond.

Index

(*Illustrations are indicated by italic figures.*)

Printed in England